ALL I NEED

JOSEPH T. JONES

ISBN 978-1-4958-0621-6

Published August 2015

INFINITY PUBLISHING
1094 New DeHaven Street, Suite 100
West Conshohocken, PA 19428-2713
Toll-free (877) BUY BOOK
Local Phone (610) 941-9999
Fax (610) 941-9959
Info@buybooksontheweb.com
www.buybooksontheweb.com

TABLE OF CONTENTS

ACKNOWLEDGEMENTS

I would like to thank Rakia Clark for the professionalism she exhibited while editing my less than professional work, the friends and relatives who provided information and pictures of our family members, and Charlie Badalati for working a miracle restoring old family pictures. I would also like to thank my wife, Carol Wilson Jones, for putting up with me during the time it took me to complete this book.

*"Tell me a fact, and I'll learn.
Tell me the truth, and I believe, but tell me a
story, and it will live in my heart forever."*
                              Native American Proverb

PROLOGUE

My father taught me how to shoot a rifle when I was about ten or eleven years old. I know that I was about that age because of a tradition that was of great significance in the Jones family. My two older brothers Jaye W and Bobby had experienced it before me, and the tradition would surely be carried on with my younger brothers Larry and Jerry after me. It was a joyous occasion and a rite of passage. Now it was my turn. The single shot, bolt action, Remington 22 rifle that had been in our family for more years than anyone could remember was being passed down to me.

My father didn't need to give me much instruction on the rifle or shooting. Just the basics: take a deep breath, exhale, hold your breath, and squeeze the trigger. According to my father, I didn't need much training because I was a "dead shot," meaning my aim was exceptional. He said I *took after* my great grandfather Peter Jones. Daddy also said that I looked just like my great grandfather. So many people claimed that I *favored* and *took after* my great grandfather that around my small town, folks jokingly referred to me as Peter. I didn't mind, though. All my life I had heard stories about what a great marksman and hunter my Grandpa Peter was with a rifle and a shotgun. During the years when he was a young man, shooting contests were very popular, well attended events in southeastern North Carolina. Men from all over Columbus County would come to witness and participate in these events. The grand prizewinner could expect to take home a turkey, a pig or maybe even a calf. According to my father, my Grandpa Peter – this is how I've always referred to him – didn't just win some of these contests; he would win every one he entered. He was such a good shot that, if he was known in the area, contest officials would ban him from entering the competitions.

Since I *took after* Grandpa Peter, there was an expectation that I would be good with a rifle. I don't know whether I inherited my shooting ability or simply rose to my family's expectations through practice, but one thing that I do know is that I was a very good shot with that Remington 22. Most men learn to excel with firearms during their military career. I, on the other hand, entered the U. S. Air Force at seventeen years of age already an expert marksman.

These types of tidbits that make my family's history unique and special to me often get forgotten over time. For all of us, our ancestors' influence is present in everything we do, but without the histories documented somehow, I worry that nobody will know that although our ancestors appeared to be just ordinary folks, their accomplishments were extraordinary in spite of the difficulty of their circumstance. They provided us with more than just a Hill or Jones name, they provided broad shoulders for succeeding generations to stand on. I not only want our family's accomplishments known, I want our family members to be known and remembered. I want colorful relatives like *Big Dan, Rabbit,* and *Gone* to be remembered. Family tree charts and even oral traditions don't feel like enough.

My children have never asked for this information. They are much too busy trying to earn a living and enjoying the fruits of their labor to concern themselves with family history. I had the same attitude about our history when I was younger. But if they are truly like me, then between the ages of forty and fifty, they are going to want to know more. This book is written for when that happens. I want them to know more about our relatives than just their names. I want them to know some of what I know.

My sense and knowledge of family comes from growing up with relatives in very close proximity to where I lived. I saw family history close up. I also grew up in a time before television, music lessons and other activities dominated the lives of our children. Without these distractions, it seems as if we had a lot more time to talk.

For example, my family spent more time than I care to remember working together on the tobacco farm. During these work periods, we also talked. Mostly what we talked about was family history. My children, on the other hand, grew up in Wyncote, Pennsylvania, far removed geographically and culturally from our family history setting of Welches Creek, Lees Lake, and Whiteville, North Carolina. When you grow up in a different village from your family and when television, computers, video games and varied activities of gifted, involved children compete with family time, how do you get the information to help you determine where you come from, and what might be your true identity?

The typical family tree that I initially began charting for my children could never tell them who they *favor* or who they *took after*. For that kind of information, you need family history. The written history of most Black families in America is either nonexistent or sketchy at best. What did and still does exist are the stories that came from our history's direct witnesses. Because I grew up in the area where most of our American family history occurred, I had the opportunity to witness some of our more recent history for myself. I was also fascinated by the family stories I heard from my parents and grandparents generation that had been passed down to them by their parents and grandparents. In passing on the little family history that I have, it is my hope that I can provide some of the knowledge my children missed because they were born and grew up in a different village than me. Just as I became a good marksman with a rifle because that's what was expected of me, perhaps their knowledge of family history will help them better assess the size and style of the shoes they are expected to fill. At the very least, hopefully, this book will give my children some understanding of their father, grandparents and ancestors and, in turn, help them learn just a little about themselves.

Since this book was written for my children, I dedicate it to them. To Sterling, Kaya and Janay, I am so proud of everything that you have accomplished in your young lives. More than the success you have had, I am impressed with the spiritual and moral people of integrity you have become. I cannot remember one single day since you were born when I was not proud that a little piece of me was in each of you. I would be honored if one day I heard someone say that you *took after* me.

Bound in,
Bonds to Welches Creek

My father was born and spent his entire childhood in the same Lees Lake community as my mother and her family. However, the first recorded ties to a community for my father's family was the Welches Creek area of Columbus County in North Carolina.

Welches Creek is a small, rural community just a few miles northeast of the county seat of Whiteville. It was named for James Welch who owned 640 acres of land in that area, which also included a creek. Early land deeds mentioned the creek owned by James Welch, namely Welch's Creek as a reference point in identifying boundaries for plots of land. It is believed that from these often used references, the township name of Welches Creek was derived.

During the reconstruction period following the Civil War, Black and mixed race people built a thriving community there. Several of the residents either owned or worked in the logging or turpentine business, but most were farmers. In addition to businessmen and farmers, Welches

Creek produced other African Americans of note. One of Welches Creek's most famous residents, George Henry White, was the last African American to serve in The United States Congress before Jim Crow disenfranchisement laws eliminated them from the halls of Congress around the end of the nineteenth century.

George White lived on his family's farm in Welches Creek prior to becoming a lawyer and being elected to Congress. He served from 1897 to 1901. He was a very effective congressman, using his office to appoint African Americans to prominent positions in his district. He also introduced the first federal anti-lynching legislation in the United States. The bill was soundly defeated by racist southern congressmen.

During the first reconstruction period following the Civil War, and the second reconstruction just before the turn of the century, several Blacks were elected to represent districts with a majority of Black voters. Mississippi, Louisiana, and South Carolina had a clear majority Black population. Some other areas and several southern states had a Black population of almost forty percent. Fearing that Blacks might acquire some small measure of equality by virtue of legislation and patronage from their elected officials, southern states enacted poll taxes, arbitrary literacy rules, residency requirements, rule variations, and other voter intimidation tactics to deny Blacks their right to the ballot box. The most insidious of these laws was the grandfather rule. This law specified that your grandfather had to have voted prior to January 1, 1896 in order for you to be able to vote. Since most African Americans grandfathers were slaves or denied the right to vote as freemen, this law alone prevented any of them from voting. Because of its effectiveness, state constitutions enacted the grandfather rule in every former confederate state. These laws were all classified as disenfranchisement laws, as they denied Blacks the franchise presumed available to all in the land of the free. Congressmen of conscience, sensitive to the plight of southern Blacks, tried to pass legislation to outlaw the kind of rules that prevented Blacks from voting, but powerful southern congressmen who gained seniority by preventing Blacks from voting, also prevented these movements from going anywhere in the House of Representatives. The bill never made it out of committee. Most of these laws remained in force until a people who were determined to be free suffered intimidations, beatings, bites from snarling dogs, fire hoses, being jailed and even being killed, during the Civil Rights Movement of the 1960s, which forced the abolishment of such laws.

The lengths that people went to deny one the right to vote, and the sacrifice people made to achieve the right to vote is the only testament I need as to its value. The right wing conservative's attempts to dismantle the voting rights act, and the new voter identification laws springing up all over the country are just an updated version of those same disenfranchisement laws we thought were just a bitter memory. I am just as determined to fight for the rights of free and easy access to the ballot as conservatives are about changing or circumventing the laws that we thought would forever assure us of those rights. Considering the sacrifices made by my people, how could I do less? The fight continues. The right to vote is a franchise that I should have inherited simply by living under the umbrella of the Constitution. Unfortunately, I did not. I inherited my franchise from the blood of my people. Like any sacred and valuable inheritance, I am prepared to defend it with my blood and pass it on to my children.

Succumbing to the disenfranchisement of his constituents, George White left Congress in 1901. In his January 29th farewell speech on the floor of the House of Representatives, White said;

> *"This is perhaps the Negroes' temporary farewell to the American Congress, but let me say; Phoenix-like he will rise up some day and come again. These parting words are in behalf of an outraged, heart-broken, bruised and bleeding, but God-fearing people, faithful, industrious, loyal, rising people – full of potential force."*

During a speech by President Obama at the Congressional Black Caucus Foundation Awards

Dinner, on September 26, 2009, the President made reference to George Henry White's departing words to Congress.

After leaving Congress, White started a law practice in Washington, D. C. He then moved to Philadelphia and was associated with the first Black managed bank in the country. He is also credited with the founding of Whitetown, New Jersey, the all-Black community near Cape May. The residents with sir names of Spaulding, Moore, and Graham that are so dominant in Whitetown, all had ancestors in the area of Welches Creek. Most of the current and former residents of Whitetown, including Oprah Winfrey's life partner, Steadman Graham, share a common ancestry with my father's family in Welches Creek.

George White's departure from Congress in 1901 left it devoid of an African American congressional representative from any state for the next twenty-seven years. North Carolina didn't elect another Black to Congress for *ninety-one years*!

Jones family kin, Charles Clinton Spaulding, a founder of North Carolina Mutual Life Insurance Company, and Asa T. Spaulding, a past president of the company and the first African-American actuary in the United States, both claimed the Welches Creek area as home. It's most well-known citizens however, were the world famous conjoined Siamese twins, commonly referred to as Millie-Christine. The twins were the eighth of fifteen children born to Jacob and Monemia McKoy in Welches Creek in 1851. I referred to them as the eighth child rather than the eighth and ninth children because their parents, spoke of them as one person. Later in life the twins also spoke of themselves as one person.

Born slaves, Millie-Christine belonged to Jabez McKoy, and their parents, Jacob and Monemia, had no control. Consequently, exploitation of the twins started at a very early age. Jabez McKoy, entered into an agreement with John C. Purvis of South Carolina to earn money by displaying the twins as curiosities in various freak shows.

Through yet another transaction, the twins ultimately ended up in the possession of a Joseph P. Smith. Then during an exhibition at the P. T. Barnum American Museum in New York, the twins were stolen and spirited off to England. Once Smith found them there, he traveled to England with Monemia and filed a suit in England's courts to retrieve them. Smith won his case and when the Englishman in the courtroom heard testimony about the terrible treatment of the girls at the hands of their kidnapper, the thief jumped out of a second story courthouse window to avoid being beaten by the locals.

Upon his return to the United States, Joseph Smith relocated the girls to his hometown of Wadesboro, North Carolina. Smith and his wife taught the twins how to read, write, sing and dance, and to speak foreign languages. They would eventually become fluent in five languages.

Millie-Christine toured the world, appeared with the Barnum Circus, and fascinated audiences with their singing, dancing, music playing, and poetry recitals. They were billed as the Carolina Twins, The Two-Headed Nightingale, and The Eighth Wonder of the World. After emancipation, the twins agreed to remain with the Smiths and continued to tour for nearly thirty years. In the summer of 1871, they again traveled to the United Kingdom and performed for Queen Victoria. The queen was so impressed with the talented Millie-Christine, that she presented the girls with diamond hairclips and a jewel-encrusted necklace.

Meanwhile, the Civil War and the loss of slaves as a valuable commodity decimated the finances of many plantations in the south. Plantations in Welches Creek were no different. Jabez McKoy was one of those owners who lost his plantation after the war. With money provided by Millie-Christine, Jacob and Monemia McKoy were able to purchase the very plantation where their children were born and where they were all enslaved. After the death of Jacob and Monemia, Millie-Christine inherited the plantation from their parents. When the twins were in their early thirties, they moved back to the place of their birth in Welches Creek. They would tour occasionally, but preferred staying at home. When Millie died of tuberculosis in October of 1912, a doctor from Whiteville gave Christine morphine to aid her in the painless ending of her life. She died some seventeen hours after her sister. They were sixty one years old.

I didn't know anything about Millie-Christine when I was young, but I do remember my father always greeting and referring to the McKoys from Welches Creek as our cousins. Residents in the area, including the relatives and descendants of George Henry White, Millie-Christine, the Spauldings, Moores, Grahams, McKoys, and my father's family, were documented and counted in the United States census of 1870. It was the first to include Blacks and listed my great, great grandfather, Melvin Jones, as being born right in Welches Creek. I suppose that any census prior to 1870, the United States would have considered my family as just property and not people to be counted. I have not found any records that would lead me to the identity Melvin's mother or father. The 1880 census records were the first that I have seen to also list the birthplace of the respondent's parents. That may have been done as a devious means of collecting information to enforce those disastrous disenfranchisement grandfather laws that affected the Black vote later on. Those 1880 records list Melvin's mother and father as being born in North Carolina, so apparently he knew of them. Unfortunately, as of this writing, I do not know who they were or where in North Carolina they may have lived. Even if I complete this project without finding them, my search will continue.

Jones family records begin in Welches Creek, so I suspect that ancestors on both sides of my father's family were held in bondage there. In all probability, they were slaves on the James Smith or James Baldwin plantations, as both plantations were prominent in the area. My great, great grandparents, Melvin Jones and Rebecca Baldwin were married in the Welches Creek area in 1850, so being held as slaves on the Baldwin plantation was a strong possibility for Rebecca or even both of these ancestors. Since no slavery records exist for my family, I have no proof that they were held at either plantation. Melvin Jones was estimated to have been born in 1825. His wife Rebecca, sometimes spelled Rebeckah, had an estimated birth year of 1832. They were both born, raised twelve children, and died in Welches Creek. Their twelve children were Aurpha, James, Sunor, Pinkney, Peter, Alford, John, Warren, Harvey, Izzadoria, Violia, and Mora Mahaly. They also raised a niece named Aurra. Seven of their twelve children were born before emancipation. My great grandfather Peter Jones, born in 1861, was one of them.

Grandpa Peter was obviously a highly intelligent, very talented and extremely handsome man, because I was told throughout my young life that I am just like him. (I can dream, can't I?) He married Nina Smith, whose family and friends called Niney, on April 6, 1883. He was about 22 years of age and she was about 20. Before the dawn of the twentieth century, Nina had given birth to six children and had died. Peter and Nina's children were Lutisia, William (Bud), Hattie, my grandfather Seymore, Henry (Jeff), and LuGene. I don't know exactly why or when Grandpa Peter relocated to the Lees Lake area, some twenty five to thirty miles from his hometown of Welches Creek. I don't know if Nina moved there with him or died before they left Welches Creek. But I do know that June of 1900 found my great grandfather widowed and living in Lees Lake Township with his six children.

YOU KNOW THEY WERE IN NEW ORLEANS?

When I began this project of family and self-discovery, I knew almost nothing about my mother's maternal Lewis family. I grew up around the Joneses of my father's family and the Hills, the paternal side of mother's family. I knew we had Lewis relatives in Whiteville, but I never understood exactly how we were related. I also knew that Grandma Bert, my maternal grandmother, had people who lived in South Carolina before they moved to the Lees Lake area of North Carolina. The Lewises in South Carolina were attractive, very dark-skinned people with curly black hair. Their short stature stood in stark contrast with the tall, lanky, Hill side of my mother's family. I didn't know any of them personally. I only saw them on the rare occasion of a death in our family when some of them would come to the funeral in Whiteville to pay their respects. After I left home, even that line of communication was broken and the gap in my knowledge of that side of the family became even greater. During my research for this project, that gap narrowed considerably. Let me tell you what I know.

I started my search for my Lewis family where I had long been told they were from – Horry County, South Carolina. During my search, I discovered a book by J. D. Lewis called *My Neck of the Woods*. Mr. Lewis lived in Horry County and had written a book about the Lewises. The book was somewhat of a history of Mr. Lewis's family, complete with statistics, records and even the Lewis family crest. To date, Mr. Lewis has researched and catalogued some 25,000 Lewises in the United States and in England. While pouring through the birth, death and marriage records of Lewises in Columbus County, North Carolina, I discovered some of my family members in his book. I was really excited. I thought, *WOW! Someone in my family has written a book about us.*

However, as I read more excerpts from the book and did more research, my excitement began to wane. I began to realize that J. D. Lewis might not be related to me after all. Several of the Lewises in his book had fought for the confederacy, and although I knew that some Black soldiers did perform in somewhat of a service capacity for the confederacy, I knew they were not *my* relatives. However, there were Lewises in his book that I knew for certain *were* my family members. I found Grandma Bert's father, Esquire Lewis, who I knew had been a slave, listed in his book. I found Grandma Bert's brother, Alexander Lewis in his book. I found his burial place and the burial place of his wife and children in the book while I was jumping back and forth through the pages of the book on the Internet. *Hold on,* I thought to myself. *I know it's the middle of the night, but I think I understand what I'm reading, and this can't be right! There is definitely a problem here.*

J. D. Lewis had listed Piney Grove Cemetery as the burial place for my great uncle and his wife and children. The Piney Grove Church in that area was a white church. I had passed it many times as I traveled the back roads from Whiteville to coastal towns in North Carolina and South Carolina. The most segregated institution in the south was then and still is the church. I'm certain that they did not bury my great uncle in Piney Grove's white cemetery when he died in 1930. In addition, I had always been told that my uncle, Alexander was killed at sea and his body thrown overboard near New Orleans. I was really confused. I needed to contact J. D. Lewis.

I had no email address or telephone number for J. D. Lewis, but after some cyber-detective work, I found a mailing address for him online. I wrote to him requesting that he please contact me about my Great Uncle Alexander Lewis. Mr. Lewis called me a couple of weeks after I had written him and although the message he left on my voice mail was exciting, it confused me even more. He stated that it looked like we had a common ancestor, as Alexander Lewis was his great grandfather.

After several attempts to reach Mr. Lewis, and what seemed like an endless rounds of telephone tag and voice mail messages, I finally got a call from Mr. Lewis on a cold, rainy, January morning while I was in my old hometown of Philadelphia. I answered the call as I was walking down the street in the Chestnut Hill section of Philadelphia. It was really difficult trying to walk, manage my umbrella and my cell phone in the freezing rain, but I was not letting Mr. Lewis get away this time. I quickly ducked into the Starbucks on Germantown Avenue so we could carry on a conversation. Mr. Lewis told me that he had been researching his Lewis family for years. He said that he even spent three years in England researching his family's origins. I thanked him for getting back to me and told him that I had a million questions for him. He told me to fire away.

Did Alexander Lewis live in Columbus County in Southeastern North Carolina?

Yes.

Was he called Zander?

Yes.

Did some of Zander's children die at a very early age?

Yes.

Are you sure Alexander Lewis is buried in Piney Grove Cemetery?

Yes.

You said that he was your great grandfather?

Yes.

Are you African American?

Ah, noooo.

Mr. Lewis really confirmed what I suspected all along. Still, we must have spent over an hour on the phone investigating the Lewises in Southeastern North Carolina and Northeastern South Carolina. He was gracious with his time and his information. Based on research I had already done and information I gleaned from Mr. Lewis, we came to the agreement that his great grandfather was not my great uncle. Believe it or not, there were two men named Alexander Lewis living in the same area at the same time. They both were married and had children who died at an early age. They both were called Zander by family and friends. One was white and his great grandfather. The other was Black and my grandmother's brother. It was his great grandfather, the white Alexander Lewis that was buried in Piney Grove Cemetery. When J. D. Lewis was gathering information for his book, I believe that he inadvertently intertwined data about my uncle Zander with his Great Grandfather Zander, thinking they were the same person. I know what you were thinking. I was thinking the same thing. This had to be a case of ole massah's Black and white descendants discovering each other some one hundred and fifty years after they left the plantation. A surprising turn of events during my probe into our Lewis family history proved that this could not be the case.

When I was thinking about my mother's work history as a cook and domestic worker, I could not remember the name of one of the white families she worked for. I called my cousin Carrie Jones Kemp for the information. I thought that she might know because her mother, my Aunt Violet, and my mother had worked for sisters-in-law. My mother and my aunt were Black sisters who worked for wives of white brothers. I was correct in my thinking; Carrie did remember. She seemed genuinely pleased that I was doing family research, so she started to give me other tidbits of family history that I had never heard before. She said that she knew all of this history because when she was a little girl, she spent a lot of time talking to our maternal grandmother, who we all called Grandma Bert. As a matter of fact, I discovered that her immediate family lived with Grandma Bert when she was a small girl. She said that when others were running around the yards playing, she always liked to hang around and talk to Grandma. Carrie said that she asked Grandma a lot of questions and was provided with a wealth of information about the Lewis family, which she still remembers.

During my inquiries about the area in South Carolina where Grandma Bert's family had once lived, Carrie said to me, "You know they were in New Orleans before they were in South Carolina?"

No, I didn't know that! It was a complete shock to me! I had always imagined that our ancestors were brought from Africa to the port of Charleston, and sold in the Charleston slave market before either being sold or migrating into North Carolina. Carrie said that Grandma told her that her Lewis forefathers came from the Virgin Islands to New Orleans and then South Carolina before eventually moving to North Carolina. This was all new information that I had to look into. Now I had to start exploring family history in an area that I would have never considered looking before that conversation. I had to start researching in New Orleans.

During my exploration for family history in New Orleans, I found what I was looking for — evidence of Grandma Bert's Lewis family being in New Orleans. As excited as I was to find Grandma Bert's family, I made another discovery that excited me even more because I was not looking for it. I discovered the Hill side of our family also came through New Orleans. (More on that later.)

Between the years of 1650 and the end of the Civil War in 1865, as many as fifteen million African were shipped to North and South America. I don't think that most African Americans consider the magnitude and impact of slavery in South America. Before this project, I know that I never thought much about it, but more people were enslaved there than in North America. As a result of so many Africans being enslaved in Brazil, there are presently more people of African descent living there than in any country outside of the continent of Africa. In addition to South America, millions of Africans were also shipped to Central America and the Caribbean. Of the approximate five million Africans brought to North America, most were first seasoned in the mines or on the sugar plantations of the West Indies before being sent to the United States. New Orleans, Louisiana; Charleston, South Carolina; and Richmond, Virginia were major shipping ports during that period, and they were the likely spots where most of our ancestors' feet first touched soil in the United States. The stories passed down from Grandma Bert to my cousin Carrie about the Lewises being in the West Indies and New Orleans before moving on to South Carolina makes perfect historical sense. There is compelling evidence however, that New Orleans may not have been the first stop in America for the Lewis family. I believe that the Lewis family's patriarch, Esquire Lewis, was also in Richmond, Virginia before being shipped to New Orleans.

The likely reason my ancestors were brought to New Orleans was because of the tremendous demand for slave labor following the invention of the cotton gin. I'm going to use the term *"invention"* of the cotton gin because Eli Whitney was given credit for inventing it, although the cotton gin was used by ancient Africans in Egypt 4000 years before the birth of Whitney or the birth of America. Anyway, that one invention had more impact on the growth of slavery in America than any other invention, institution or ideology.

Although slaves had always been valuable assets to slave owners, the cotton gin made slaves even more valuable. Before cotton can be spun into yarn, the seed must be removed from the cotton fibers. Separation of the cotton from its seed was a labor-intensive process. So labor-intensive in fact, that planting cotton to sell was not a profitable enterprise. The cotton gin changed all of that. While a human could separate perhaps a pound or two of cotton per day, the gin could separate over fifty pounds of cotton per day from its sticky seeds. The cotton fiber could then be spun into yarn and the seeds used for oil, lotions, soaps, animal feed and even high-quality fertilizer. The invention credited to Eli Whitney made cotton a very profitable crop for those who had the land to plant it and a low-to-no-cost labor force to harvest it. The planters of the lower south had the land, so they planted cotton on every acre of land available to them. Even thousands of pristine forest acres were cleared and or drained and planted with the crop that had by now been crowned King Cotton! The dramatic increase of cotton acreage in the lower southern states created such a huge demand for slaves that it was directly responsible for the greatest forced migration in American history. To satisfy the insatiable demand for low-cost laborers to work those cotton fields, upwards of one and a half million slaves were forced to march hundreds of miles over land, or transported by ships to the slaves market in New Orleans. My relatives were a part of that migration.

Long after laws were passed ending the importation of slaves from Africa, there was still a brisk and very profitable slave trade within the United States. In addition to captured Africans still being smuggled into the southern ports of America, the sale and transportation of human cargo between slave states was big business. Our ancestors were not only sold through one-on-one transactions as depicted in Alex Haley's groundbreaking novel <u>Roots</u>, but they were also sold to agents and brokers who resold them to other agents and brokers. Our forbearers had value. Although they were not valued by their owners in a human sense, their owners certainly valued them as an instruments of wealth. According to Yale history professor, David Blight, by 1860, enslaved African Americans were worth approximately $3.5 billion dollars to the individuals, corporations and institutions who owned them. They were the largest single asset in the entire U. S. economy, worth more than all manufacturing and railroads combined.

The income generated from slavery was so important that precautions were regularly taken to prevent an interruption of the revenue stream. To protect slave owners from the loss of revenue resulting from the death of a slave, insurance companies such as Aetna and New York Life wrote life insurance policies to compensate the owners in the event one of their slaves died. Slaves were even mortgaged, and occasionally those mortgages were packaged and resold to banks in financial centers such as New York, London, Paris, and Amsterdam. Lehman Brothers actually got its start by financing the slave business. J P Morgan Chase, AIG, Wachovia, Rothschild's & Sons, Barclay's, Fleet Bank's predecessor, Provident Bank, Brown Brothers Harriman, and other giant financial institution were also complicit in the financing that helped to turn the slave trade into an economic juggernaut.

Like any other commodity, slaves were traded or bought and sold for any number of reasons. They could be sold to satisfy a debt. They could be sold as property is divided in a divorce settlement. They might be sold or transferred through a will upon the death of an owner. They were purchased by traders who, just like the stock market traders of today, made their living by buying low and selling high. Due to all of the activity in this peculiar American enterprise, an individual could have been sold and resold several times in a matter of weeks. Simply put, slavery was big business.

The ports of Richmond, Charleston and New Orleans, and the slave markets in those cities, were crucial in facilitating all of this trade in human misery. Of the three cities, New Orleans' role was most crucial. In addition to having a bustling port, New Orleans was the greatest center for slave trade in America. In the area that is now the business district of New Orleans, there were nineteen slave yards where human beings were held in pens like cattle before being prepared for New Orleans' enormous slave market.

The law against the importation of captured Africans that took effect on January 1, 1808, required a manifest listing the names and point of origin of any slaves aboard ships docking in the United States. In addition, the ship's master and the owner or agent for the owner of the slaves aboard, were required to sign a declaration printed on the manifest, stating that they were in compliance with the law against the importation of slaves from outside of the United States. Abolitionists claimed the law's passing as a partial victory against slavery, but in the early years, there was no serious enforcement of the law, so the slave traders continued to smuggle nearly as many Africans into the United States as were brought in before the law was passed. The law also did nothing to eliminate or even reduce the slave trade within the United States, so when the flow of new slave labor finally stopped, people already held in bondage in America became even more valuable. Slave owners saw their property increase in value due to the simple law of supply and demand. It is my belief that wealthy plantation owners who had powerful friends in Washington, or were legislators themselves, allowed this law to succeed not because of a fit of conscious, but because they saw this as a way to increase their status as slave owners and to increase their personal wealth. No matter their intent in allowing the law to pass, its compliance helped me identify ancestors held in bondage in New Orleans.

The barque ship Phoenix sailed from Richmond, Virginia, into the port of New Orleans on February 16, 1846. The kind of vessels described as barque were wooden, three-mast types of ships, commonly used as a deep-water cargo carrier during the middle of the nineteenth century. The captain of the Phoenix during that voyage was Nathaniel Boush. Listed among its passengers was my great grandfather Esquire Lewis. The signed manifest indicated that he was sold by A. M. Lyons of Main Street in Richmond, Virginia. I suspect that A. M. Lyons was a slave brokerage firm in Richmond.

The manifest further indicated that the shipper/owner was David Cume. I believe that he was my ancestor's owner in Richmond, Virginia, as a separate column on the manifest indicated that my great grandfather's owner at the time of the ship's docking was John Hagan. John Hagan was a slave trader.

Slave trading was a dirty business, and usually the people who made their living trafficking in human beings were not the pillars of white society. There were hundreds, maybe even thousands of people who dabbled in the slave trade just to make a quick buck if the opportunity arose. A slave trader may have been the local shopkeeper, a bartender or a blacksmith, but these were not the professionals. Most of the pros were hard-drinking, tobacco-spitting, whore-mongering men who lived on the edge of the societies with which they did business. While many white homeowners and owners of small farms may have held one or two slaves to do house and farm labor, it was the wealthy planters with dozens or even hundreds of slaves who were at the top of the social ladder in the antebellum south. To obtain the slaves who facilitated their wealth, they had to deal with some of the dregs of white society, the slave traders. The wealthy plantation owners did not mind using the services of the slave traders, but more than likely would not have invited one of them into their gentile setting for a sip of Kentucky bourbon or for a Sunday dinner. They could purchase slaves and reap the benefits of slavery without getting their hands dirty with that messy trading stuff. The high-society planters were spared from having to navigate through the filth of those retched slave pens where human souls were reduced to something lower than a prized animal. That was the job of the traders. White, southern, high-society took advantage of the inhumane treatment of a people without really having to see inhumanity at its worst. The slave traders provided them with the product to obtain and maintain wealth without getting down and dirty in those slave pens, which would have been offensive to their "Christian" values.

I'm not claiming that the trade or ownership of slaves would have been against *their* Christian values. That was certainly not the case. In addition to the Christian church turning a blind eye to slavery, the Catholic Church in New Orleans was actually slave owners themselves. Although the Christian church and men of so-called high moral standards were complicit in the trade, it was most often the slave traders who bore witness to the day-to-day inhumanity suffered by people in bondage. Despite their not-so-genteel profession, a few of these slave traders became part of the societal class and enjoyed the same benefits of the people their businesses served. Due to the success and the scale of their business, some in the profession rose above the status of the ordinary slave trader. They were very successful businessmen. John Hagan was one of these traders.

Hagan was from South Carolina, but he ran slavery operations in Virginia, South Carolina and in New Orleans. He most often purchased slaves in the Charleston and Richmond market, and sold them in largest slave market in North America – New Orleans. For example, John Hagan purchased my great grandfather Esquire Lewis in Richmond and likely sold him in New Orleans. I have not been able to determine how long Esquire Lewis remained in the New Orleans area, as I have been unable to find any of John Hagan's slave sales transaction that included names. Was my great grandfather sold to someone in the New

Orleans area and resold into South Carolina? Did he migrate to South Carolina after emancipation? Those are just a few of the hundreds of questions I have about my family history. Unfortunately, like millions of other people who had their American history stolen, I may never be able to get those answers.

I don't know why, but I have always loved New Orleans. The first time my eyes saw her and my feet touched her during the early eighties, I wasn't just in love. I was instantly addicted.

When I first went there, it was in the middle of the summer. It was hot and humid, but I didn't mind. The Big Easy had the culture, nightlife, and activities that lured me to the big cities, but the warmth, pace and southern comfort that I still loved. Since that first trip, I have always been excited about returning to New Orleans for vacation or for business. I even traveled there five times in 1991 for conventions, for business and for vacation. I've never been able to get enough of the city's architecture, food, music, people, and even the summer heat. Looking "up" at a river, I did not love so much!

Most of all, I love the way the city celebrates life. I remember calling a major hotel there one year to make reservations for a business trip. I could hear all of this noise in the background while I was trying to make my arrangements with the desk clerk. I didn't mind the constant interruptions in our conversation, but it just seemed to me that the clerk that I was trying to conduct business with was just having too much fun while I hung on the phone. Finally, the clerk said, "Can you call us back later? We are trying to have a party here!"

That's New Orleans. They don't even let business interrupt the party!

I'm far from being an African-American historical expert. I consider myself an interested student, but just a student nevertheless when it comes to our history. I knew New Orleans had a slave history, but my view of that history was somewhat sanitized until I began this research. It turns out that New Orleans was the epicenter for slave trade in America, so every degrading act associated with the enterprise happened there a thousand-fold. Now that I know my people were there, New Orleans is personal. I now wonder if I will ever be able to look at New Orleans the same way again. When I see one of those high walls of the beautiful courtyards downtown, will I wonder if they was built to keep slaves from getting out, or the genteel citizens of New Orleans from seeing in? Every time I see one of those historical buildings in the financial district, will I wonder if one of my ancestors were sold there? Will I begin to hate New Orleans for what my family likely experienced there, or love her even more because I know now that we are connected? Will I have to forgive New Orleans before I can enjoy it again? Then again, should I blame New Orleans for the crime committed against my ancestors?

New Orleans didn't commit the crime; it was just the scene of the crime. Why should I harbor any resentment against The Big Easy? I would only be harming myself by doing so. To quote Nelson Mandela; *"Resentment is like drinking poison and hoping it will kill your enemies."* However, people like John Hagan and everyone that were silent benefactors of his crimes do need to be forgiven, although they have never asked for it. My faith requires that I forgive. I have gladly honored my faith and the faith of my ancestors by doing so long ago, but my ancestors who survived the horrors of the middle passage, the humiliation of the auction block, and the hammer blows delivered by Jim Crow, continue to softly whisper to the conscience of my soul; *"never forget."* I never will.

New Orleans, Louisiana, Slave Manifests, 1807-1860 record f
Squire Lewis

Record Index   Source Information

Name: Squire Lewis

***** Listing of my mother's maternal grandfather, Esquire "Squire" Lewis on the manifest of the Phoenix when it docked in New Orleans on February 16, 1846.

Shortly after the end of The Civil War and after slavery was abolished, thousands of former slaves were legally married and had their marriages recorded by the state, although they may have already been married for several years under the slave system. Since slaves did not own their bodies, they had to obtain permission from their owners to marry. Marriages were permitted, ordered or dissolved as dictated by owners of couples held in bondage. After emancipation, many slaves rushed to the altar to legally demonstrate their commitment to each other. They were guided only by their love for each other and for the first time, by their own *free will*. There is no way to tell if my great grandparents were married during slavery, but shortly after emancipation, on February 28, 1867, Esquire Lewis and a young lady with family ties in Greenville County, North Carolina named Dolly A. George were legally married in Lees Township, North Carolina. Dolly George Lewis was in all likelihood the first freed woman in our family. She retained a skill passed on to her that could have possibly linked her all the way back to Mother Africa. Our family's oral history claims that Dolly was a very capable herbalist. My mother told me that her grandmother Dolly often spend hours in the local forest and would emerge with tree barks, plant roots, leaves and berries of all sorts that she mixed to cure everything from bad breath to influenza.

Esquire and Dolly's children were; Mary, Lewis Jasper, Rahova, Sena, Arrena, Susanna, Bessie, Lizie, Ella, Hattie, my grandmother Buelah, and Alexander. Several of Esquire and Dolly's children died long before I was born. One of their children, Sena was the subject of several anecdotes from my father's side of our family. You will read more about her later. I vaguely remember just one of my grandmother's other siblings who lived in the area when I was young. I recall a relative we called Aunt Reni, so she must have been Arrena. I don't remember any of the others.

Alexander Lewis was another of my grandmother's siblings who died many years before I was born, but because I had heard so many stories about him, I knew I had to explore his life as I researched the history of my Lewis family. He was born in 1892. He was my grandmother's baby brother, and as is common with the youngest male of a family of several females, his sisters loved and doted on the younger brother they called Zander. He grew up in the family household with his many siblings, and at the dawn of the twentieth century, his sister Sena's children were also living with them. Sena's children must have seemed like siblings to Zander since his niece Anna was just three years younger than him, and his nephew Steadman was his exact same age. According to legend, Alexander was of a very dark complexion and sported a mop of dark curly hair. He grew into a confident, defiant and what local white folks called an arrogant young man. Today those attributes might be admired – even valued – in a young Black man. But when Alexander Lewis was a young man, being Black and having that kind of attitude was very dangerous.

Sometimes near the end of the first decade, or near the beginning of the second decade of the twentieth century, Alexander Lewis married Roxie Skeeters. Roxie was born in Darlington County, South Carolina in 1894. The couple may have married in the area of her birth, but I'm not sure. I could find no records of their marriage in Columbus County, North Carolina. I did find a record of their unnamed, two-day old infant dying on February 28, 1924, so it may be, just *may be* safe to assume that they were married sometime before the child's birth, short life and subsequent death. He must have commanded a modicum of respect in the community because he had been appointed by Columbus County as a committeeman representative for the Mill Branch School which my Hill family had started. To make a living, Zander did farm work in the area, but he also traveled to New Orleans during the late 1920s to work on the fishing and shrimp boats there. The setting of the story of his demise passed down in our family took place on one of those shrimp boats in New Orleans. I had heard for years that Zander was a proud and confident Black man who would not submit to the subjugation demanded by white people. The white crew on the boat, growing weary of his attitude toward white racial authority, murdered him and threw his body overboard. His body was never found, and my grandmother grieved his death and bemoaned the fact that nothing was done about his murder until the day she died. I had heard of others in the family also saying that "Zander was killed on that shrimp boat and nothing was done about it!" Just like other family stories, some of it is probably true and some of it is definitely not.

After I had exhausted all of my avenues of research about Alexander Lewis, I started doing research on his wife Roxie Skeeters. It was during my research of her that I discovered something that is a family history researcher's dream. I found a picture of my great uncle Zander and great aunt Roxie.

It all started with Eyvonne Skeeters Crawford of Florence, South Carolina researching the history of her family and posting the information and a picture on the Internet of her grandmother Roxie Skeeters Lewis and her grandmother's husband Alexander Lewis. I was floored! I had never seen a picture of any of my grandmother's siblings, let alone one who had died so many years ago. Of course I had to contact Ms. Crawford. She told me what she knew about her grandmother, and I since she didn't know anything about Alexander's family, I told her what I knew about my great uncle's family. I asked Eyvonne if she knew the circumstances surrounding Alexander's death.

She said that she had been told by her older family members that several white men had come to Alexander and Roxie's home in Lees Township and had dragged him out in the middle of the night. They took him into a wooded area near Lees Lake, where he was killed. Although Eyvonne Crawford's version of the story is different from my family's version, I believe her version is closer to the truth because I have a copy of Zander's death certificate. It shows that he died on January 29, 1930 and he was buried on January 31, 1930. The location of his death is listed as Lees Lake, and not New Orleans. Perhaps he was taken by boat onto Lees Lake and killed by the men who had dragged him out of his house because the cause of death listed on his death certificate was "drowning accident". His body was not lost at sea, but is buried in the same place as my other Jones, Hill, and Lewis ancestors. He is buried in what once had been a part of Aunt Viola Hill's field but later became the Hill Family Cemetery.

Like so many other family stories, some of Alexander Lewis's story was true and some of it was not. I remain convinced however, that the part of the story about him being murdered is true, and another abiding truth is no one did anything about it.

Momma's Family, Joys and Sorrows

M ost of what we know about my family's history was passed from one generation to another by word of mouth. Oral history, as important as it is, sometimes adds and loses detail as it travels from the lips of one generation to the ears of the next. For most African Americans with a lineage of slavery, family history is a combination of a small amount of documented fact, what we have personally witnessed, and what we have been told by reliable sources. What I know about Momma's family is a combination of research by me and other family members, what I have seen, and just as important, what I was told.

My mother's family history odyssey obviously did not begin in the Lees Lake area of Columbus County North Carolina. But until I began this research, my knowledge of their history was limited to their Lees Lake years and beyond. This area was the genesis of most of the legends, stories, and traditions of both sides of my mother's family. Of all the stories handed down by the paternal side of my mother's family, the one that made the earliest impression on me as a young boy was about my great-great grandfather Henry Lewis. I had heard of his extraordinary accomplishments after emancipation, but the family narrative about his refusal to take his former slave master's last name was the one most interesting to me. Henry Lewis is the first person known on the parental side of my mother's family, and Esquire Lewis is the first person known on the maternal side of her family, so both sides of my mother's family was named Lewis. I had known that fact for years and had thought that perhaps both sides of her family coincidentally had slave owners named Lewis and took the Lewis name after emancipation. *Not so,* says family lore! The story passed down about my great-great grandfather claimed that his owner was not named Lewis. Our oral history contends that Henry married an unrelated Mary A. Lewis and chose to take her name rather than the former master that he so bitterly disliked.

I had imagined that after emancipation, Henry Lewis had not wanted to be chained to someone by name that had possibly held him in chains during slavery. Not taking the name of the person who owned you could have had serious consequences, and I thought that Henry Lewis must have understood those consequences as he stood his ground. White American literature and lore gave the appearance that the taking of the master's name after emancipation was done out of love and respect. That was not the case. It was done for a much more practical reason. The name that you took from your master not only identified you, but it also gave some indication of where you came from. After emancipation, former slaves roamed all over the south searching for family members who had been sold away to other locations. The classified sections of newspapers all over the south were filled with advertisements seeking information on lost children, siblings, parents and other relatives. One of the many tragedies of slavery was that hundreds of thousands of freed slaves grieved and searched for loved ones for years, never finding them. Finding a former slave with a common name like John, who could be in any former slave state, would have been close to impossible. However, if you knew that John had been owned by Master Smith on the Smith plantation, you might start your search for John Smith in the area of the Smith plantation location. If you had the name of your former slave relative and the location of the plantation where he was enslaved, you had information to assist you in your search. Most freed slaves could not read or write. Some had never set foot off of their master's plantation, yet with little or no resources, many of our ancestors sought desperately to reunite with loved ones scattered at the slave owners' will. During the period of the great American tragedy which my family called "slavery time," we were separated from our culture. We were human beings reduced to chattel whose only purpose was to make slave owners, the families of slave owners and the countries of slave owners rich! We suffered the humiliation of knowing that the physical bodies of what was most precious to us, our mothers, sisters and daughters were actually owned by another person who could do with them what he pleased. The emotional pain of having no control over your life or the lives of you family may have been greater than the pain of being chained or the pain of the whip. With all of the imagined and unimagined horrors of slavery our families endured, no horror, no act so cruel, no sin of slavery was greater than the separation of families. Slave history tells us that our ancestors would go to any lengths, including killing their children and themselves to avoid separation. Today we sometimes anguish over a short separation of a mate or a loved one. We struggle when our children decide to leave home, even if we know where they are going. Imagine having someone else making the decision to separate a mother from a child without regards to the feelings or welfare of mother or child. Separation of father or mother from family could be done at the will of the slave master. It could be done as retribution for a minor offense, financial gain or just on a whim.

Once slavery was finally over, many Americans felt that freedom itself was the balm that healed the wounds of slavery. Many still harbor this belief today. I believe that every act of slavery, every crime against humanity committed during the period impacts all of us even to this day. The separation of families had such a devastating effect on our people that the vestiges of that offense dramatically impacted us from the post-slavery period to the present day. Imagine the effect slavery had on a people in the immediate post-slavery period who heretofore had known no life other than one of bondage. Freedom itself may have provided the balm that healed many of the pains of slavery, but how does one get over the pain of losing his family and not being able to find them?

An early and very vivid description of the agony endured by the separation of slave families in America was published in 1844. It was an extremely important publication, as it was written by Moses Grandy, someone who experienced this painful separation first-hand. Moses Grandy was born into slavery in Camden County, North Carolina. After purchasing his own freedom three times before finally being set free, he wrote of his family being torn apart in his autobiography, *The Narrative of the Life of Moses Grandy*.

> "Of my other children, I only know that one, a girl named Betsy, is a little way from Norfolk in Virginia. Her master, Mr. William Dixon, is willing to sell her for 500 dollars.
>
> I do not know where any of my other children are, nor whether they be dead or

alive. It will be very difficult to find them out; for the names of slaves are commonly changed with every change of master: they usually bear the name of the master to whom they belong at the time. They have no family name of their own by which they can be traced. Owing to the circumstance, and their ignorance of reading and writing, to which they are compelled by law, all trace between parents and their children who are separated from in childhood, is lost in a few years. When, therefore, a child is sold away from its mother, she feels that she is parting from it forever: there is little likelihood of her ever knowing what of good or evil befalls it.

There are thus no lasting family ties to bind relations together, nor even the nearest and dearest, and this aggravates their distress when they are sold from each other. I have little hope of finding my four children again."

This story about the surname of my great-great grandfather was the first about him that I remember. Although he and the family he started have gone on to do and accomplish other great things, it was the story of this simple act of rebellion against the norm that caused me to stick out my chest and proudly proclaim that I was from that stock! Unfortunately, like so many other family stories, this one is not exactly true.

When I was directed to New Orleans by my cousin Carrie Jones Kemp to do research on the maternal side of my mother's family, I found evidence of my mother's maternal grandfather Esquire Lewis having been there. As I stated before, I found his name on the manifest of the ship in which he arrived to the slave market of New Orleans. I was so encouraged at finding his name on a manifest that I started searching the manifest records for slave ancestors from each of my family lines. After several days of carefully mining those manifest records, I finally struck gold. I could hardly believe my eyes! I found another ancestor!

A ship named Bachelor sailed into New Orleans Harbor on February 20, 1847. This ship also sailed from Richmond, Virginia just like the Phoenix, which brought Squire Lewis to New Orleans in February of the prior year. The Bachelor was also a barque type of ship just like the Phoenix. The two ships were likely owned by the same company, as their names appeared together in advertisements in Richmond newspapers during that time for the service of transporting enslaved human beings during the mid-1800's. The Bachelor's captain was Hiram Horton. My great-great grandfather Henry Lewis was listed with dozens of other men and women on that ship's manifest. From the description of the men and women held on that ship, they all appeared to be in the prime of their lives. The fact that they were healthy young men and women made them a valuable commodity for the bastion of antebellum commercialism: the New Orleans slave market. They would have likely been advertised as "prime number 1 Negroes" in the New Orleans slave market. Henry Lewis's description on that manifest was no evidence of his humanity. He was just "catalogued" with a description to satisfy the mandates of the 1808 law against the importation of slaves from Africa. Nevertheless, Henry Lewis was listed as male, age; 19, height; 5'6 ¼", color; black. He was owned by R. R. Beasley.

As is the case with most slaves, written records are rare. I could find no records of Henry Lewis in Richmond, Virginia, the demarcation point of The Bachelor, nor could I find any records in New Orleans other than the ones on the manifest. While the manifest told us that he was there, why he was there was another matter I could not help but contemplate. His prior owner could have sold him for any number of reasons. He could have been part of an estate settlement after his owner's death. He could have been the linchpin of a business deal, or at the prime age of nineteen, he may have represented a profit to his owner that just could not be passed up, even if it meant separating him from his family and sending him to market in New Orleans. He may also have been one of those "bad Negroes" who had to be sold before his influence infected the "good Negroes" his previous owner held in Virginia.

Slaves numbering in the hundreds of thousands – maybe even millions – were held at a location called the Lumpkin Jail, located in an area of Richmond called Shockoe Bottom, before being sold in the Richmond slave market or before being shipped to slave markets in New Orleans or Charleston, South Carolina. Rebellious, strong-willed or "bad" Negroes were sent to the specially designed whipping rooms in that prison where they were bound for twenty-four hours a day, starved and whipped into submission. Many slaves were beaten to death and buried at that location because they would not submit to their slave masters will. So infamous was the brutality in the Lumpkin Jail that it was nicknamed "The Devil's Half Acre." This area that saw so much human misery – the ground that still holds the blood and bones of captive people – now lies under a portion of I-95 and the campus of Virginia Commonwealth University.

Since most slaves in Richmond were held in Lumpkin's Jail before being sold, it is highly likely that my ancestors who were shipped from

Richmond to New Orleans were held there. There is no way to know what Henry Lewis experienced on The Devil's Half Acre or even why he was being shipped from Richmond, Virginia to the infamous New Orleans slave market pens. I most likely will never know. His travails in bondage from those slave pens to Lees Lake also may never be known. I have never heard stories of daily slave life being passed down by members of our family. What's the sense of passing down pain? While it was important for us to know our history, I guess that the pain associated with that history, they just wanted to forget.

New Orleans, Louisiana, Slave Manifests, 1807-1860 for Henry Lewis   Page 1 of 2

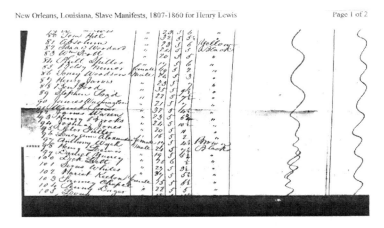

***** Listing of my mother's paternal great grandfather Henry Lewis on the manifest of The Bachelor when it docked in New Orleans on February 20, 1847.

44

The ship manifest records that I found in New Orleans provided some invaluable information on our family history and helped me set the record straight on one piece of family lore. As I had stated earlier, I discovered that the family legend about how Henry Lewis got his last name could not have happened. My great-great grandfather already had the Lewis surname when he arrived in New Orleans at nineteen years of age. His full name, Henry Lewis, is listed on the ship's manifest. He married Mary A. Lewis in 1866, so he had been a Lewis long before he married her. It's possible that he refused to take an owner's name earlier in Virginia, or maybe at some time later, he refused to take a name other than Lewis after emancipation. Perhaps after years of telling and retelling, the story was changed. Maybe the story that I admire so much has no truth in it at all. I now know for sure that Henry Lewis did not take his last name from his wife Mary A. Lewis. Another thing I know for sure is that Henry Lewis had to have had a defiant spirit to accomplish all that he did later in his life. I love his spirit. I also love the spirit of the story, and even though I now know the truth, in this one instance, I still hate to see the facts get in the way of a good family story.

Henry Lewis fathered a son who was born in the Lees Lake area on May 7, 1859. Now here is where the family name really gets confusing. Henry Lewis' son was named Henry Hill. Our family has no written or even oral record of Henry Hill's mother. We can only assume that her last name was Hill. Henry Hill's mother could have possibly died or was sold away when he was a very young child because he was raised by his aunt Viola Hill who was most likely the sister or aunt of his mother. When he was older, perhaps after emancipation, he moved to his father's house. He remained with or in close proximity to his father until his father died, but he retained the Hill name.

A common practice after emancipation was for freed slaves to remain on or near the plantation where they had been slaves and even work for their former slave masters. Since the south was in economic ruin and there was no money available for white farmers and plantation owners to pay for the labor that they had been getting for free, former slaves were often compensated with land of their own. Henry Lewis continued to work in the Lees Lake area, more than likely doing the same kind of work he had done while being enslaved. He worked until he had acquired one hundred fifty acres of land in the same area where he had once been a slave. When Henry Lewis died, his property fell to his son, my great-grandfather, Henry Hill.

On September 23, 1878, twenty-one year-old Henry Hill married seventeen year-old Fannie Parker. Fannie was the daughter of Riddick (Redie) and Winnie Parker. Their post office address was listed as Peacocks Store, Whiteville, Columbus County, North Carolina. Their wedding ceremony was performed by Manson Gore in the home of Henry Hill's father Henry Lewis. By the time their ten children – Lucy Jane, Albert, Eliza, my grandfather Luther, Calvin, Roland, Mary, James, Gertrude and Bertha – were adults, fifty of the one hundred and fifty acres owned by Henry Hill was cleared for planting and for the building of a home for each of his children. He flourished in the community and apparently was well-respected. He was the principle, founding member of Mill Branch Baptist Church. He also started a school in that church, and at one point, he was the census taker for the Black community of Lees Lake. Copies of the census information he gathered were in the possession of our family for several years before being turned over to the state of North Carolina for its historical significance. Some of the information I have viewed from census records in preparation for this book could have very well have been gathered by my own great grandfather, Henry Hill.

On December 26, 1907, Henry Hill's fourth child, my grandfather Luther Hill, married a beautiful young lady from the area by the name of Lilly Beulah Lewis. My grandfather Luther was 21, and my grandmother Lilly Beulah was 18. The wedding took place in the parlor of her father Esquire Lewis and was witnessed by Luther Bellamy, Will Davis, and my paternal great-grandfather, Peter Jones. My grandfather Luther Hill fathered ten children, just as his father before him had done. Luther and

Beulah's children were Carl Lester, Emma, Robert, my mother Lillie, Violet, Willie, Eva, Catherine, Nathaniel, and Mazie. Luther Hill was a minister by profession, but the economic realities of the time dictated that he also be skilled in other areas. Luther worked on the farm and he also did some work as a carpenter. I don't know if he ever made any money as a carpenter, but as late as 2003, I was able to see the results of work that he had done more that seventy-five years earlier. During an outing with my mother in the Welches Creek area, she directed me to an area of a church where her father Luther had pastured at one point during his young life. We entered the church's driveway and drove around to the rear of the fairly new brick church. Situated behind the new building was a very old, wooden structure. It looked out of place and I sensed that the only reason for it still being there was for some kind of historical significance. My mother, almost in tears, pointed at the structure and said, "My father built that church with his own hands."

The history of Columbus County written in the book *Recollections and Records*, published in 1980, made reference to Luther Hill cutting the logs into lumber for the building of the church in 1947. While the book did provide me with historical information on Whiteville and Columbus County, most of the information in the book comes from interviewing members of the Columbus County community, so some of the information in it is incorrect. The book also treated the rich history of African Americans in Columbus County as little more than just a footnote. My grandfather Luther Hill not only hewed the logs into lumber, but the book also fails to mention that he built the church, as my mother often said, "with his own hands." Members of that church have said for years that he was the builder. The information about the year the church was built is also incorrect. The church had to have been built in the nineteen twenties. By 1947, the year *Recollections and Records* states that the church was built, my grandfather had been dead for 19 years.

One after another, my grandfather's siblings moved from Lees Lake to places of different horizons and the promises of the warmth of other suns. His sister Bertha married and moved to Wilmington, North Carolina. His brother Roland and sometime later, his sister Mary began the migration of our family to Philadelphia and other northeastern cities, that caused more of our family to reside there than in North Carolina. My grandfather Luther, my grandmother Beulah, and their ten children remained on the family farm in Lees Lake, and according to my mother, they flourished there. Although they had little money, the hard-earned land that they believed that God had given to them provided everything that they needed. I was not aware that you could grow rice in that area, but my mother said that in addition wheat, sugar cane for molasses and every variety of vegetable, they also grew rice. Meat for their table was provided from the farm animals that they raised and an abundance of fish from nearby Lees Lake. Farmers, who did not have the ability to grind their own corn and wheat, could take it to the mill to be ground. The miller would take a portion of the goods as payment for turning corn and wheat into corn meal and flour. According to my mother, the only food that her father had to buy was an occasional bag of sugar, which he would bring with him when he returned from one of his preaching assignments. She said that all of the children would eagerly await their father's return to the farm because of the joy he would spread when he brought them a very special treat of peppermint candy.

My mother received a basic primary school education while living in the Lees Lake area. The two-room school that she attended at Mill Branch Baptist Church provided the only education available for children of color in that area. Grades one through four were taught in one room and grades five through seven were taught in the other. The teachers identified through historical church narratives were Mother Julia Baldwin and Miss Annie. I believe Miss Annie was my mother's cousin Annie Lewis-Jones who later married Jim Cato and became Annie Cato. My mother's father, Luther Hill, following in his father's footsteps became the principle and superintendent of the school. My mother said that since her family founded the school, taught in its classrooms, and was in charge of the school, she and her siblings believed that they should have been entitled to special privileges. She said that they got none! As a matter of fact, she said that she and her brothers and sisters got the "board of education" more than any of the other kids. The school at Mill Branch most likely only taught the very basic skills of reading, writing and arithmetic on an elementary school level. I don't think education for women was a high priority in Lees Lake during the second decade of the twentieth century when my mother would have been in school. After my mother completed her basic education, she left before completing middle school.

Additionally, local whites made it difficult for my mother and any other young Black people to attend school. Momma said that she and her young sisters and brothers had to walk several miles to and from school, while the local whites were bused. I imagine that her older brothers had completed or left school to work by this time, so these young children walking alone were an inviting target for the local white racists and mischievous young white kids as well. On almost a daily basis, as she and her siblings walked along the country roads leading to their schools, the bus carrying the white children would try to run them down. The Black children would run in terror, screaming to the delight of the driver and the children on the bus. The only way they avoided the bus was to run off of the road in the trees where the bus could not follow, or to jump into a ditch and soil their special school clothes. Escaping the bus did not mean that the fright and humiliation for the day had ended. The road that my mother had to walk to her school took her directly past the white school that the children on the bus attended. The white children knew the Black kids were coming, so they would prepare and lay in wait. Each day as my mother and her siblings passed the white school, they had to run the gauntlet with sticks, rocks and mud being hurled at them. After school had ended, my mother had to face the same hostilities she experienced that morning as she walked home from school. This was one of the many stories that were more painful for me than they were for my mother when she told them. These kinds of attacks did not seem to leave my mother with any ill feelings toward white people, nor do I believe that they were particularly traumatic for her. She seemed to shrug off those events without letting them harden her heart toward white people. She maintained an attitude of, *that's just the way it was.* It seemed to be just one of those things that you had to deal with twice a day in Columbus County, North Carolina if you wanted to learn to read and write.

I don't think that my mother ever believed that her education was adequate. Much later in her life, I remember her attending evening literacy classes taught by James Clarence Davis at Central

High School in Whiteville. She also caused quite a sensation when she enrolled in a class at Southeastern Community College at the age of eighty.

Although stories of my mother's attempts at obtaining an education troubled me more than it troubled her, she did relate one story to me that seemed to cause her great distress. She didn't speak of it often, but each time she did, I could see more than a half century of pain on her face every time she thought about it. When she was a very young child, my mother and her very best friend were playing a game of hide-and-seek in her yard. I don't know what the typical age would be for girls playing hide-and-seek during that time period, but I can imagine that they must have been very young. It was my mother's turn to cover her eyes and count to ten while her friend hid. Immediately after she finished counting, my mother started the search for her friend's hiding place. She searched all of the usual hiding places to no avail. After searching for several minutes, she alerted adults who began a wider search. An alarm went out to the community who expanded the search to an even greater area. Every place a child could possible hide was searched, but her friend was never found. To this day she was never seen or heard of again. My mother believed that her friend disappeared at the hand of someone who brought unspeakable harm to her. Every time Momma told this story, I could see in her face the suffering this event caused her. When I imagined what her little childhood friend endured, it filled me with rage. However, the story never filled Momma with rage. I don't know if she was capable of experiencing that through the pain she felt.

I know that my faith requires me to love and forgive even the vilest offenders. Even when someone commits one of those "difficult sins," God still commands us to love them. I admit that this tenant of my faith is a challenge for me. I don't think that there is any punishment too harsh for someone who harms a child. My sinful nature even longs for a chance for me to inflict the punishment. I know that it is wrong for me to feel this way and I pray for God's help with my failure to love someone so evil as to do harm to God's precious little ones. There is a famous scriptural reference of Christ's distain for offences against children. The Apostle and Biblical scripture writer Mark, wrote about Christ's feelings on the subject in Mark 9:42: *"And whosoever shall offend one of these little ones that believe in me, it is better for him that a millstone were hanged about his neck, and he were cast into the sea."* In short, God does not like it when you mess with His children, and neither do I.

From the first time I heard this story until I was well into adult life, I never considered the possibility that anyone other than a white person could have caused that child's disappearance. Growing up in the somewhat sheltered environment of my family village, and seeing my people in a mostly positive light, I believed that Black people just didn't do things like that. It had to be a white person who caused that child's disappearance. Of course I know better now. Evil is not a hallmark of or restricted to any race or class of people. We are all capable of it. It is only our relationship with God that determines our relationship with our fellow man. Christ's instructions to us in His new commandment is simple and very clear: love one another. When we sever a relationship with man, we sever it with God. When you harm a powerless child, you offend an all-powerful God. Final justice for such an offence will be much worse than the offender trying to tread water with a millstone necklace.

Recalling and writing what my mother told me about this unfortunate event, I had a chilling thought that I now realize was a blessing for me. When my mother played hide-and-seek with her best friend so long ago, if it had been my mother's turn to run and hide instead of count and seek, I might not be here to retell this story to you, and my children would not be here to read it.

Although many of my mother's remembrances of her Lees Lake childhood were of challenges suffered by all African Americans in the rural south during that period, there were far more stories that seemed to fill her with delight as she told them. One event that caused her to beam with pride when she spoke of it was the education of her father. Her comments about his schooling conveyed more admiration than boast or pride when she reminded us that her father was "the only colored preacher around here that went to seminary school." She said that he went to Shaw University. Of course I was intrigued by the notion of a man from Whiteville, North Carolina, married with at least five or six children at that time, pasturing a church, also going to Shaw University, over one hundred miles away in Raleigh. How was that possible? This was the early 1920s. I had to investigate this claim myself.

I knew that North Carolina State University had digitized old university catalogues from schools all over North Carolina because I had found the catalogues from The State Normal School that my father had attended on their website. The 1921 to 1930 catalogues from Shaw University proved to be very interesting reading, as I was able to find evidence that my grandfather had indeed attended Shaw University. Listed under "SPECIAL THEOLOGICAL" were twenty students. Among them was R. L. Hill from Vineland, N.C. R. L. was the initials for Robert Luther and Vineland was the original name for Whiteville. Scanning the catalogues also gave me an historical peek at the university the Black church in Whiteville looked on with such pride and claimed as their own. Shaw University was a Baptist school and they made it clear in their literature how the students were to conduct themselves. The requirements for attending church and the rules against arriving on campus or departing from campus on Sundays showed how serious Shaw University was about the demonstration of its faith. Excerpts that I took from the catalogue's school restrictions and the requirement for girls, which are reprinted below, also made for some interesting reading:

Restrictions

The following practices are forbidden: dancing, profanity, the use of intoxicating liquors and tobacco, card playing, betting and gambling.

No student is allowed to have in his possession pistols or other weapons, fireworks, gasoline, benzene or any flame-producing stove, candle, or heating devices.

REQUIREMENTS FOR GIRLS

Students are expected to dress neatly and modestly. Silk, satin, velvet, or expensive and showy coats, dresses and waists of any kind are not suitable for school wear, and will not be allowed.

A dark blue coat-suit should be provided. A plain, dark crepe de chine or plain pongee waist may be worn with the suit.

The restrictions on activities such as dancing, and the bold capital print heading for the requirement for girls indicated that my grandfather was unlikely to encounter rowdiness or any hoochie mamas during his time at Shaw.

Instead, the environment at Shaw was conducive to theology study by a serious, married pastor with children, but how could someone in his position manage going to college? To their credit, Shaw University recognized the need for pastors and other Christian workers to obtain the knowledge offered in their theology courses, but with the requirements of family and church duties, these pastors were unlikely to become traditional college students. To solve this problem, Shaw developed a course of study to accommodate those individuals. Students like my grandfather would travel to Shaw, spend three weeks in intense study, then return home for two weeks. They would then return for another three weeks of study to complete a semester. My grandfather followed this course of study each school year from 1921 through 1926. Again, to Shaw's credit, there was no tuition for this course of study; just the princely sum of $5.00 per week for room and board.

Researching Shaw University was very rewarding to me for several reasons. The first of which was my ability to confirm that my grandfather was a student there. Secondly, I made one of those discoveries that are always exciting to history researchers. I discovered that the history of my family and the history of my wife Carol's family intersected at Shaw University in 1921. After I found my grandfather listed in the catalogs at Shaw, I started to review the hometowns of all of the students to see if any other students were from Whiteville. I found students with the sir names of Pridgen, Peacock, and Powell who had listed Whiteville as their hometown. All three of those family names are still common to the area today. During my review of the students' hometowns, it surprised me to see so many students from out of state. Some had hometowns as far away as Providence, Rhode Island, New York and Philadelphia. I did not expect to see African Americans students traveling so far to attend school in the early twenties. The fact that they did travel such great distances shows how determined our ancestors were to be educated, and it also indicated how important Shaw was to the Black community at that time. As I continued my scan for the hometowns of my grandfather's classmates, I spotted Ocala, Florida. The sight of that city piqued my interest because I had visited Ocala twice. I traveled there in 2005 scouting areas in Florida to relocate, and again in 2011 to explore my wife's exciting and extensive family history there. Relatives of my wife's mother had immigrated to Ocala from Bermuda around the turn of the century and became very successful and wealthy businessmen there. When the family business patriarch, George Giles was refused admittance to a movie theater because of his race, he built one for people of color and named it The Metropolitan Movie Theater. He also owned The Metropolitan Cotton Gin, which provided services to the multitude of cotton growers in the area. They were owners of The Metropolitan Knitting Mills, which employed 75 people and manufactured knitwear to fulfill orders by the thousands for clients as far away as New York and Boston. The family in association with other Black business partners owned The Metropolitan Hotel with 25 guest rooms on the upper floor and stores and a barbershop on the lower floor. Their vast real estate holdings were controlled by The Metropolitan Real Estate Company. Until the Great Depression reversed their fortunes, my wife's Bermudian immigrant family members were successful and wealthy businessmen by any standard. By the way, to safeguard their wealth, they deposited their money into the family owned Metropolitan Bank. As my eyes traveled from the right side of the computer screen displaying the Ocala, Florida hometown, to the left side with the student's names, I could hardly believe what I was seeing. The student from Ocala was G. Kenneth Butterfield. Butterfield was the first cousin of my wife's grandmother, Winifred Giles Todd Ratteray. His family and my wife's grandmother's family were among those immigrants from Bermuda to Ocala. After his education at Shaw, Butterfield remained in North Carolina, married and became a dentist. His son, G.K. Butterfield, became a lawyer, and later a judge. He is currently the representative from the first congressional district in North Carolina to the congress of the United States. In 2014, he was elected chairman of The Congressional Black Caucus. G. K. is also an avid and passionate family genealogy researcher, and since he regularly speaks with his cousin, my wife Carol, I look forward to telling him that his father and my grandfather were students at Shaw University at the same time.

While doing this research, I gained a tremendous amount of respect for Shaw University. My admiration for that institution is now even greater than it was when as a child, I heard members of Mill Branch Baptist Church speak so reverently of it as they collected a few nickels, dimes and quarters to send to the school. I now have a better understanding of their love for the University. When we look back on our history and the crucial part that Shaw and other Historically Black Colleges and Universities played in the uplift of a people, we should look at them not only in awe, but with profound reverence. More importantly, knowing what we now know, how could we possibly withhold our support from them? We must do better. I must do better.

I also gained a higher level of respect for my grandfather, Robert Luther Hill. He was obviously a hardworking and determined man. He maintained a farm, supervised the school that the family started, constructed church buildings, preached the Gospel, took care of his family, and yet traveled back and forth from his home in Lees Lake to Raleigh all of those years to attend school. Perhaps that's why he died so young. Maybe he just flamed out! The story of his life should make all of us who carry his blood ashamed to think that we don't have the talent, time or resources to accomplish any goal for which God has given us vision. When we juxtapose our opportunities and achievements with his, we don't measure up. We've got huge shoes to fill. I promise R. L. Hill from Vineland, North Carolina that I will do better.

Life was changing in Lees Lake as all of Henry Hill's descendants, with the exception of my grandfather's family, were leaving. Still another change was coming to Lees Lake and the Hill family that would forever alter life as they knew it.

The late 1920s ushered in one of those bad clouds that just loomed over my family and the area they called home. That cloud signaled coming storms in the life of the Hill family that just hung out there on the horizon and presented a serious threat to their very way of life. On New Year's Eve 1928, my grandfather, forty-two year-old Robert Luther Hill died. I can just imagine the impact his death must have had on the family and the entire area. He was one of the few, if not the only educated Black minister in the community. He was the school principal, carpenter, farmer, community leader, and a church pastor. The long procession of family and friends walking behind the mule drawn wagon that carried his body from the family home to the Hill Cemetery was ample testament to his status in the family and in the community. At the head of the line was my forty year-old newly widowed grandmother, followed by her ten children. The age ranges for the children went from Carl Lester at twenty years to Mazie Bell at twenty months. My mother's age fell somewhere in the middle. My grandfather was buried on January 2, 1929 in the family cemetery among his Hill ancestors and his wife's Lewis relatives. With its leader now gone, the Hill family now faced the real possibility of having to give up their homestead in Lees Lake. My great, great grandfather Henry Lewis' sweat purchased every inch of the one hundred and fifty acres that made up our family's property in Lees Lake Township. My great grandfather Henry Hill cleared fifty acres of that land for planting and provided for his ten children on that land. My mother and all of her siblings were born on that land and were fed from the bounty garnered from it. This land had been passed down from two generations. The ancestors were buried there. Racial hostilities and common everyday hardships caused others to move on, but this family did not. This was their home. This was their world. They did not want to leave, but the coming storm that blew a strong bitter wind all over the nation damaging, changing, and even taking lives, was blowing across Columbus County, North Carolina and forcing the Hills from their land. Just as with the wind, they could do nothing about it! The bitter wind we colloquially called Hoover Time.

When I was young, I never heard my parents, my relatives, or other Black people of their generation refer to that extremely difficult period in American history from 1929 to 1940 as the Great Depression. Since President Herbert Hoover's administration ushered in the depression and he is widely blamed for it, they referred to that period as "Hoover Time." The Great Depression, or Hoover Time, signaled a death knell to our family's existence in Lees Lake Township. The precious land owned by my family had always provided for their needs. They had an abundance of food at a time when people in America's cities were starving. They had shelter when many others who did not own their land were homeless. The one thing that they did not have was money. Back taxes were overdue on the one hundred and fifty acres that the family owned and they could not pay. Hoover Time was a tough and frightening period. My family had no money, their friends had no money, and there was no work, so they could not earn the money. Thousands of African American families have had millions of acres of land stolen – yes I said stolen – because they could not pay some small debt or a few tax dollars. This story is not unique to the Hill family. I have heard this same haunting reframe from Black friends and acquaintances who had valuable family real estate lost in the same manner. Their family inheritance was lost in places like northern Virginia, which is now an expensive metropolitan area; the low country of Hilton Head South Carolina, which is now a very expensive resort area; Savannah Georgia; and the coastal areas of northeast Florida. The landscape in all of those places may be different from my family's American homeland, but the stories of land lost are the same as the Hill family story in Lees Lake.

To prevent the family property from being taken by the county, my family sold the ground earned by the sweat of Henry Lewis. The same ground that now held the bones of Henry Lewis, Henry Hill, Luther Hill and many other family members and friends who had gone on glory. From the proceeds of the sale, the family purchased a much smaller but suitable piece of property for their family to live. The money that was left over after the purchase of the new property was to be divided between my mother and all of her siblings. My mother told me that as long as she lived, she would never forget the sorrow she felt at that time. This land was made possible by the sweat of her great-grandfather; it was made fertile by the sweat of her grandfather, and it was the inheritance of her father. One might think that my mother should have been happy and excited. She was a young girl about to move to a new area, and her share of the proceeds of the sale would have been considered a windfall for someone so young.

She was neither happy nor was she excited about leaving Lees Lake. I don't think she ever got over the sadness of losing her family home. From the sale of her family inheritance, my mother's share was twelve dollars.

With the proceeds from the sale of their farm in Lees Lake, Grandma Beulah, who by then everyone called Bert, purchased property in the Cherry Grove section of Whiteville, North Carolina. This area of Whiteville is about eight to ten miles north of Lees Lake on Highway 130. During the late 1920s or early 1930s when my mother's family moved to the Cherry Grove, it was far from being as developed as it is today, but it did not have the open spaces and large farms that they knew in Lees Lake. Their new home might have some country roads to walk, but not the well-beaten footpaths that led to the homes of aunts, uncles, cousins and friends. It might even have a place to fish, but it would not have the secret locations so familiar to them at the lake. Their new home had a pecan tree, but not the room for the grove of walnut trees, and all of the fruit trees that they were accustom to. The new home had land for gardening and for raising a few hogs, but nothing like the acreage they owned in Lees Lake. That life was now gone.

The Cherry Grove section of Whiteville, North Carolina was now their new home and they would begin a new life. They would have to make do. They still had the most important thing in life. They had family. Even the hammer blows of Hoover

Time could not change that. With a loving family, maybe the new home and new land would yield wonderful memories just as Lees Lake had done. Maybe it would produce pleasant memories of a warm home, memories of a loving community, a very special village, and memories of a father who would always return home to excited children with a gift of peppermint candy.

Every person that I have ever known who experienced the Great Depression seemed to be of a different breed. They are just different from the generation that followed them. When they speak of life, finances, and the general conditions of that time, you get a genuine since that they have really been through something extreme. The depression generation of my family members became savers and perhaps even hoarders. They are careful with every dime earned and careful not to be wasteful of what they had. They insisted that the generation that followed them buy property, educate themselves and save their money. If you listen carefully and observe closely, you will hear in their speech and see by their actions some signs of paranoia. It may be a healthy paranoia, if there is such a thing, but they seem to be a little obsessively cautious. They believed that the depression not only could happen again, but that it *would* happen again. Whenever there was a downturn in the economy, my parents would fear that we were "getting ready to go through Hoover Time again." I listened to their stories and I understood their fear. Hoover Time had a dramatic effect on their lives.

While they were not in a position to prepare for and could do little about the effect of the depression on their lives, they wanted to be ready for the next Hoover Time. As the children and grandchildren of the depression era generation, whatever giant steps we have taken or achievements we have made were largely due to guidance of our people who experienced Hoover Time.

SACRED GROUND

～✦～

"*H*eavenly *father, I just wanna thank ya this mornin that I woke up in my right mind. I thank ya Lawd that the walls of my room were not the walls of my tomb, that my bedclothes were not my winding sheets and my bed was not my cooling board.*"

As a child, I heard those phrases repeated over and over as part of the rhythmic, passionate, and fervent prayers sent up from the pews of the church in our community, Cherry Grove Baptist Church, and from our family church, the beloved Mill Branch Baptist Church. While I always listened intently, I had no idea what the deacon uttering that prayer was talking about. What was a winding sheet? What was this cooling board? Ever inquisitive, I eventually asked my father what they were talking about when this prayer was prayed. His explanation led to my understanding of the way of life for the family that came before me, and also a way of death.

The practice that even predates America was to bury the dead in a sheet or a shroud rather than an expensive dress or suit of clothes. The deceased would be washed and in some cases massaged in oils and perfumes, wrapped or *wound* in a sheet as preparation for burial. The body would then be laid out or displayed on a wooden board sometimes overnight to cool before being transferred to a plain, wooden box for burial. Store-bought or manufactured cooling boards could be adorned with ornate sheer materials to add a measure of status and class to the viewing of the deceased. It is unlikely that the kind of cooling board referenced in the prayers I heard, and the kind used for my ancestors were anything fancy. They were more likely to be just wooden slabs. Thus the terms of winding sheets and cooling boards were the plain but necessary instruments used to prepare a body for eternal rest.

The death certificates that I have seen for my family members indicate that some of them were buried with the services of an undertaker, while some were not. It was likely that even though the services of an undertaker were acquired, embalming did not take place during those early years. In many of the recorded cases, burial took place the day after the date of death. That would indicate to me that embalming was not a common practice, or a quick burial made the expense of embalming unnecessary. Our ancestors' wound bodies likely were displayed overnight in the family's home as relatives sat up through the night guarding the remains of their loved ones. The next day, they were buried in the Hill Cemetery, always facing the rising sun of the east and their Mother Africa.

The one hundred acres of land that Henry Lewis had carved from the forest and thickets of Lees Township provided the means for his descendants to make a decent living. A small portion of a cleared field on that land provided a decent place for their bodies to rest when their lives were over. Most of the current living descendants of Henry Lewis and Henry Hill could not point to the exact location of that plot of ground that holds the bones of their honored ancestors. They just know that the Hill Cemetery is somewhere on the land that once belonged to our family.

Many years ago, my mother and I were touring the area in Lees Lake Township where both sides of my family had once lived. As we drove the back roads of Lees Lake Township, she was constantly pointing out the areas where several relatives had lived including the homestead of my father's family. The driving tour and commentary by my mother of where she spent her childhood was interesting, but after a while, we both wanted to feel that historic earth under our feet, so we stopped the car and walked around while she continued to reminisce. It was during this time that she pointed in a northeastern direction from where we were standing and informed me that the Hill Cemetery was over in that direction. Some twenty years after that outing with my mother, I discovered that the cemetery was not located in the clump of trees where I assumed she was pointing. After an exhausting all day search that included speaking with several members of the presently all-white community, and with the help of my brother Jerry, I finally located the Hill Cemetery. The site is in a thicket adjacent to a cleared field just off of Highway 130 in Lees Township. While I found it to be in the direction that my mother had pointed out to me, it is situated about a mile from the point where I thought my mother had indicated.

No one knows the exact number of family members buried in the Hill Cemetery. The identities of everyone buried there is also unknown. Hill family descendants had assumed that only members of the Hills of my grandfather's family and the Lewis' of my grandmother's family were buried there, but I know that non-relatives are buried there also. The death certificate of my great-grandfather Peter Jones indicates that he was buried there. The death certificates of my father's mother, Maggie Jones, just indicate that she was buried in Lees Township. It makes no reference to The Hill Cemetery, but I am almost certain that my mother told me that she was also buried there. The list that I have created contains the names of people that I believe are buried in the family cemetery. There is no documented proof of some of the names on the list, but they were added because it would have been impractical to bury them at any other location. For example, there is no oral or written record of the burial place of Henry Lewis and his wife Mary. It is a safe assumption, however, that they were buried in the family cemetery on their own land. Henry Hill and his wife Fannie Parker had a child that they named Lucy Jane. The child was stillborn or died the same day of her birth, August 26, 1881. Zander Lewis and his wife, Roxie Skeeters, had the same experience with an unnamed child on February 26, 1924. Although there are no records stating where their children were buried, it is only logical that they would have been buried in the family cemetery on the farm where they were living at that time.

The Hill Cemetery was not only the place where family members were laid to rest, but it also served as a final resting place for others in the community who needed a place to bury their dead. As I indicated earlier, my paternal great-grandfather Peter Jones is buried there. He no longer owned his farm and was living on rental property when he died on October 22, 1940, so it's understandable that his family would have needed a place to bury him. When my maternal grandmother, Maggie Jones died on October 10, 1918, she was living on the Jones family farm. As it was a common practice to bury people on their own land at the time, there is a possibility that she could be buried on what was then Jones family property instead of The Hill Cemetery. Since I believe my mother told me she was buried in The Hill Cemetery, I have listed her with others that I have determined through research, oral history and logical conclusions are buried in the place the Columbus County courthouse records first described as Aunt Viola Hill's field.

The Hill Cemetery located in the little patch of earth in a clump of trees just a short distance from Highway 130, in Lees Lake Township has gone unattended for more that seventy five years. The owners of the land have respected what they assume are the boundaries of the cemetery by not clearing the trees and underbrush and adding the land to their income-producing acreage. That's about all of the respect it has received. There is no marker denoting its historical significance or even common signage indicating its existence. You won't see manicured grass, tombstones or even grave markers there. You won't even see the symbol of the cross my ancestors rejoiced in bearing. There is nothing to indicate that people who were loved and respected are buried there. There are just trees and a dense briar thicket. Although that little plot of land goes primarily unnoticed, our current family came into the world and into Columbus County, North Carolina through those vessels who lay beneath the rich black earth there. Even though it has been largely neglected, it is still sacred ground.

	NAME	DATE BORN	DATE DIED	SPOUSE	FATHER	MOTHER
***	Henry Lewis	1827		Mary A. Lewis	Unknown	Unknown
***	Mary A. Lewis	1835		Henry Lewis	Unknown	Unknown
***	Lucy Jane Hill	8/26/1881	8/26/1881		Henry Hill	Fannie Parker
*	Dollie Ann Lewis	1850	10/22/1914	Esquire Lewis	Unknown	Unknown
*	Esquire Lewis	1837	6/10/1917	Dollie Ann Lewis	Unknown	Unknown
**	Maggie Yeoman Jones	5/18/1890	10/11/1918	Seymore Jones	George Yeoman	Ellen Baldwin
***	Unnamed Baby Lewis	2/26/1924	2/26/1924		Alexander Lewis	Roxie Skeeters
*	Hattie Lewis Hemmingway	1888	11/19/1925	Manson Hemmingway	Esquire Lewis	Dollie Ann George
*	Robert Luther Hill	6/16/1886	12/31/1928	Lilly Buleah Lewis	Henry Hill	Fannie Parker
*	Henry Hill	5/7/1859	7/3/1929	Fannie Parker	Henry Lewis	Unknown
*	Alexander Lewis	6/12/1897	1/29/1930	Roxie Skeeters	Esquire Lewis	Dollie Ann George
*	Fannie Hill	1860	6/6/1934	Henry Hill	Reddick Parker	Winnie Parker
*	Senna Lewis Jones	1873	2/6/1935	Peter Jones	Esquire Lewis	Dollie Ann George
*	Peter Jones	7/5/1861	10/22/1940	N. Smith / Senna Jones	Melvin Jones	Rebecca Baldwin
**	William "Bud" Jones	08/06/1885	2/18/1943		Peter Jones	Niney Smith
	* Death Certificate					
	** Oral History					
	*** Logical Conclusion					

Family members buried in The Hill Cemetery

LEES LAKE, BIRTHPLACE OF FAMILY AND FAMILY LEGENDS

Lees Lake Township is about ten miles south of the town of Whiteville, North Carolina, and about three miles south of the Mill Branch church so prominent in my family's history. Lees Lake Township was not then nor is it now a metropolitan area or even a small town. No central commercial area exists now or when Peter Jones moved there. As far anyone knows, it has always been rural farmland. It had a lake for fishing, abundant hunting areas, and rich soil for planting, but I imagine that Welches Creek also had all of those attributes, so we really don't know why Peter Jones relocated some twenty five to thirty miles from Welches Creek to Lees Lake Township. Perhaps it was just kismet that led him to Lees Lake. Maybe he just fell in love with the area, or maybe he fell in love with someone who lived there.

Peter Jones, the forty year-old widowed father of six children, married Ann Sena Lewis on January 19, 1901. Perhaps moving from Welches Creek to Lees Lake was a condition that had to be met before Sena would marry Peter. Since she was twenty-five years of age and already had a nine year-old son named Steadman and a five year-old daughter named Annie, she could have needed the moral and physical support of her family to take on the responsibility of an older husband and a readymade family. Why Peter moved to Lees Lake is one of the many questions I wish I had asked family elders before they passed on. Since anyone who would have that kind of information has already made their transition, many family history questions like this one may never be answered.

My step-great-grandmother, Sena Lewis was a legend in the Jones family. Members from every branch of the Jones family tree has their own stories about how this woman loved, protected, and cared for children who were not her own. Sena had to be a mother to Peter's oldest daughter Lutisia, who at fifteen years of age was just ten years younger than she. Next, at fourteen was William, who the family called Bud. He and others with his malady were referenced as "deaf and dumb" as he could neither speak nor hear. The other children were Hattie, eleven; my grandfather Seymore was ten; Henry Jeff was eight; and a baby named LuGene was just two years of age. In addition to caring for her own biological children, Sena's dedication to her husband's children and family won for her the love and respect of everyone in the Lees Lake community.

All of the children of Peter Jones, including my grandfather, Seymore Jones, grew to adulthood in Lees Lake Township, but they in all likelihood, maintained ties to the Welches Creek community. At some point during my grandfather, Seymore's early adult life, he met Maggie Yeoman, who was a native of the same area near Welches Creek where he and his family had once lived. They were married on September 30, 1910. My grandfather was twenty-one years of age. Official documents list my grandmother's age in the year she was married as twenty. I don't believe that was the case. I believe that she was much younger. During those years Black folks were issued no birth certificates, so a person's official age was based on what was reported to the authorities. What was reported in some cases was an estimate. In other cases it may have just been what the person doing the reporting wanted to tell the officials recording the information. Such a system left room for a multitude of errors. My father always said that his mother and his Uncle Willie (Yeoman) were twins, yet his birth year is listed as 1886 and his sister's birth year is listed as 1890. If they were indeed twins, I believe both of those birth years are incorrect. My conclusion comes from two sources. The first is from statements made by my grandfather Seymore for several decades. He had always said that he married at twenty-one but that my grandmother was a young teenager. Secondly, I believe she was younger based on information I received from my mother's Aunt Gertrude Hill Bellamy. Aunt Gert told me that my grandmother was her best friend. She said she was with her when she died. She said that my grandmother was in her very early twenties when she died. (Not almost twenty nine, as her death certificate states.) Based on this information, I believe that she was about fourteen or fifteen when she married and was about twenty-one or twenty-two when she died.

Maggie Yeoman Jones had long, straight hair and a very light skin color that conveyed Native American or Caucasian ancestry. My grandfather said that her skin was so light that she was often mistaken for white. Being Black and mistaken for white could have been more than just an inconvenience or an embarrassment in Columbus County, North Carolina in 1910. Being mistaken for white and associating with a Black man could have brought harm to the woman and death to the man. To give the allusion that they were not a couple, my grandfather said that he sometimes walked behind her when they traveled by foot so he would not be beaten or even killed by the self-appointed racist enforcers of American apartheid.

The marriage of Seymore and Maggie produced four children. My father, James Wayland, was the oldest, followed by Henry, Ellen and Adell. Before my father was ten years of age, history had repeated itself and another young mother in the Jones family had died. My great-grandmother Nina died as a young woman leaving behind young children, and less than twenty years later, my grandmother Maggie died and left young children. Her death certificate list the cause of death as congestive chills. I was told by my father that she died of pneumonia. If antibiotics had been discovered by that time, they certainly were not available to poor rural Black people, so pneumonia was often fatal. Whether the family was told it was congestive chills or pneumonia that took her life, it was probably just an educated guess as she was not being attended by a doctor. Sena, the wife of my grandfather, Peter Jones, had fulfilled her role as mother, raising her stepchildren after their own mother Nina had died. She was once again called upon to fill the role of mother to her step-grandchildren following the death of my grandmother Maggie. My father was the oldest child at nine, his brother Henry was about seven, his sister Ellen was about three, and the baby, Adell was the youngest at about ten months of age. While my father and Uncle Henry remembered and loved their biological mother, it was the woman they called Aunt Senni who they adored for her motherly love and extraordinary sacrifice for their well-being.

My father's step-grandmother, Sena Lewis Jones, was also the sister of my maternal grandmother Lilly Beulah Lewis Hill. My grandmother Lilly, or Bert as we called her, had ten children while she lived in Lees Lake. To Grandma Bert's ten children and their multitude of cousins, Sena Lewis was simply their Aunt Senni. Since my father and his brother and sisters were neighborhood children, they also referred to her as Aunt Senni. Everyone in the community had grown accustomed to hearing my father address my mother's aunt as Aunt Senni, so they assumed that he was related to her also. My mother even told me that when the news of her impending marriage to my father was made public, several people in the little community asked with amazement, "you are going to marry your cousin?"

Of the many stories that I have heard about members from both sides of the family, the most have been about Aunt Senni. Her niece, my mother, told me that she really loved children and dedicated her life to them. When she was visiting others in the neighborhood, she would always be in a hurry to get back to the children. When someone gave her fruit of or some other small gift, she would make sure she had enough for the children. She seemed to always be on the lookout for something, no matter how small or seemingly insignificant to take back to my father, his brother and his sisters. It was this dedication to the care of her step-grandchildren that caused my mother and father to speak of her with a special reverence. During one of my many conversations with my mother about Aunt Senni, she paused and said, "Wait a minute." She then left the room and returned a few minutes later with an old faded, dilapidated picture. I was shocked when she said,

"This is Aunt Senni." Wow, all of the years of talk about Aunt Senni, I never imagined a picture of her existed anywhere, especially hidden away in a bottom drawer in my mother's bedroom. After a costly process of having the picture restored, I made a comment to the photographer that this woman was a legend in my family. The photographer, sensing that the woman in the picture was special to me, said "Oh really, tell me about her." I was glad he asked as it gave me another opportunity to honor her. After spending more time than he had intended listening to me go on about who she was, where she came from and what she meant to both sides of my family, I could tell by the expression on his face that he wish he had never asked. Several times a day I am reminded of Lees Lake and that great lady as I gaze at her picture on the wall of my home office. I can tell. I can see it in her face. That woman was somebody special!

After my grandmother Maggie died, my grandfather Seymore left his four children in the care of his father, Peter Jones, and his second wife, Sena, and moved back to the Welches Creek / Bolton area. In 1922, he married a young woman named Laura Lillian Belle Peacock. I understand that she, like my grandmother Maggie, was a very attractive woman. My grandfather was small in stature, not practically handsome, and did not have a lot of prospects for a bright financial future. In spite of his shortcomings, during a thirteen year period of time, he somehow convinced two very beautiful women to marry him. He and his wife were living in Wilmington, North Carolina, when their son Walter was born. Seymore, his new wife and six month-old son Walter, moved to Philadelphia around 1923. I was told that he moved there because construction jobs building the Philadelphia Subway System were plentiful. He readily found construction work in Philadelphia during the expansion of the subway system. He also worked as a longshoreman on the docks in Philadelphia. The toughest men in the city worked on the Philadelphia waterfront. As I stated earlier, my grandfather was short with a slight build, but he must have been a rugged individual, because he worked those docks for many years.

In Philadelphia, my grandfather and his wife had three more children, Juanita, Isabella (Kitty) and Rudolph before they divorced in 1930. Although his North Carolina family knew he was living in Philadelphia, his children in Whiteville had no contact with him until my father made his first pilgrimage to Philadelphia in the mid 1950s. Prior to that visit, my grandfather Seymore had not seen or had any contact with my father for well over thirty years. When they finally met, Seymore had no idea who my father was. During that trip, my father learned about his father's life in Philadelphia, and although he never got to know them very well, he learned about his Philadelphia born siblings for the first time. Of all of the discoveries my father made on that first trip to Philadelphia, there was one revelation that made the journey worthwhile for him. Before that trip, I had sensed a feeling in my father of total abandonment by his father. His father had left four children who ranged in age from about one to ten years, to be raised by their grandfather and step-grandmother. Long overdue conversations between my father and grandfather that went well into each evening produced not only a wealth of knowledge, but may well have produced some measure of redemption. For the first time, my father learned that there had been communications been his father and grandfather during his childhood. He learned that his father had sent money home at least once. My grandfather had remembered sending money home during the mid-1920s to have my father's tonsils removed. My father had remembered being gravely ill with tonsillitis when he was about twelve years old. He remembered that there was no money for doctors or the hospital, so his condition just got worst each day. My father also remembered when his grandfather acquired the money for the procedure, although my father never knew how his grandfather had gotten the money. In my father's eyes, this meant that his father had not totally abandoned him and his siblings in North Carolina. My father felt good about that. I guess when you are searching for a reason to renew a thirty-year lost relationship, you take what you can get.

Seymore Jones never returned to North Carolina. According to Jones family history, there had been an issue between him and some white person back in Columbus County. During the early 1920's, if a Black person had an issue with a white person, the Black person usually *became history!* The prevailing attitude and rule of law in the Jim Crow south at that time was that A Black man had no rights a white man was bound to respect. Philadelphia may have been a safe haven for my grandfather. I'm certain that my father was not aware that there may have been extenuating circumstances that caused his father to leave North Carolina and never return. Had my father known this, I'm sure the thirty year separation would have been a little more palatable for him. For whatever reason, my grandfather remained in Philadelphia until his death in July of 1973. He is buried in the Philadelphia suburb of Bala Cynwyd, Pennsylvania.

My father completed all of the secondary education available to him while growing up in Lees Lake. He attended the school at Mill Branch started by my Hill family as it was the only school available for Blacks in the area. There were no forms of higher education available to my father in the Columbus County area, so after he completed the Mill Branch School, he left home to attend The State Colored Normal School in Fayetteville. Years later, the normal school my father attended became The Fayetteville State University. Normal schools were established to train young people to teach in North Carolina schools. If you signed a pledge to teach school once you had graduated, your tuition was free. If you did not sign the pledge, the tuition was ten dollars. I don't know if my father signed the pledge to teach that would allow him to attend for free, but I do know that he sought higher education because he had wanted to be a doctor. I had always assumed that he wanted to be a doctor because of all of the sickness, including his own sickness, and death he had witnessed as a child due to the lack of medical care. The State Colored Normal School and the city of Fayetteville opened up a whole new world to the country boy from Lees Lake. James Troy, a cousin from back home in Columbus County, was already a student at the school, so he was invaluable in helping my father adjust to the new environment, and helping him find work. My father always spoke fondly of the time he spent there learning, playing football, and courting the girls. Although he came from a far different background than some of the other students there, he said that he was well liked and well treated while there. But as much as he enjoyed school life, he did not complete his education. He dropped out of The State Colored Normal School in Fayetteville that had broaden his horizons, and returned to the familiarity of Lees Lake.

Dropping out of school was a decision my father regretted all of his life. Although the normal school learning experience served him well, he could not to become a doctor or a teacher without completing his education. Long after he was married and had children, he would wax nostalgic about his days at normal school and often spoke about going back to school again. He would calculate the age he would be if he went back to college and then completed medical school without talking about the unlikely probability of being able to complete such a task with a family and no money. I once asked him why he dropped out of school if he loved it so much. I expected him to tell me about the racial prejudice of the time that made it difficult to get an education. I thought perhaps I would get a story about a country boy from Lees Lake having an insurmountable problem with a powerful professor. I expected to hear that the expense was too high; his family just could not afford it. I heard none of these things. He simply answered, "Back then, I thought school was too hard, I just didn't want it [an education] badly enough."

YEARS LOST, LOVE FOUND

After my father left The State Colored Normal School in Fayetteville and returned home to Lees Lake, the next few years of his life were, to put it mildly, nonproductive. He was a young adult, without much direction, who filled those years mostly with drinking and riotous living. During that period, he also forged a reputation for being strong, tough and a good fighter. The teetotaler Christian husband and father of four children that I knew always seemed to be very careful of how he spoke of this period in his life. The drinking, and comical things that happen as a result of drinking, he would talk about. The fighting, he would not talk about. His stint in prison, he would talk about. What he did that landed him in prison, he would not talk about. Since his life during this period was not an open book, and we all know that Black families are very good about keeping secrets, what I know about this phase of his life is mostly a patchwork of what he told me, combined with information I've gathered from conversations with folks outside of the family.

The folks in Whiteville, where we lived, referred to the towns of Welches Creek, Clarkton, Bolton, and a few other small communities northeast of Whiteville as "Across the Marsh." A swamp or marsh separated that area of Columbus County from Whiteville, so efficient southern linguistics dictated that we label the entire region Across the Marsh. If you wanted the best homemade wine that could be found anywhere in North Carolina, you went Across the Marsh to get it. In dad's opinion, the best wine available from Across the Marsh, was found in Welches Creek. As a young man, my father loved to drink wine, and he loved the wine from Welches Creek. Whenever his weekend scheduled allowed, he and his friends would head to the area where at least three generations of his family had lived. He knew many of his relatives still living in Welches Creek and his folks made the best wine in the area. If they did not have a good supply themselves, they knew where to get it. Once he and his friends acquired the best local wine, they would drink until they were "fall down drunk." My father said that he and his Across the Marsh buddies loved the wine so much that they would sometimes put down their drinking cups, lie directly under the open tap on the wine barrel, and let the wine flow directly from the tap into their mouths. Can you imagine the wild partying that went on in Welches Creek following one of those drinking sessions?

My great-grandfather, Peter was well aware of my father's rowdy reputation and his love of the grape. Sometimes during the late twenties or early thirties, Grandpa Peter was somehow able to purchase a new Model A Ford. On second thought, I don't know if it was new, as in the current year's model, or if it was just new to them. Realizing their economic condition, it was probably just new to them. My father wanted to barrow the car for a Sunday excursion to the beach in South Carolina. After listening to my father's incessant pleas, Grandpa Peter finally gave in and agreed to let him take the car. There was one condition. Because of my father's reputation for getting drunk, my father's younger brother Henry had to drive the car. With the driving arrangements agreed upon, the two Jones brothers set out for the beach with their girlfriends. (I don't think that my mother was one of the girls) What Grandpa Peter failed to realize was that my Uncle Henry had by this time developed his own reputation as one who loved a good time. The party apparently started soon after they left their home in Lees Lake, and continued on their way to the South Carolina shore. When they finally reached the beach, the group was filled with jubilation and alcohol. In fact, Uncle Henry was so drunk that he could no longer control the car. When he reached the shoreline, he could not stop the car, so he drove Grandpa Peter's new Model A Ford directly into the ocean. My father would howl with laughter when he would tell us this or other hilarious stories about his youth. He really enjoyed telling us about his younger years even though they painted a picture so different from the person he had become. Maybe that was the reason he enjoyed telling them.

My father told me far too many stories about his young adult life to mention here, but some events, although not off limits, were not discussed with the openness as others. Any information about violence during that period, he seemed to hold close to the vest. I had to get the stories of his fighting from others in the neighborhood. It was through an afternoon visit to my barbershop that I first learned that my father had even been capable of violence.

A true sign that you are moving from childhood into young adulthood, is when you are allowed to go to the barbershop on your own. At about twelve or thirteen years old, I considered myself a big boy, and I was glad I no longer had sit in my aunt Eva's kitchen and get my hair cut by my uncle WM. My uncle's first and middle name was William McKeithan. He was called WM, either the abbreviation for his first name or the initials from both names. All of the locals who knew him, still truncated his initials, and pronounced his name "Doubem." Although not licensed, he was a very good barber, who used a double edge Gillette razor blade, carefully balanced between his thumb and index finger to shave hairlines as expertly as any licensed barber with a straight razor. The twenty five cents a head that he charged was also a bargain, but just like all young Black boys, I wanted to be in the barbershop with the grown men.

As a young teenager, I was excited to be at Godbolte's barbershop on Franklin Street in Whiteville. Franklin Street separated the business section of downtown Whiteville from the Black residential community in the city we simply referred to as The Hole. I had several school friends who lived in The Hole, but since we lived out of the city in rural South Whiteville, I was not allowed to go there. Two local juke joints, Punk's Place and The Black & Tan were located in The Hole. On almost every weekend, it was not unusual to hear that someone had been cut or shot in one of those clubs. The whole area was considered dangerous and my mother just didn't want me down there. My cousin, Rodney Bell had died in a suspicious fire while asleep at his girlfriend's house in that neighborhood. A rumor that the house had been deliberately set ablaze by a jealous suitor quickly spread all over town. Because my mother considered The Hole so dangerous, I could go no further in its direction than Godbolte's Barber Shop on Franklin Street, which bordered the neighborhood. One Saturday afternoon, during what had to be one of my very early visits to the shop, I was sitting in one of the shop's side chairs, waiting my turn to have my hair cut by my barber Charles Burris. If your barber was skilled, there was bound to be a wait for his services on a Saturday afternoon. Most folks didn't mind the wait because while you waited, you sat and listen to or participated in "man gossip." A major reason boys like to visit barber shops is because of the back and forth bantering, the sports talk, the jokes, and the outright lies about one's past exploits and sexual conquests. On this afternoon, the gossip was hot and heavy. Using barbershop language, I would say that *"the shit was flying."* During one of their conversations about who was a bad ass back in the day, my barber Charles Burris, pointed to me and said, "Your daddy was one of them." I was surprised at his comment because Charles was not of my father's generation. As a matter of fact, he was just a few years older than my brother Jaye W, so I shot back the question, "What, you knew my father when he was young?"

"Sure, I knew him," Charles answered. "I knew his whole family. He and your Uncle Henry were some tough fellas."

He went on to say that although my father was not that big, he was very strong and nobody messed with him. He said that people were scared to death of him. Charles told me that my aunts Ellen and Adell were very pretty young girls, but no boys wanted to talk to them until they were almost grown because their overprotective brothers, my father and Uncle Henry, would beat the hell out of them! Although I knew that my father had been to prison when he was a young man, this was the first time I had ever heard that my father had ever fought anyone at any time. The stories I heard that day were about a man I certainly didn't know. The behavior of the young tough Wayland Jones were totally different from my father's gentle demeanor at that time.

The stories that I heard about my father were of contrasting personalities even during those rough-and-tumble years. One on hand, I heard he was a tough guy that beat up a lot of people. On the other hand, I heard that he was not a bully at all. He was self-assured, quiet and for his size he was very strong, so nobody bothered him. One story that I heard about the demonstration of his strength involves, of all things, a foot tub and an anvil.

Before we had bathtubs for bathing and washing machines for washing our clothes, we used large galvanized tin tubs for both purposes. We also used a smaller multi-purpose tin tub, which was about fifteen inches in diameter. It was sometimes used for washing feet as it was just large enough to fit both of your feet, the soap and the water. I imagine that's why it was called a foot tub. As a demonstration of their strength, my father and his young friends would stand with both feet in the small foot tub and attempt to lift an anvil. The first rule of weight lifting is, you always lift with your legs. If your feet are together in a foot tub, lifting with your legs is impossible. These young men would attempt to lift a 150 to 250 pound anvil with just upper body strength. Not a very smart thing to do as it could wreak havoc on your lower back. Of all the young men who attempted the feat, only my Uncle Henry and my father were able to do it.

My father had a small brown scar on the top of his head that stood out when you looked closely because of his baldness and his light complexion. I remember asking him how he got the scar, and his answer would always be the same. "I got it from being a bad boy." Although he never told me how he got the scar, my brother Bobby said that dad had revealed to him how he got it. Maybe Bobby was older than I, when he asked and maybe my father felt comfortable telling him the story when he did not feel comfortable telling me. Perhaps it was because of this special relationship that my father had with my brother Bobby. I was never envious or jealousy of this relations because I have always felt that my father would give his life without hesitation for any of his children, but I always thought that Bobby and my father had a special relationship, so maybe that's why he told him this story. Anyway, according to Bobby, my father's brother Henry, my father's first cousin Rayford Jones, another first cousin's husband Theodore McAllister, and some other locals, were all drinking at a house in the Mill Branch area, when, of all things, a fight broke out. Henry and Rayford were the instigators, but for some reason Theodore McAllister hit my father in the head with a jar of bootleg whiskey. My father said that the attack surprised him. He didn't expect Theodore to bash him with that jar. When the dust and the room had cleared, my father was bleeding profusely and angry. Without treatment for the gash in his head, and covered in blood, he found

Theodore about three or four miles northwest of Mill Branch in a rugged little community called Cut Tail. A fight between my father and Theodore ensued, and my father slashed Theodore McAllister in the face with his knife.

Apparently, in later life, the two men had resolved all of their issues and there was no bad blood between my father and his first cousin Rebecca's husband. I would have never imagined that violence between these two men caused the scar on Theodore McAllister's face and the scar on my father's head, when I would see the two impeccably dressed, and well respected deacons sitting next to each other in the amen corner of Mill Branch Missionary Baptist Church.

Nearly every member of our family, and most of the people in our community knew that my father had served a few months in prison when he was a young man. My father spoke openly about the experience. However, every inquiry about the crime that landed him in prison was always met with the same pat answer. "I went to prison for being a bad boy." Just as my brother Bobby solved to mystery of the scar on daddy's head, he also said that he knew why our father had gone to prison. How did he know? Again, he said that daddy told him. Bobby said that when he was young, daddy also gave him that same "bad boy" answer, but he said that through persistent questioning, Daddy finally told him. (What else did Daddy tell him that I don't know about?)

As I said earlier, my father was a young roughneck who loved to drink. On one occasion when he had been drinking, he went to his step-uncle, Steadman Lewis to borrow money to continue his weekend of partying. Uncle Stead, as everyone called him, refused to loan my father the money. Apparently my father became enraged, strong armed Uncle Stead and took the money. For his crime, my father was sentenced to a few months in prison.

During those years, prisons in the south were segregated. My father was in a Black prison with white guards. He said that the brutal racist guards would flog incorrigible prisoners with a bullwhip to the point that they would lose control of bodily functions and almost die. While he was incarcerated, he had no issues with fellow inmates, or with the white guards. He followed the rules, served his sentence, left prison and returned to Lees Lake. Although my father only spent a few months in prison, what the State of North Carolina really gave him was a life sentence. The effect of that relatively minor indiscretion against his step uncle when he was about nineteen or twenty years old, deprived my father of a valuable and fundamental right that should be guaranteed to every American citizen. He lost the right to vote. The State of North Carolina didn't need the poll tax or Grandfather Rule to deny my father the right to vote. They disenfranchised him and others in his situation for life with just the stroke of a pen.

Following my father's marriage and Christian conversion, his life went in a totally different direction. He was a hard working respected member of his community. He was a founding member of several originations in his community. He not only held leadership positions in his church he was also a leader in the umbrella organizations such as, The Brunswick Waccamaw Association, and the Deacon Brotherhood, that supported the needy as well as other area churches. He encouraged people in our community to vote, and on Election Day he drove those without transportation to the polls. He was politically active, but because of one petty crime, like so many other young Black men in North Carolina, he had been labeled a felon and he never cast a vote during his entire lifetime.

Growing up together in the Lees Lake community, my parents had known each other all of their lives. My mother's aunt Sena Lewis, the second wife of my great grandfather, Peter Jones, had raised my father and his siblings, so there had been strong interaction between the families. I don't know at what point in their lives that the two of them fell in love. Perhaps they were childhood sweethearts or maybe Cupid didn't whack them until they were adults. At some point they fell in love, but decided to keep their plans for marriage a secret. My mother said that "the cat was let out of the bag" on one evening when my father came to visit at her home. My father was welcomed into the house and was invited to sit in the place reserved for honored guest, the living room. When Grandma Bert informed him that my mother was in her room bathing, my father calmly got up and headed for my mother's bedroom. Grandma Bert jumped up, blocked his path, and shouted "YOU CAN'T GO IN THERE!" My father replied, "It's okay, we're getting married." To which, Grandma Bert then said with motherly authority, "I don't care what ya'll fixin to do; you're not going in there until I *see* a marriage license."

On February 17, 1935 the handsome young tough guy, James Wayland Jones and the ebony-skinned beauty, Lillie Mae Hill made their way to Marion, South Carolina and were married. Accompanying them and serving as witnesses was my mother's sister, Violet Hill and my father's sister Adell Jones. How in the world could this marriage ever work? My mother was the daughter of a well-respected minister, and a descendent of the founders of Mill Branch Baptist Church and school. My father had dropped out of The State Colored Normal School, he was a drinker, prone to violence and he was an ex-convict.

My parents first home as a family was on the farm of M. D. "Duff" Watts. The farm was just a few miles from the former homesteads of both my mother and father's families. Living on the Watts farm was my parent's first experience with living on land belonging to someone other than their own families. The house was a rundown, unpainted, clapboard shack that sat at the edge of an open field. The house, of course, had no insulation, so to keep the wind at bay, they covered or stuffed holes in the walls with whatever material they could find. One of my father's favorite jokes about that first home was, "The holes were so big in that place that the wind would blow into the house and blow the blankets clear off of the bed."

The little shack, barely large enough for one family, soon became the home of two families when my father's brother Henry and his wife Estelle moved in. My parent's first child, and Uncle Henry and Aunt Estelle's first child, were born while they lived in that house. My parents named their son James Wayland Jones Jr., after his father, but they called him Jaye W. My Uncle Henry and Aunt Estelle named their daughter Maggie, after the child's grandmother. Now a one-room shack had to suffice as home for two families with infant children. To give each family a sense of their own space, a blanket hung on a line that stretched across the room, dividing it into separate living quarters for the two families.

When my brother Jaye W was a very young child, he had a condition that would occasionally cause him to suddenly stop breathing while he slept. When this occurred, my mother would quickly pick him up and pat him rapidly on the back. She said that following that procedure, he would let out a loud gasp, and then start breathing again. Because my brother had this condition, my mother was afraid to sleep at night for fear of not knowing when my brother might stop breathing. On most nights, she would sit on her family's side of the blanket room divider and watch over her baby while he and everyone else slept.

Despite the hardships of working as farm laborers and sharecroppers during those Great Depression-era years, my parents not only endured, but looked fondly on the time when they were a new family. I believe that this period also provided the cornerstone for building the rest of their lives together. The hard work on the Watts farm prepared them for the hard work that they never seemed to mind doing for the rest of their lives. It also showed them what could be accomplished when husband and wife worked as family unit. Most important, those times proved once again, that trusting in God will see you through anything.

Being a husband and father in such arduous times was certainly bringing huge changes to my father's life. The married Wayland Jones with a family, bore little resemblance to the tough young man he had been just as few short years earlier. My mother told me that throughout her life with my father, even during their courtship, she had never seen any violence from him toward her or any other person. Those days were forever gone. What was not gone was the drinking. He still loved the grape, and he still loved to travel to Welches Creek to get it. My mother said that it was nothing but help from the Lord that got them back home after some of my father's drinking excursions to Welches Creek. After a few drinks, my father would sometimes put the three or four year old Jaye W on his lap, and let him steer the car as they sped from Welches Creek to their home on the Watts farm in Lees Lake. I suppose that when my father let my brother take control of the steering wheel of his Model A Ford at the age of four, and burn up the road from Welches Creek to Lees Lake, it instilled in him a lifelong love of driving, and a love of speeding.

Although my father's life was radically changed after his marriage, the most significant change in his life came after his profession of faith in Jesus Christ. Like many other facets in the life of my parents, the details of my father's conversion were never important to me when I was young. It is now, though, one of those events that I certainly would love to know details. What life event caused him to make such a drastic change? What was his breaking point? Did he have some kind of epiphany? Did he kneel at the moaners bench in Mill Branch Baptist Church, with other sinners who had never confessed, pleading, "Oh Lord save me Jesus, oh Lord save my soul while the saints of the church sing and prayed for his deliverance." I don't know how his change came about, but I know that he did make a change. After his conversion and his declaration that he would be a follower of Jesus, I don't think he ever touched another drop of alcohol the rest of his life, not even for a champagne toast at my wedding. The father who would never touch a drink of alcohol and worked for the cause of Christ is the only father that I knew. I was also told many stories about my father's devotion to his service to God. My Boy Scout master, Isaac Jones told me that my father was a founding and instrumental member of The Deacon Brotherhood. The Deacon Brotherhood is a prestigious organization of deacons in Southeastern North Carolina, who provided services for the region, that deacons provided for their local churches. In additional to what I have been told, I was also a personal witness to my father's service on behalf of Christ. I tagged along with him as he visited the sick in their homes. I sat in the car when he visited sick in the colored section of Columbus County Hospital as children under the age of twelve were not allowed in the hospital as visitors. I also sat in the car when he visited the prison in the Brunswick section of Whiteville. From the car, I could still see dad sitting along the wire prison fence as he visited and prayed for prisoners sitting across from him on the other side. The primary image that I have of my father is one of him always in a leadership position at Mill Branch Baptist Church. He was a deacon there before I was born. The Wayland Jones that drank wine and beat up people, I only know from those stories that I have been told.

Another event in the life of my father has remained with me all of my life, and it defined my father's

Christian service in my own mind. I was about thirteen or fourteen years old because that was about the time I began to pay attention to the Civil Rights Movement, and think seriously about racial issues. This event involved white folks. My father had agreed to a part-time job of helping a local white woman care for her aging husband in home hospice. The elderly woman said that she needed help, because she could not lift her husband to change the bed and keep him clean. My father was the rugged outdoor type, who knew about farming, wildlife, and hunting. He knew nothing about changing beds and washing sick people, but he agreed to do it. Three or four times a week, after my father had come in from his work on the farm, he would clean himself up and head to his part-time job. Since the white lady's pension check came on a monthly basis, my father was to be paid at the end of the month. One day after a couple months had passed, as he was preparing to leave for the lady's house, I started to quiz him about his part-time work.

Were they white or colored?
They were white.
Where did they live?
I don't remember the answer.
How much do they pay you?
He did it for no pay at all.

Now that was an answer that I did not expect to hear, and it almost knocked me off of my feet! When the time had come for the woman to pay my father the compensation that they had agreed upon, he refused to take it. I would have never questioned the judgment of my father or any other adult at that time. That's something Black children just didn't do. That is, I would have never questioned his judgment out loud, but I certainly questioned it in my mind. What was he thinking? He *must* be crazy! I understood the racial discrimination in Whiteville that relegated most Black folk to menial jobs, but here my father was spending his precious free time doing the menial job of cleaning up after a nasty white man for nothing! That's what I was thinking. All I said was *why*? His answer provided for me one of those life lessons that parents often impart by simply talking with inquisitive children. My father said that the old white man was very sick and needed help. He said that what they needed was something that he could do. He continued to explain to me that he thought that you had to do more to serve God than just going to church; He needed to do something with his hands. He was serving God by helping those people. He then asked me, do you understand that? Un-huh, I nodded that I understood. *You are working for white people and they are not paying you! I don't get it,* is what I was thinking.

I had the opportunity to witness what I would consider greater acts of service by my father to his church and to his community than helping the white women with her sick husband, but for some reason, when I think about my father's Christian life, I always remember this incident. Every time I think of it, I am reminded of who my father was as a young man and who he had become by this point in his life. By this time he had become the man that I will admire for the rest of my life. Did my father have faults and failures? Sure he did. He was not perfect, he was human. Because of the perfect sacrifice of Christ, I believe that imperfect people, who love and follow him, have their service made perfect. My father's service record was perfect.

This picture is a composite taken from two different photographs. The original picture of my grandmother, Lilly Beulah Lewis Hill was taken when she was in her late fifties or early sixties. The original picture of my grandfather, Robert Luther Hill was taken when he was in his mid to late thirties.

My maternal grandmother Lilly Beulah Lewis Hill
(Grandma Bert) Circa 1950 Photo source: Marvin Hill

My great grandmother Fannie Parker Hill

Sena Lewis Jones, my maternal great aunt and my paternal step great grandmother

My great uncle Alexander Lewis and his wife Roxie Skeeters Lewis.
Photo source: Eyvonne Skeeters Crawford

My great aunt Gertrude Hill Bellamy

Willie Yeoman, the `brother of my father's mother, Maggie Yeoman Jones

Shaw Hall on the campus of Shaw University when my grandfather R. L Hill attended the school from 1921 to 1926

Marriott, Charles A. .... Raleigh
Melton, John E. .... Spencer
Perkins, Andrew .... Concord
Standback, Robert B. .... Raleigh
Sapp, Isaac B. .... Dunbarton, S. C.
Sykes, Carl M. .... Decatur, Ala.
Thompson, Walter J. .... Hertford
Williams, Yarborough .... Elberton

SPECIAL THEOLOGICAL

Alexander, L. J. .... Wise
Alston, Peter S. .... Henderson
Currie, W. T. .... St. Paul
Davis, Peter C. .... Warrenton
Devane, D. J. .... Fayetteville
Finger, W. L. .... Winston-Salem
Henderson, T. S. .... Manson
Hill, J. D. .... Raleigh
Hill, R. L. .... Vineland
Kindell, N. B. .... Raleigh
Madkins, G. F. .... Raleigh
Mardica, Napoleon F. .... Auburn
Pair, Hardie .... Clayton
Posey, E. W. .... Winston-Salem
Smith, S. W. .... Clarkton
Steale, F. S. .... Raleigh
Tisdale, J. W. .... Wendell
Todd, G. W. .... Zebulon
Williams, John T. .... Mt. Holley
Williams, James .... Louisburg
Williams, Yarborough .... Elberton
Wright, Mallory .... Tarheel

* Six weeks' course.

MISSIONARY TRAINING SCHOOL
Hunter, Mrs. Hettie A. .... Winston-Salem
Mitchnier, Eura Lee .... Raleigh
Patterson, Emma G. .... Laurinburg

Sewing and Millinery
Brown, Bessie .... West Raleigh
Fenderson, Susie .... Raleigh
Foster, Dazelle B. .... Raleigh
Harris, Mrs. Thomas .... Raleigh
Higgs, Mrs. James .... Raleigh

My grandfather R. L. Hill was listed as a student in Shaw University's catalog each year from 1921 to 1926

Harris, Dallie P. ....Raleigh.
Henderson, Rosalie ....Raleigh.
Holmes, John M. ....Clinton.
Horton, William H. ....Raleigh.
Lewis, Duffie ....Manson.
Lytle, James E. ....Marshville.
Mangrum, J. P. ....Franklinton.
Marshall, William Y. ....Norfolk, Va.
McElrath, William M. ....Johnson City.
Perkins, Andrew W. ....Concord.
Robbins, Clayton A. ....Ahoskie.
Scott, Callie M. ....Pratt City, Ala.
Scott, Claude C. ....Method.
Smith, Jacob E. ....Virginia, Va.
Stallings, Verta M. ....Edenton.
Stephens, A. Omega ....Lumberton.
Sykes, Carl M. ....Decatur, Ala.
Turner, Julia M. ....Raleigh.
Wall, Richmond ....Rockingham.
Williams, Almeta J. ....Florence, S. C.

SPECIAL

Baker, Henry W. ....Raleigh.
Mitchell, Maude M. ....Gatesville.

ACADEMY
Fourth Year

Alexander, Zachariah ....Charlotte.
Artis, Mary E. ....Franklinton.
Avery, James T. ....Gastonia.
Baker, Lillie J. ....Raleigh.
Ballard, John C. ....Elrod.
Banks, Archibald L. ....Hampton, Va.
Barnes, Vina ....Goldsboro.
Benton, Thressa M. ....Hamlet.
Berry, Selena E. ....Clinton.
Bowser, Jesse S. ....Leeds, S. C.
Broadnax, Geneva J. ....Reidsville.
Butler, Mabel A. ....Love Grove.
Butterfield, G. Kenneth ....Ocala, Fla.
Cardwell, Gladys L. ....Elizabeth City.
Cheatham, Susie C. ....Oxford.
Clark, Beatrice D. ....Greensboro.
Clark, Corena V. ....Henderson.
Cooper, Alice C. ....Windsor.

G. Kenneth Butterfield, the father of my wife's cousin, Congressman G. K. Butterfield, and my grandfather, R. L. Hill were students at Shaw during the same period of time.

Mill Branch Missionary Baptist Church founded by my Hill family in 1864, situated at its third location on Harrelsonville Road in Whiteville, N. C.

My birthplace, located on Highway 130 in the Mill Branch section of Columbus County, North Carolina

Mr. Ben Robinson, a fellow tobacco farmer and family friend, circa 1976

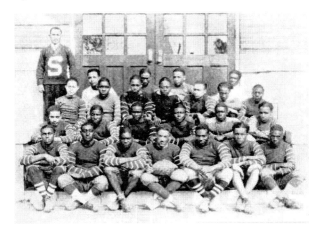

The State Normal Colored School football team in Fayetteville, N. C. when my father attended and played there. Retired NYPD forensic artist Weldon Ryan concluded that the first player, second row right, is my father.

Picture of my parents, James Wayland and Lillie M. Hill Jones. The picture of my father was taken on July 9, 1977. The picture of my mother was most likely taken during the late 1940's or early 1950's.

My mother, Lillie M. Jones and her five sons, on the evening that she was honored by The NAACP for service to her community. (L-R): Jerry, Larry, Bobby, Jaye W, me

ANOTHER CHILD, ANOTHER MIRACLE

My mother was a woman of great faith. I believe that her Christian walk and way of life had its beginnings in the Lees Lake home of her family. The Lewis side of her mother's family and the Hills of her father's family were both rooted and grounded by a tradition of strong Christian faith. Mill Branch Missionary Baptist Church and School had begun in the home of her family. Her father had been a church pastor, well respected throughout Columbus County. She was raised in the conservative southern Black Baptist tradition. As a child, that was the only life she knew. Her faith however, was another matter. Strong faith is not derived by being raised in a Christian home or because your family kept the faith. Not even a university-educated minister father can give you faith. Faith is personal. It is a "what I know for sure" belief, knowledge and connection to God without any physical evidence of Him. It is also derived from your personal witness to the power of God. How you have seen Him move in the life of others, in the life of your family, in your own life. Faith comes from the witness that God still performs miracles that our ancestors simply described as "he has made a way out of no way." My mother believed that she had had several experiences in her life that could only be explained by a for-certain and direct intervention by God. It had to be a miracle, and if God had delivered her in the past, if she trusted Him, He would certainly deliver her from any present predicament. This was the cornerstone of her faith.

Some years after all of her children were adults and living on their own, my mother confided to my father that she thought that she had been called to the ministry. She did not stand before her church congregation like some holier-than-thou sanctimonious Christians and give the impression that somehow God made her better than most folks because He had called her. No, she did not do that; she just discussed with her husband the calling that had for some time been a stress and burden on her heart. A woman being called to the ministry in the rural Black church was a serious issue that came with some serious challenges at that time. Unfortunately, it is still a serious issue even today. It is a blessing to the Black church when women perform most of the work necessary to keep it functioning, but some of those same Black churches still harbor the archaic notion that God forbids women from ascending to positions of leadership. In those kinds of churches, the pulpit is strictly forbidden to them. My father counseled my mother about the difficulty she could expect to face but told her if she felt that she had been called by God to preach the gospel, she had no choice but to do it. No, you've got it all wrong, my mother informed my father. I have not been called to PREACH! I think that I have been called to a ministry of prayer. She had seen evidence of God's favor by her prayers being heard and answered. She had kept the faith. She believed that she was being called to make intercessions on behalf of others. And so with that declaration, my mother's ministry of prayer began.

On one occasion, while I was visiting my mother, she got a telephone call, went into her bedroom and closed the door. When she returned, I asked her who had called. She said that she didn't know, but she thought the caller was a white man. Someone had told the man that she prayed for people and he said that he needed prayer. "You do that?" I asked, meaning that she prayed for people on the phone that she didn't know. Yes, she informed me. She did it all the time. She said that soldiers even called her from Iraq and asked for prayer. Apparently, someone from the Whiteville area had given out her number to other soldiers in the Iraqi war zone, so she got calls from young men requesting prayer that she had never met and never would meet. I had become accustomed to seeing people come to the house and my mother go into another room for council and prayer, but the telephone prayer thing was something that was new and surprising to me.

My mother believed that she had experienced miracles in her life, and perhaps it was the miracles she witnessed that gave her the strength and faith for her prayer ministry. She knew that the hand of God had guided her family through the trials and tribulations of bondage and the racial oppression that followed. She also had to overcome tribulations in her own life that left her with the impression that only God could have brought her through that. She saw God's hand in her extraordinary lifesaving events to the mundane reminders that He lives. She believed that it was an extraordinary occurrence that she was spared while her childhood friend disappeared, never to be found as they played together in Lees Lake. There were other phenomenal life events that I will discuss later, but first let me tell you about a mundane incident that my mother believed occurred so God could just remind her of who He is.

"After the same manner also he took the cup, when he had supped, saying, This cup is new testament in my blood: this do ye, as oft as ye drink it, in remembrance of me

For as often as ye eat this bread, and drink this cup, ye do shew the Lord's death till he come.

I Corinthians 11:25-26

Remembering Christ by the taking of Holy Communion was very serious business at Mill Branch Missionary Baptist Church, even though they only followed the scriptures that remembered

Him in that manner just four times per year. The saints of Mill Branch Baptist Church used Welch's Grape Juice as a symbol for the wine referenced in I Corinthians 11:25-26 as tee totaling Baptists would never use real wine. The bread was not the quarter-sized thin, fancy wafers that are widely used today, but real store-bought bread. To distinguish it from home baked bread, we referred to these commercial loaves as light bread. The bread was broken into tiny pieces, and served with the grape juice for the communion service. Following the quarterly communion service, the communion glasses and the silver serving set were removed from the church and taken to the home of one of the church members to be cleaned in preparation for the next service that was to occur in three months. The communion service set was removed from the church because of the fear that someone who feared neither man nor God, would break into an isolated church under the cover of darkness and steal the only thing of value remaining there. For most of my childhood, it seemed that my mother had the responsibility of taking care of her church's communion set. Following the service, she would bring the serving set to our home, clean it and stored it under my bed. On the Saturday just before the next communion service, she would remove the set from under the bed, clean the set again, and prepare the sacraments to be served the next day. On one such Saturday, when she removed the set from its usual place of storage, she discovered that she had forgotten to clean it and had stored it with the leftover grape juice and bread from the prior quarter. "Oh my goodness!" she shouted. That's as close to cursing as she was willing to go. She realized what she had done so she expected to see ants and mold everywhere. To her amazement she saw neither. The grape juice and the bread were as fresh as the day they had been served. How could that be? How could elements that one might expect to spoil in just two days be as fresh as it was when served three months ago? This could only be the work of God she surmised. She counted this as one of her mundane and simple miracles, but a miracle nevertheless. What was God trying to show her with this phenomenon? She thought that God was just showing her who He was and what He could do. I don't know what God was saying to her. We may never know for sure. Perhaps the message wasn't for her at all. Maybe God was showing a little boy just a minute portion of His unlimited power in a manner and with elements that the little boy could understand.

Another miracle that she believed she experienced was associated with her belief that a married woman should give birth to as many children as possible during her lifetime. Twenty one children had been born to her parents and grandparents, so I imagine that the *be fruitful and multiply* scriptural command had real meaning for her, but my father said that his ideal family was four boys, born about four years apart. I guess they were both overjoyed when they conceived a second child almost six years after their first child Jaye was born.

By the time my mother was pregnant with her second child, the family had moved to a larger home a few miles north of Lees Lake, on Highway 130, in the Mill Branch section of Columbus County. It was the same house where I was born. Perhaps the expectation of having another child was the reason for the move to the larger house. That little shack on the Watts farm could not possibly accommodate a growing family.

Most African American children in our area were born at home during this period. They were usually born with the assistance of older women from the mother's family circle or a midwife. There was a midwife of legend in Columbus County during the time of my mother's pregnancy, and for many years afterwards. I'm sure all of the grown folks knew her full name, but the children only knew her as Miss Millie Ann. Children were usually unaware that their mother was expecting until Miss Millie Ann dropped in for a visit while making her rounds. If Miss Millie Ann attended your mother during your birth, you were referred to as a Miss Millie Ann baby. Most of my friends and relatives in my age group were Miss Millie Ann babies. When an expected mother's water broke and she started having contractions, it was time for someone to go find Miss Millie Ann. The only reason to bare the expense of a doctor or hospital instead of using the services of Miss Millie Ann was the expectation or prior history of complications during childbirth. My mother was seeing a doctor on a regular basis during her second pregnancy, and she expected to deliver the baby in the Columbus County hospital.

Apparently, my mother was having serious complications with this pregnancy as she was receiving an unusual amount of prenatal care. She told me the name of her physician, but I won't mention it due to the sensitive nature of this story. On one of my mother's visits, the doctor sat her down for a serious and private conversation. She was told that she could not deliver the baby she was carrying. She had delivered one child five years earlier, so I don't know what medical reason the doctor gave her for not being able to have this second child, but she was informed that there were complications with the pregnancy. Her doctor gave her the dire warning that if she carried the baby to term and tried to deliver it, she could possibly die during the delivery process. The doctor's advice was to terminate the pregnancy. It could be done in the doctor's office, no one would ever know, and she would be fine, the doctor promised.

As a young man, I was shocked when my mother told me this story. In retrospect, I'm even more shocked that her doctor offered that advice in the heart of the Bible Belt, thirty four years before Roe versus Wade. Had that doctor been discovered doing abortions in North Carolina in 1939, I'm sure the doctor's license to practice medicine would have been revoked, and the doctor jailed. There must have been serious concerns about my mother's welfare to make such a suggestion. My mother had a decision to make. She could terminate her pregnancy and live, or possibly die during childbirth.

With my mother's moral compass already set, there was really no decision to be made. Her response to the doctor's advice was immediate. "I can't do that! I can't get rid of a child. If it kills me, it kills me." Those were the exact words she said that she told the doctor. Her decision was not a surprise to me at all because I was well aware of how she felt about termination a pregnancy. She had expressed her position to me one day while discussing a rumor about someone in the community having an abortion. In addition to her belief that a woman should have as many children as possible, she believed that any woman who had an abortion would be tormented with the sounds of babies crying as they laid on their deathbed. This punishment at the time of death and possibly even after was not a theory or a rumor she had heard, she said that she had seen someone go through this agony before they died. By contrast, she believed that anyone dying during the process of childbirth would go straight to heaven. My mother preferred death during childbirth to an abortion, so she carried her baby to term, and entered the colored section of Columbus County Hospital to deliver her second child. Just as the doctor had feared, there were severe complications. Fathers were not allowed in the delivery room in those days, so my father just stood in the hallway, hour after hour and watched doctors and nurses race back and forth, to and from the delivery room where my mother suffered. His mother and grandmother had died at an early age, leaving children behind. I wonder if my father was praying that history was not repeating itself. The prediction my mother's doctor made some months earlier almost came true. My mother nearly died. It was only a miracle that she did not die. I am certain that the experience of this troubled birth served to strengthen her faith even more because this was a miracle that produced a miracle. On March 27, 1940, her second child came kicking and screaming into the world. They named him Robert, after her father the minister, and her older brother who also shared the name.

As a young man, I had heard my mother testify so many times about yet another particular spiritual phenomenon that the story naturally remained with me. I have often repeated what my mother had told me during the discussions about experiences that could only be explained as a direct intervention by God.

During the middle to late 1950s, my mother said that she discovered a lump on one of her breast. As people without any kind of health insurance are prone to do, she tried to ignore it, hoping that the lump would go away and the family would be spared the expense of a visit to the doctor or the hospital. The lump did not go away, it got worse. When she finally decided to seek medical care, the lump had increased in size and discoloration around it had begun to occur. When she finally made a visit to her doctor, he was so concerned with her condition, that after a very brief examination, he ordered her to go immediately from his office to the hospital. Her doctor had telephoned the specialist my mother was to see at Columbus County Hospital and he would see her as soon as she arrived. When my mother heard the urgency in her doctor's tone and saw the concern on his face, she was terrified. As instructed, she went straight from the doctor's office to the hospital and was immediately ushered in an examination room. The doctor entered shortly after my mother was taken there and the slow, methodical inspection of her breast began. The few minutes of scrutiny by the physician must have seemed like hours of offence to the sensibilities of an African American southern Baptist mother, but this was serious business. Finally the doctor is finished and he throws his hands in the air in what appears to be utter frustration. I can't find it, he yells! He then picks up the phone and dials my mother's referring doctor. This woman doesn't have anything abnormal on her breast, he tells his associate. My mother's doctor assures him that when she left his office, she had a significant mass and discoloration around it. Well, she doesn't have it now, I'm going to order an x-ray, but she appears to be perfectly fine. The x-ray confirmed the specialist's diagnosis, he informed my mother. There is nothing there, and he did not know why her doctor had sent her to him. My mother assured this physician that she had the lump and the discoloration long before she had seen her doctor, and her doctor had seen it less than an hour ago. With the doctor's voice now elevated, and a quizzical wrinkle on his brow, the doctor asked; well, if it was there, where did it go? The doctor's question began what was for my mother a lifelong testimony about her belief in God's healing power. She just smiled and informed the doctor that she knew exactly where it went. She said that she had prayed every inch of the drive from her doctor's office to the examination room of the hospital. Yes, she absolutely knew where the lump went. God had heard her prayer and healed her. That's where it went! The doctor then nodded his head, lifted his eyes up and to the right in disbelief, and left the room.

Those of us who profess to be Christians say we believe in miracles. We sing that we are looking for a miracle. We expect the impossible, feel the intangible and see the invisible. Do we really? We may say we believe in miracles but when we experience one, we often seek a logical explanation for the supernatural. Surely we know that God is powerful enough to do these things. We pray for them, and we sing about them, but perhaps we don't receive them for what they are because we feel that we are not worthy of God's supernatural favor. Well we are not, but God gives them to us anyway. It was God's supernatural favor, a miracle that our family and other families like ours, not only have survived, but have flourished. My mother always said that some people didn't believe her when she relayed those stories of the miracles in her life. Their unbelief did not matter to her because she certainly believed that they happened. She believed that nothing but the hand of God could have done those things. I agree with her. I believe in miracles. I receive them for the blessing that they are, and continue to expect more miracles every day of my life.

SCENES OF MY BIRTHPLACE AND OTHER PETTY CRIMES

The earliest event in my life that I can recall is playing in the driveway of the house in which I was born. There was nothing dramatic, traumatic or momentous about this event. I have no idea why I recall it so vividly. I don't remember anything else about that house during the period that we lived there. I just remember sitting and playing in the sandy soil of the driveway. When I was well into my twenties, I told my father that I remembered this event. He laughed and assured me that I could not possibly remember living in that house as I was a mere two years old when our family moved from that house in the Mill Branch section of Columbus County to the Cherry Grove section where my family built the house in which I grew up.

The house in Mill Branch where I was born was a small, wood-framed structure with a front porch typical of the houses of rural North Carolina. I was surprised to see that the house had recently been torn down, as it always appeared to be in fairly good condition. It sat back well off of the rural road

Highway 130 south, due to its large front yard. It had farmland to the left and the house originally belonging to our landlord on the right. Years after we moved from that location, I learned that the house was owned by Tom Hill who lived in the much nicer, much larger house next door to us. An irony that I had difficulty understanding was that in the strictly segregated south, even during the fifties and sixties, when it was economically advantageous, Blacks and whites lived mostly segregated lives right next door to each other. Next to the house where Tom Hill lived, he maintained a store. Locals from Mill Branch shopped there. The nearby tobacco farm laborers would descend on the store during their lunch break to purchase the fixings for their sandwiches, to purchase sardines, Vienna sausages and the ever-popular honey bun! This store was also the scene of many petty crimes. My older brother Bobby often tells the story of how he and my oldest brother Jaye W would visit the store, and while one brother distracted the owner, the other would pilfer some Baby Ruth candy bars or Nab cookies. They would then go to a secret location and divide the booty. Thank God my parents never found out about my brothers stealing from that store. A well-known rule of Black (colored back then) southern culture was that *you do not steal*. It was as if the commandment against stealing was somehow greater than some of the others. It was certainly held in higher regard than the prohibition against adultery, or beating up each other. It seemed that the guardians of morality looked the other way as some residents acted as if they lived in Peyton Place, but stealing was a no-no. Perhaps the lack of sexual ethics was accepted behavior to alleviate the boredom of a small rural town. Fighting, even cutting up each other on a Saturday night didn't bring down the raft of the community as hard as stealing did. Perhaps the reason stealing was so frowned upon was because it is usually a crime of the have-nots taking from the haves. In that southern North Carolina society, that meant Blacks taking from whites, and that was just plain unacceptable. Had my brothers been caught stealing, there would have been hell to pay. Both my parents were devout Christians. They would not have spared the rod for such an offense against God, our white landlord Tom Hill and the Jones family name.

In the late fifties, long after we had moved from that location, the owner of the little store and our little house died. My memory of his death is not based on when or how he died or the circumstances surrounding his death. The flood of memories about Tom Hill's passing comes from all of the whispers immediately following his passing. It was rumored that Tom Hill not only had lived as a sinner, but apparently he had died without ever professing faith in the Lord and Savior Jesus Christ who was the object of all of that praise I had witnessed on a weekly basis at Mill Branch Baptist

Church. I don't know how his wife Penelope felt about her husband's relationship or lack thereof with God, during his life, but the condition of his soul became a burden and constant worry for her after his death. We in the Black community were, of course, not part of Penelope Hill's inner circle, but we heard that she was seeking help in the form of spiritual consultation from her local white religious community. I was just a small child and don't remember how she was led to a *spiritual* or *religious* person from somewhere outside of Columbus County. This spiritualist had the reputation of being able to affect the souls of those who had passed on. Three things were required if you wanted to be assured that your loved ones would not spend eternity in the place of the dammed. Those three things were faith in the preacher, a lot of prayer and a lot of money! After consulting with the widow Hill, this man of faith convinced her that he could help. You see, even though Tom had died an unrepentant sinner, he was not yet in full-fledged hell. The preacher Penelope had consulted assured her that there was still hope for Tom Hill's soul. Tom was now residing in purgatory. Black Baptist children had no idea what that was, but it was described as an awful place because it was one of the outer chambers of Hell. Without intervention he would most assuredly go to hell. The preacher said that he was sure that through prayer, he could change her husband's direction and send him to Heaven.

Once Mrs. Hill had paid the required fee, the preacher began the prayer to reverse the direction of Tom Hill's soul. He prayed all day but alas he had to inform the widow that even though there had been movement, he had not been successful in moving her husband from purgatory into Heaven. Mrs. Hill became frantic in her search for a solution, any solution, even a temporary solution to her husband's eternal problem. Was there anything that could be done? The preacher had to help her. Okay, okay the preacher said, I can stay another day and try to help you if you can come up with the money for another day of prayer. Was there any amount of money worth her husband's soul? Of course she would get the money to keep the preacher praying another day. The second day brought a lot more success for the preacher. He informed Penelope Hill that her husband was almost out of purgatory. Now, he was sure that if he could just remain for one more day, he could pray her husband into Heaven before the three-day time limit had expired on her husband's position in purgatory. Penelope gladly gave the preacher a third day's wages and was overcome with joy when the preacher informed her that he had been successful. Her husband Tom now had a permanent home in Glory, Hallelujah!

The community gossip about this event, whether it was true or untrue, just served to reinforce the notion of the kids in our community, that white people were surely some strange folks. One thing that every child in Sunday school at Mill Branch Baptist Church knew for sure was; if you die in sin without Jesus, no amount of prayer or money will save you from going straight to hell.

After Tom Hill had died and went to wherever he went, the property was sold. I don't recall the name or anything significant about the new owner. I do remember that an appliance store was built next to the little general store where my family sometimes purchased food, the farm workers bought lunch, and my brothers stole. The most exciting product sold in the new appliance store was the television. Televisions were fairly new to our community at that time. Early TVs were also very expensive. You could only get large console models that cost from seven hundred to over a thousand dollars. That would be several thousands of dollars in today's money. I can only remember one brand of that large console being sold. If you had the means to purchase a television in those days, you got an American-made Dumont. Although the television consoles were over three feet high and over two feet wide, the viewing screen was only thirteen inches square. There was, of course, no color TV at that time, however you could simulate color by placing a plastic sheet over the thirteen-inch screen. The see-through sheet was green on the bottom, simulating grass and vegetation, red in the middle, for people, (no Black people were on TV at that time) and blue at the top, simulating the sky. Television in those days was not the source of twenty-four hour entertainment that it is today. The televisions stations signed on at seven in the morning and signed off with the playing of the National Anthem at eleven PM. You had your choice of two stations to watch: channel 3, the NBC station in Wilmington, North Carolina, and channel 8, the CBS station in Florence, South Carolina. To watch either, you needed a very large antenna mounted to the side of your house that in most cases had to be rotated manually when you switched from one channel to the other. When we finally got a television some years after they were fairly common in the area, we had the luxury of having a control box that sat atop the television that was used to change the channel. We would simply rotate the knob on the control box from E (east) for the Wilmington station to SW (southwest) for the Florence station. You would then hear a slow, rhythmic tick, tick, tick as a small motor turned the outside antenna.

A limited number of white people and almost no Blacks in the area owned a television during the period of time when the new appliance store first opened in Mill Branch. To advertise this new and exciting product, the owner of the store placed a television in the display window and tuned it to one of the two stations available for viewing. This advertising stunt produced unexpected and unwanted consequences. Since there was no other evening entertainment for saved and sanctified people in the Mill Branch area except listening to radio, some residents would bring chairs from their homes and sit outside the store in the parking lot and watch the television on display through the store's window. They would just watch the picture as very little to no sound could be heard through the large thick glass window. That was not what the storeowner wanted. The talk of the neighborhood was that the storeowner did not want these colored people sitting in the parking lot outside of his business. Sometime later however, the storeowner must have realized the potential of this kind of advertising as he rigged a small speaker outside of the store. Now the colored people sitting in the parking lot on their lawn chairs could see as well as hear the television.

A House by the
Side of the Road

Although I was born in the Mill Branch section, I did not grow up there. My childhood was spent in the Cherry Grove section of the county. Cherry Grove had a village-like atmosphere, and almost everyone who lived there was either related or somehow knew every other resident. For most folks living in the area, Cherry Grove Missionary Baptist Church was the center of their lives. Newborn babies were brought there for the congregation to fawn over as soon as they were able to leave their homes. Neighborhood children attended Sunday school with or without their parents each week, and they attended preaching service the first Sunday of each month. When someone in the community died, a slow dolorous clang of the church bell notified the community of their transition even when it occurred in the middle of the night. They were memorialized at the church, and their bodies found eternal rest in The Cherry Grove Cemetery at the end of an unpaved road nearby. I went down on my knees at Cherry Grove church's moaners bench during their fall revival when I was fifteen years old. The saints of Cherry Grove and all of the surrounding churches, sang and prayed over the seven or eight of us seeking a relationship with God that would be officially recognized by the church, and knowing no other way to find it other than following the custom of repeating the prayer "Oh Lord save me Jesus, Oh Lord, save my soul." The moaners bench ritual of the church revival that occurred from Monday until Friday, ended for me on Thursday night, when I received an unquestionable visitation of the Holy Spirit. Following that experience, I was submerged in the baptismal pool in the churchyard and joined the Cherry Grove Baptist Church of my community instead of the Mill Branch Baptist Church of family legend. The majority of my parent's siblings were also members of Cherry Grove, but my parents never joined the church in their community, preferring to remain at the church of their ancestors, Mill Branch.

My father had purchased the land in that community where our house was built from my maternal grandmother, Bert. It was a prime piece of land because it was next to the primary community thoroughfare, Highway 130. Daddy's ownership of the property at one point caused some disharmony among my mother's siblings. When my grandmother's property was divided among all of her children, my mother was entitled to be included in that distribution. Some of my aunts and uncles thought that unfair as my parents already owned choice property by the side of the road. My father pointed out that he and my mother had purchased the land that they owned from my grandmother. Grandma Bert was asking $33.00 for the lot at that time. Of course that amount of money is only a pittance now, but it was a fair price for the property during the Great Depression when cash was extremely hard to get. Since the land on which our house had been built was purchased by my parents, my mother was included in the distribution of the additional land owned by her family in the area.

The original house on that property was built when I was not quite two years old. As I stated earlier in my recollections from that same time period, my father told me that I couldn't possibly remember the house being built, but I remember it very clearly. I have vivid memories of us going to check on the progress of the construction of our new house on several evenings after finishing working on the farm. My father would pack up the Ford Model A, and hand crank the engine to start it up. If it was raining or threatening to rain, he would tie a piece of tarp across the leaky roof of the car to keep us dry. He would then drive the five or six miles to the sight of our new house. While my mother visited her mother and other family members in the area, my father would confer with the carpenter about the progress of our new house. Zeno Davis was the carpenter who built our house. He was the same man known for stirring the souls of the saints with his singing at Mill Branch Church. I think he may have been a distant relative of one flavor or another. Unfortunately, Mr. Zeno was better at spirited singing than he was at carpentry. After the house was completed and we had lived there for many years, my father often complained about studs not being properly spaced or some other malady resulting from the work of a "jack-legged" carpenter. But even with the problems, both of my parents loved that house. My father and my mother had grown up on land and in houses owned by their families in the Lees Lake area of Columbus County. Home ownership was then and still is an integral part of the culture of the area, and certainly a part of my families' culture on both sides. Living in a rented house on someone else's land must have been very uncomfortable for them. I know they were extremely proud to be in their own house. Whenever the subject of home ownership came up, my mother was fond of saying, "It ain't much, but it's ours. It's on our own land and we don't owe anyone a red cent on it." The most valuable property asset was its location near the property of other family members, thus I grew up with several of my cousins around me. My Aunt Emma lived just up the highway, on a hill near Cherry Grove Church. Great-Uncle Stedman lived directly across the road from us. Aunt Vi (Violet) lived directly behind us. Uncle Willie owned a rental house next to Aunt Vi, but he lived about a tenth of a mile just south of us. One of my mother's gardens separated our house from her mother, Grandma Bert's, house. Mom's garden was on land owned by her oldest brother Uncle Les. Uncle Les and his family lived in another area of the county for several years before building his house between ours and Grandma Bert's in the late fifties.

My father was so in love with our house and its location that he would occasionally honor our home by reciting the Sam Walter Foss poem: A House by the Side of the Road

> Let me live in a house by the side of the road, where the race of men go by.
> They are good, they are bad, they are weak, they are strong, wise foolish – so am I.
> Then why should I sit in the scorner's seat, or hurl the cynic's ban?
> Let me live in a house by the side of the road, and be a friend to man..

He always placed special emphasis on the last line. *"Let me live in a house by side of the road and be a friend to man."*

The modest wood-framed house had three bedrooms aligned in a row on one side of the house, and the living room, dining room, and kitchen on the other. Although we had three bedrooms, most of the time, we only used two of them. My parents slept in the middle bedroom, while my three brothers and I occupied the back bedroom. While the four of us slept cramped in one bedroom, the front bedroom was reserved for guests. We only started using it on a regular basis when my brother Jaye would come home to visit from North Carolina A & T College on semester breaks. The same rules were in effect for the living room in our house. It was always kept in pristine condition and used primarily when we had guests. Although I don't think that many people have rooms in their homes reserved for guests today, my mother's rules about the living room were not unusual at that time. All of my friends lived by the same rule in their home. The house had no running water, just running children, whose job was to keep the house supplied with fresh water from the pump in the back yard. The pump was installed by Aunt Vi's husband Uncle Dan whose primary profession was drilling wells. He drilled the pipes so deep in the ground that the water pumped pure and cool. My father loved that water so much that when he traveled, he carried his own water supply from home. When his water ran out, it was time for him to return home.

My mother had what seemed like every variety of flower known to man somewhere around that house. She loved flowers and the sisterhood of local women who grew them. When she visited one of her fellow flower lovers and saw a flower she admired, she would always ask, "Can I have just a little piece of that?" With the owner's permission, she would break off a stem and wrap it in a paper napkin or piece of newspaper soaked in water. Once she was home, she would place the broken plant stem in one of her Mason jars half filled with water and place it on the windowsill. When the stem began to grow roots, she would transplant it to her garden, and in a short period of time she would be admiring the flower she had seen at her friend's house in her own yard.

While visiting her many years ago, she was lamenting about the fact that the FBI had come to one of her church sister's homes, ripped out all of her flowers, put them into the trunk of a car, and took the flowers with them. Now why would the FBI do such a thing, she wanted to know. I asked her if she knew what kind of flowers her friend had. She said that she did, and she also said that she had a garden full of the same plants. I'm thinking that my mother is inadvertently growing marijuana plants, so I asked her to show me. She took me to one of her many flower beds and pointed them out. Whew, it wasn't marijuana. "What is it?" I asked

"They're poppies," she replied. "Ain't they pretty?"

"They sure are," I responded.

No, I didn't bother to explain the probability that the sap from the variety of poppies she and her friend were growing was used to make opium. I just commented once again on their beauty.

In addition to the flowers, my mother had a garden at the end of our back yard where she grew the best vegetables I have ever tasted. She grew every variety of vegetable in her garden. She would grow tomatoes so sweet and juicy that we would eat them directly from the vine as one might eat a ripe apple. She had a special talent for growing things. I still joke that my mother could stand in the doorway of our house and throw seeds in the yard one day, and just like Jack's beanstalk, the next day vegetables would appear. They may not have appeared that fast, but because of her talent and love of gardening, she planted a garden in every season. As a result we were always very well-fed year-round. Occasionally the meal on our table would have been gathered from my mother's garden just minutes earlier. Vegetables taste so much better when they are consumed within minutes of being gathered.

Our house had a kerosene heating system for the living room, but the rest of the house was heated by a wood-burning heater centrally located in the dining room. During the winter, the heater was stuffed to capacity with wood before everyone went to bed. Sometime during the night when the wood had burned, the fire would go out and we would awake to a cold house the next morning. After my father banged on the wall to wake us up, my brother Bobby and I would lie in our warm beds and argue about whose turn it was to get up and start the fire. My brother Bobby would always swear that it was he who had gotten up to make the fire the day before, so it was my turn to start the fire that morning. My father didn't care who was responsible for starting the fire, one thing was for certain, the issue had to be resolved, the fire started and the house had better be warm before my mother got out of bed or someone was going to get it!

More important than the physical shelter of our home was the psychological shelter that living in a safe, spiritual environment provided. I have a difficult time even trying to imagine what life would be like in the absence of that kind of shelter. I first became aware of people living in the modern world without shelter when I was about ten years old. I will never forget the Saturday evening as my mother stood at her ironing board, expertly preparing my father's white shirt for the next day's church service. I sat next the wood-burning heater in our dining room reading an article from one of the old *Reader's Digest* magazines my mother had brought home from her employer, Mrs. Marks. The article described the lives of people being born, living their entire lives and dying on the streets in Calcutta. Never during their whole lives did they have any comfort from the elements. Never did their children have a certain place of refuge to hide after committing some minor act of mischief in the neighborhood. Never did they have a safe cave to run where they could be sure of protection from all manners of vicious attacks designed to destroy them. They had no place that shielded them from race, class, or caste distinctions. Never did they experience a place where only their mother and father were the ultimate authority. Unlike me, they never had a safe haven in a hostile world. Boy was I lucky! My family had a home. It wasn't much, but it was ours. It was on our own land, and we didn't owe a red cent on it.

My youngest brother Larry was born while we lived in that house. I was about four years old when Larry was born so I had no idea that mom was even expecting a baby. Had my friends or I seen the area's midwife Miss Millie Ann making regular visits, we would have known something was up, but I don't remember seeing her come to our house before Larry was born. I recall spending the night prior to his birth with my cousin Ralph, and his parents Uncle WM and Aunt Eva. That was certainly not unusual, as I often spent nights there. The next day when I returned home, as soon as I got out of Uncle WM's car, the neighborhood kids were running up to me saying "you have a new baby brother!"

The friends and relatives of my parents all had one opinion of my new baby brother. That opinion was that he was one beautiful baby. The prevailing sentiments about her baby delighted my mother and she did everything she could to keep him looking as her neighbors expected. Larry was always massaged in Vaseline and his thick curly black hair slicked down with Royal Crown Hair Dressing. As an infant, he was always well dressed and looking good. When he was old enough to run with the other neighborhood kids, my mother always sent him out of the house impeccability dressed, what he looked like when he came home was another matter. He would often draw the ire of Momma for the way he looked after playing with his cousins in the neighborhood. My mother's favorite line when describing her dirty child was, "You look like you have been playing in a hog pin."

This was a time and a place where it was safe for children to leave the house in the morning without even asking, came home for lunch and leave again to play all afternoon, and return home just before dark. Parents were always secure in the knowledge that if they wanted to find their children, they could. That was not the case with Larry. As a little boy, Larry was rough and adventurous. He was also a wanderer and an explorer that could not be found where he was expected to be. I recall one day when we were looking all over the neighborhood without being able to find him, someone just happened to look up in a tree that was in Grandma Bert's yard. Perched on the tiniest of limbs, at the very top of the tree, my baby brother sat quietly looking down on everyone searching for him. When we got him out of the tree, my mother asked him why he was sitting in the tree when he knew we were looking everywhere for him. She got the same reply that she always got when her baby boy did something unexplainable; the same reply she had gotten in the past when she asked why he looked like he had been playing in a hog pen; the reply she would get when she would ask why he would come home with his legs scrapped up; the same reply when she had asked in the past how did he get that cut on his face. Larry just did what he would always do. He hunched his shoulders and said, "I don't know." Larry always marched to the beat of a different drummer, even as a child.

My nephew Jerry was also born during the time when we lived in that house. He spent most of his childhood there being raised by my parents as their son and as one of my brothers.

Jerry's father, my brother Jaye W, was in the Air Force and had left the States on a two-year deployment just before Jerry was born, so his mother Catherine lived with us for almost a year when he was an infant. Our family's attachment to him and his to us was immediate, so it was difficult for us when Catherine relocated with him to New Jersey. Jerry never forgot us and was overjoyed to see us when his mother brought him home for a visit. We were overjoyed when we convinced her to let him remain with us for a short period of time when his mother returned to New Jersey.

Jerry was to split his time between the Joneses, his father's parents, and the Brights, his mother's parents. Early on, it became apparent that this arrangement was not going to work out. While Jerry didn't have a problem going to visit the Brights, he did not want to live there. There were no other children in the Bright house, and the nearest children were too far away for Jerry to visit them.

Consequently, he spent most of his time sitting in the house with older grandparents. Conversely, there were three boys living in our house, and probably a dozen other kids nearby to play with. In addition, by this time he was addressing my father as daddy, while he followed him around trying to do everything that my father was doing. When Jerry was scheduled to spend time with his other grandparents, we would have to assure him that he was just going for a visit, and would be returning with us. During these visits, our whole family would remain at the Brights until Jerry had fallen asleep. Only then would we quietly leave before he awake. On one occasion, Jerry woke up while we were leaving, and we could hear him screaming even when we got into our car. My father said nothing on the long drive home.

The Mount Olive area of the county where the Brights lived must have seemed like a million miles from where we lived because Jerry never saw anyone there that he knew from the Cherry Grove section where we lived. One day as he was playing in the yard of the Bright's home, he spotted a car passing the house that he thought belonged to Aunt Violet's husband Dan Jones. He was correct; Uncle Dan was drilling a well for a pump at a residence about a mile away. Jerry, who must have been close to four years old at that time, saw this as a chance to get a message to my father. He stood in the yard next to the road until he saw Uncle Dan's car coming down the road again. He then stepped out close to the road and flagged down the car, and gave Uncle Dan a message for my father. When Uncle Dan returned home, he went straight to our house to deliver the message. He told my father that Jerry had stopped his car and asked him to tell his daddy to please come and get him. That was it! My father said that he could no longer endure the crying when he dropped Jerry off at his other grandparents knowing that he wanted to live with us. He informed the Brights that Jerry had to live with them or us on a permanent basis. Jerry wanted to be close to the other boys in the house and cousins in the neighborhood. He promised them that he would bring Jerry to visit them on a regular basis, but Jerry should live with us. The Bright reluctantly agreed. Jerry then became my brother instead of my nephew, and spent his childhood in that house. He continued to live in that house or in the new house that my parents built until he married and built his own house next door.

The house that Jerry had built is located on the lot where an old rental property had sat for as many years as we had been there. Before Jerry's house was built, a dirt access road leading to Aunt Vi's and Miss Annie Smith's house ran between my parent's home and the old rental house. Instead of building his house in the center of the lot, Jerry's contractor laid the foundation just inches from the access road between the properties. We believe the contractor thought by building Jerry's house so far to the left of his lot, he would have enough room to build another house just to the right of Jerry's house. My mother and Jerry *convinced* the contractor of the error of his ways, so he closed the road between the houses, and built another access road to Aunt Violet's and the other homes behind our house. Once the access road was closed, Jerry's yard was joined to the yard of my parents.

The little house by the side of the road was not only a sanctuary for me, but for most of my young years, it was also a joyful place to be. My father had the sons he had wished for when he got married, and in spite of the occasional fight common with a family of boys, our house was place full of laughter. In fact, a family friend once commented to me that she had never seen anyone who laughed as much as we did. The time when there was the most joy and laughter in our house was the Christmas season. To prepare for the season, the first item on the agenda would be to go in the wooded area where you had been watching the growth of that young pine tree since you spotted it the prior summer. You may have determined months ago that the tree would be a perfect one for Christmas. Even if the tree was growing on your own property, there was no assurance that it would still be there when you went for it, so you needed to go and harvest your prize before someone else beat you to it. While we were on our tree cutting expedition, we also would cut some holly branches from the trees that grew wild in southeastern North Carolina. If we were lucky, we may have even found some mistletoe to hang over the simple French doors that separated our living room from the dining room.

Once the prized tree was brought home and erected, it was adorned with decorations that had been in our family long before I had. With the decorations complete, the simple pine tree was transformed into one of the most beautiful things that my young eyes had ever seen, and we had not spent one dime.

I never knew if purchasing a tree and new decorations would have been a luxury that we could not have afforded because it was never a consideration. Cutting your own tree was just the way it was done. Everyone that I knew decorated the same way we did. I could not have possibly wanted anything better. I still don't.

We did not have a tradition of exchanging gifts at Christmas time. My brothers and I did not buy gifts for each other, and our parents never expected even a token gift from us. The season was all about the children as far as my parents were concerned. This was a time for them to shamelessly dote on us. Of course that meant my parents found a way to provide toys for us even during the most difficult financial times. A week or so before Christmas, we would reasonably assume that our parents had purchased our toys, so we would set out on a frantic search to find them every time my parents left the house. There were just a few places in our home where something could be hidden, and my brothers and I knew every one of them. If the toys were not located in one of those obvious hiding places or in the storehouse in the back yard, they had to be in trunk of family car. If access to that car trunk was closely guarded, we knew the toys had to be there.

In the southern Black tradition, everything was celebrated with food. The Christmas season was no different. Long before the holiday itself, my mother would line her china display case and the rear of her dining room table with every variety of homemade cakes and pies. She would swear that she was not a good baker, but she never missed the opportunity to delight her family and everyone else that walked through our door with a slice of her lemon supreme cakes, her coconut cakes or sweet potato pies. My dad's contribution to the holiday cuisine began about the same time as my mother's. No, my father couldn't cook anything, but each year about the same time my mother was doing her cooking, he would bring home a large wooden crate of apples, a crate of oranges and several bags of nuts. I can't remember a poor farming year or bad financial times altering this tradition that we looked forward to each year. When I look back on those joyous celebrations, what we did and what we had was really quite modest by today's standards. I think the concern showed and effort put forth by my parents during the holiday season was one of the reasons I felt such warmth for that house.

One of the greatest memories of living in that house was our early Sunday morning ritual of family prayer. On Sunday mornings, my parents would awake as early as or perhaps even earlier than they did during the work week. They would prepare to attend Sunday School at Mill Branch and on the second Sunday of the month, their church service would follow. If it was not the second Sunday, they would attend one of the other local churches for services following their Sunday School service at Mill Branch. My mother cooked breakfast with freshly made biscuits every day, but on Sunday mornings her breakfast meals would be far more elaborate. While those meals were great, it was not the food that made these mornings so memorable, it was the family prayer. Our house was a Christian home, and prayer was a common practice. We were instructed to say our prayers before bedtime, and always say grace before meals. We were accustomed to seeing our parents praying before they went to bed and sometimes early in the morning we often saw them on their knees through the open door to their bedroom. On Sunday morning prayer was different. This is the one time when our whole world would stop. Because it was customary for neighbors to just walk into a friend's house unannounced, we would lock our doors prior to stating the prayer so that we would not be interrupted during this special time. I think it would be safe to assume that our parents included us in the silent petitions that they each sent up from the floor of their bedroom. I know for sure that when my father led us in prayer on Sunday mornings, my mother, my brothers, and I were all included in his prayers.

After I left home, my father decided to have a new house built in what was then our backyard. I never got to watch the new house being built nor did I get to say goodbye to the old house. On my first return visit home, the old house was gone and my parents were already living in the brand new ranch style brick home with running water, two bathrooms and even a small den. As happy as I was to see my parents in the new home, I was still a little nostalgic for the home in which I grew up. My mother then informed me of a way to scratch my nostalgia itch. Just as my parent's new house was being finished, a home in the Spring Hill section of Columbus County was completely destroyed by fire. Just as the construction workers were about to tear down our old house, the owner of the house that had burned in Spring Hill, purchased our old house from my parents. The new owner then had a house mover cart our old house away, moving it some five of six miles to the location where her previous house had burned. Now when I am in Whiteville, and I want to reminisce about the house by the side of the road, I just drive to the Spring Hill section and look at it as it sits by the side of the road there.

A Church That's in Me

Although we had moved the five or six miles from the Mill Branch area to the Cherry Grove area by the time I was two years-old, Mill Branch still remained a very important part of my early life. My brothers Jaye W, Bobby and I were all born there. We had many relatives who still lived there. The tobacco farm we worked was there. Most importantly, our church was there. While we lived only a stone's throw from Cherry Grove Baptist Church, my family maintained their membership at The Mill Branch Missionary Baptist Church. They loved that church. The founding members of the church were in my mother's family, and my father's ancestors were also there when the church began. The church was organized in 1864, and services were first held in one room of the home of my great grandfather, Henry Hill. The congregation grew to the point where they needed a church building. That first church was built on Hill family property. It was built on land owned by the woman believed to be Henry Hill's aunt, Viola Hill. The second site for the church is the one of my childhood memories. The land for that church and school was acquired from the estate of Tom Smith, and constructed about two hundred yards off of Highway 130. Although the deed was first recorded in 1928, I am certain that the property was purchased and the church built long before that time. A vivid recollection of early church life was revealed in a short narrative by an early church member named Kitsie Brown. This account is from an eyewitness to the formation of the Mill Branch Baptist Church that was so dear to my family. The date of the interview with Mrs. Brown is not mentioned, but since she was referred to as Mother Brown, she must have been an elderly and well-respected member of the congregation.

Mother Brown said: *"The first church was on Uncle Henry Hill's sister's land. I remember Reverend Sam Stevenson was the pastor when I joined the church. I was fourteen years old then. Uncle Squire Lewis was a deacon then. We had a schoolhouse down there. I went as high as the fourth grade. Miss Annie and Mother Julia Baldwin taught us. We had to walk to school in the rain or shine. Eli Bell was a deacon down there at the church too. The road was bad, but we went on anyhow; did what we had to do. Everybody brought wood or splinters to kindle the fire. I remember Reverend Jessie Kelly built the first church seats. They was benches with no backs on them. People used to come from all around to visit our church. We had some good ole times down there. The church was full at every meeting time. The church mothers would sit on the front. Some of us walked, some drove surge buggies with fringes and a lantern on the side, they was the fancy buggies. Other people drove mules and wagons or horses and buggies. We just enjoyed the Lord. I remember we used to sang 'Gimme That Old Time Religion.' I remember Reverend Sam Stevenson, he was a short man, he would sang 'Father I Stretch My Hand to Thee,' and it would set the church on fire. We used to sang another song, I don't know the name of it, but the words was something like this: 'Lordy take me to ride, ride, ride; Lord knows I'm gonna ride; oh take me to ride, ride, ride; Lord knows I'm gonna ride."*

The Henry Hill Mrs. Brown spoke of was my mother's paternal grandfather. Squire Lewis was my mother's maternal grandfather. The teacher referred to as Miss Annie was the daughter of my mother's Aunt, Sena Lewis. Although Mrs. Brown, states that the land on which the first church was built was owned by Henry Hill's sister, I don't believe that the owner of the land was his sister. I believe that the land was owned by Viola Hill. My research points toward her being the sister or aunt of Henry Hill's mother.

The Mill Branch Baptist Church that I remember as a child was located just south of my birthplace and a few miles north of the Lees Lake area where both of my parents were born and spent most of their early childhood. The access road to the church was unpaved and during rainy weather it was so muddy and slippery that it required careful navigation by drivers to avoid getting their car stuck in the mud or suffering an even worst fate by sliding completely off of the road into the ditch.

The careless or unlucky driver could get stuck in mud that could reach all the way to the car's chassis. A car stuck in that manner would require more than just a push from fellow churchgoers. To be freed from that kind of dilemma, the stuck car would be chained to another car or truck and pulled out of the muck in order to proceed to the church for services or to the paved Highway 130 after church services. The church's access road opened to a cleared area in a wooded enclave with enough room to park church goers cars, for children to play and for the wood framed church building that sat alone in the center of the clearing.

Although it was a small, simple, wooden structure, it seemed very large and stately to me at the time. To my knowledge, churches were the only independent organization in our area that was owned by Black folks, and as simple as the church was, the fact that Mill Branch Missionary Baptist was our church gave me an enormous sense of pride. For some of the Mill Branch saints, the winter's chill in the church was no match for the heat generated by the moving of the Holy Spirit. A big, wood-burning stove was required to warm the rest of us. The hot summer air in the church was conditioned only by rapidly moving hand-held cardboard fans picturing praying hands or a beautifully attired Black family on one side and an advertisement for Shaw Funeral Home on the other. Open windows throughout the building could not have provided much relief from the

Carolina heat, but somehow I don't remember ever being very hot or uncomfortable. The sanctuary was built in the shape of a "T" or the cross that was common for Baptist churches of that day. Young church goers and the general population of the congregation entered from the rear of the church and sat in the center of the building. My mother always entered the sanctuary from a side door at the front of the church and sat on the left of the pulpit with the deacon's wives and female leadership. My father always entered from the side door on the opposite side of the church and sat on the right of the pulpit with Eli Bell, Ben Robinson, Manson Hemmingway and other Mill Branch deacons. That area of the church was commonly referred to as the amen corner.

Once-a-month services were a common practice for rural community churches at that time and Sunday preaching services were held at Mill Branch on the second Sunday of each month. Cherry Grove Baptist Church had services on the first Sunday. Mill Branch had services on the second Sunday. Diamond Branch Baptist Church would hold services on the third Sunday, and New Mount Zion would have preaching on the fourth Sunday. Most of the members of the other churches in the area were neighbors and or related, so on the Sundays when their home church was not in service, they would attend one of the other local churches. My father seemed to always be in a position of leadership at the church.

His position as superintendent of the Sunday school required that he sit at a table in the front of the church every Sunday morning as individual Sunday school classes were held in different parts of the sanctuary. When I was a very young child, I really felt important when he would allow me to sit at the table with him as he went about his duty of maintaining order in the midst of all of that activity.

On the second Sunday of the month, I was always with my family for our church's "preaching" service. My father seemed to be the perennial chairman of the deacon board, so he was usually involved in the worship services and often led devotion before the service. Although my father was not a singer himself, he would sometimes lead the singing through something called "lining." With no musical accompaniment, He would read a line in a singing cadence from a small hymnbook. Once he had completed this read / singing of a line, the entire congregation would then join in and sing the line that he had just read. The congregation would sing the lines in common meter, so the arrangement or style of all of the hymns would be common or the same.

I remember asking my father why they sometimes sang in this manner. He told me that during slavery time and for years afterward, colored people (*his description, not mine*) would perhaps have one precious hymn book and no musical instruments. During their church service, someone who might be literate would read a line from the book and the other worshippers in attendance would sing what was just read in common meter. Occasionally the congregation of Mill Branch Baptist Church would sing in this manner to honor the tradition.

On the second Sunday, or Mill Branch's preaching Sunday, the members must have felt as if they needed to dress their best to give God their best. The tradition of dressing up for church in the Black community goes all the way back to the period just after slavery in this country. We have always been a spiritual people so church was the most important institution we had. When we were in bondage, we had to have permission to attend worship services on Sunday and all we had to wear on the Lord's Day were the rags we had toiled in day and night for the prior six days. After emancipation we demonstrated our freedom by worshipping faithfully, dressing up to present ourselves to the church and our Lord and Savior in our finest attire. For the ladies, nothing but your very best Sunday outfit would be worn on this day. Of course the outfit had to be accessorized with the best of care. My mother would always make sure that she had her very best stockings, with no runs, even during the hottest dog days of summer. Going to church "barelegged" as she used to say, was unthinkable. Of course they had to have the matching shoes, handbag and even gloves. The head of every woman was adorned with hats so elegant that in another place and time, they could have served as glorious crowns. The men also came in their finest double-breasted suits and at that time most men wore hats. They appeared stately and important as they headed into the sanctuary, even though the day before they may have been covered with the unavoidable sticky gum from working the tobacco fields or the dirt and grime from Sledge's Saw Mill. Quite often, their white employers would have no idea that the Black men who they employed were very important members of the Black church community. Yesterday one of our Christian brothers may have been a poor, struggling sharecropper but today he is superintendent of our Sunday school. Yesterday he may have been a janitor but today he is chairman of our Deacon board. Yesterday he may have been someone's gardener but today he is our church pastor.

Once the men had greeted each other with a handshake, after the women had greeted each other with a heavenly hug and after nearly every child's cheek had been pinched, (I had dimples then, so I got pinched a lot) we all entered the church and the service began. It didn't take long for the faithful to get into a posture of praise. Seemingly, the saints entered the church with an expectation and anticipation of pouring spiritual kerosene all over the sanctuary and setting the church on fire with the Holy Ghost. The church did not have a musician or a choir during my very early years so the service would begin by someone in the congregation starting an old, soul-stirring song. The songs were not the traditional Negro spirituals or even gospel. These songs definitely were not the *Guide me, O Thou Great Jehovah* kind of music. It was more of a *The Lord Will Make a Way Somehow* variety. The pain, the tone, spirit and soulfulness of the music conveyed a message of "you don't know what I know" or "you don't know what I've been through". Even without musical accompaniment, the songs also delivered a powerful message of comfort, hope and redemption. They were more than the standard requirement for worship service. The Mill Branch saints sang those songs as a testimony to their years of experience of The Lord actually making a way out of no way.

At some point during the service, the tempo and tone was changed from worship to that of church business. The business of the church meant that announcements of all upcoming events had to be made. The announcements would end by informing the church of where the Pastor was to have dinner. Since churches had preaching services only once per month, preachers were typically pastors of more than one church and usually came from other communities. On the Sunday that they preached at your church, he and his family were always invited to a member's home for Sunday dinner. More often than not, the person reading the announcements would end by saying, "The Pastor will be the guest of Deacon

Wayland and Sister Lillie Jones today for dinner."
After all of the scheduled activities of Mill Branch
were announced, members in attendance from
other area churches, *every* area church, would
stand and inform our congregation of what was
going on in their church. Since there were no social
media computer sites, no email and since many in
the community didn't even have telephones, the
church also served as a place where information
was dispensed. With all announcements complete,
it was now time to call on two brother deacons
to *lift* an offering. I never understood why the
deacons lifted instead of collected an offering,
but they would always *lift* the offering. Another
inspirational, hand-clapping song was rendered
as everyone filed around the church and dropped
their money on the offering table. The deacons
would busily count the money while the collection
process was still in effect. Once everyone had an
opportunity to contribute and the counting was
complete, the deacons would make a declaration
of what had been collected. The disclosure of what
was lifted often came with a plea for more money.
"We have collected twenty six dollars and eighty
five cents. Now Mill Branch, we can do better than
that. Can we get thirty dollars for the Lord?" With
that request, members who had already made
a contribution would sacrifice even more until
finally the goal was achieved. Occasionally, our
church would also collect an offering for Shaw
University in Raleigh, North Carolina. I remember

my father or one of the other deacons making a plea to the congregation by saying, "Shaw is our school and we need to send them something." I suppose that the fact that it was Black, founded immediately following the period when most African Americans were held in slavery, and the fact that they had Baptist affiliations gave poor Black Mill Branch Baptist a sense of pride, ownership, and more important, a sense of responsibility. Following the request, the already financially stretched congregation would again dig deep into their pockets and purses for more nickels, dimes and quarters for Shaw University. The five or six dollars collected would then be set aside to send to Shaw.

With the business of the church complete, the focus returned to worship. The return to worship would begin with a song followed by the deacon's prayer and then the most important song of the service because it set the mood for the Word to be delivered. This had to be one of those emotionally stirring songs that moved not only the spirit but also the body. The song would echo off the walls of the church and was somehow naturally amplified through the trees as it wafted out of the surrounding church enclave. You could hear that joyful sounds of the Mill Branch saints at least a half of a mile from the church. The vocal exclamations of praise were often accompanied by Holy dances which we called shouting. That's what happened when someone in the church *got happy.* When the spirit came over them and they got happy, some of the Holy Ghost filled sisters would do the Holy dance or shout to such an extreme that they had to be supported or restrained by fellow female members so they would not lose their beautiful Sunday church hats or their modesty.

Just when you thought that the song was about to end and the excitement subside, so the preaching could begin, a deacon named Zeno Davis, who was known for his singing all over Columbus County, might pick-up the song and take it to an even higher level of praise. When Zeno Davis sang, someone was bound to get happy. The waving of hands, the shouting, and everything that accompanied spiritual euphoria would start all over again. Everything that is except speaking in tongues. We didn't speak in tongues. Mill Branch was a Baptist church. Speaking in tongues was something done by those strange Pentecostal folks. When the singing would finally end, quite often the spiritual euphoria had not, but it was preaching time. The pastor would take his position in the pulpit even as the congregation continued to shout their praise to their Lord and Savior. The difference now was that they were being exhorted to do so by the pastor.

Slowly, and after the Spirit had its way, order would be somewhat restored and attention would now be focused on the preacher. The preacher might start his sermon by saying something like "Today I'm going to take my text from Luke chapter 15, verses 11 through 32." Taking a text meant that his message would be derived from that particular part of scripture. The preacher may have begun his sermon with the story of the Prodigal Son, but to me it seemed that by the time he had finished, he had repeated every cogent point at least three times and had run through the entire Bible from Genesis to Revelations. Unless the preacher had done some powerful wailing and whooping he had not really preached, so with a lot of vocal encouragement from the congregation, the pastor usually gave the Mill Branch faithful what they came for. The call-and-response style of preaching was very common in Black churches during those days. It is still popular in some of our churches today. When the preacher started wailing or whooping during his sermon he was certain to get a favorable response from the congregation. Every time the pastor would pause during this whooping-style preaching, the members would respond with spiritual encouragement. "I heard a voice say, hah, (preach on brother) you can't cross that old river Jordan, hah, (that's right) unless you been born again, hah, (hallelujah!)."

Almost every member of the congregation is on his or her feet with hands extended and shouts of praise lifted toward Heaven that seemed to invite the visitation of the Holy Spirit. The electricity in the air and a holy dance by one of the sisters getting happy was testament that the Spirit had indeed made a visit.

When the singing, praying, preaching and shouting was over for this second Sunday of the month, many Mill Branch members often lingered in the churchyard to converse with each other. Ignoring my whining and persistent objections, my family would also linger to socialize with the other congregants, unless we were scheduled to host the pastor at our house for dinner. In that case, my mother would insist that we beat a hasty retreat up that dirt road to Highway 130 and break all of the speed limits in Columbus County to get home as soon as possible. If the preacher was coming to our house for dinner, Lillie Jones was going to be prepared!

When the announcement was made during the church service that the pastor and his family were to be guest at our house for dinner, my expectation was that our dinner table would be straining to hold all of the food my mother was to place on it that afternoon. We were not a wealthy family by any means, but since we and most other families in our community grew much of what we ate, we produced great quality and quantities of food. When my mother had guests, she spared nothing. We would have two or three different vegetables from her garden. Of course, one of them would be collard greens that had been "looked" twice, meaning checked for bugs and worms, and washed three times before they were expertly cooked in fatback or ham hocks. We would have two or three meats, perhaps beef and one dish of fried chicken and yet another of stewed chicken and dumplings. We always had my mother's famous freshly baked biscuits as she made them every day for every meal. Desert would not be pie or cake; it would be pie, cake and perhaps a delicious banana pudding. My mother had a reputation for being a great cook and she reveled in the opportunity to display her talent for cooking, or as my father would say to "show out." She would never disappoint. The dinner would taste as if (to use more of my father's words) "she put her foot in it."

The announcement in church of the pastor as our dinner guest also meant that we could expect to have several uninvited members of the congregation stopping by our house for dinner. They did not disappoint either. About thirty minutes after we would get home from church they would start to just show up knowing that southern tradition demanded that when dinner is served, anyone present is asked to join in. The additional guest never concerned me as my mother always prepared enough for everyone and enough for leftovers for the coming week. Following these wonderful Sunday dinners, the family, friends, and fellow church members who just happened to stop by, would sit around and fellowship with each other. If I was not running wild or playing baseball with the other neighborhood kids, I would spend those special Sunday afternoons listening to the conversations and to all of the stories the grown folks told. As a child, I would have never considered participating in adult conversation. Merely asking a question during one of these Sunday afternoon chats would have signaled that I was sticking my nose into grown folks' business. After all of our guest had departed, I would have paid dearly for such a serious breach of southern Black etiquette, so I just lingered inconspicuously within earshot and heard talk of tobacco crop concerns, family members remembered, Republicans reviled, and Jesus praised.

It was in this environment that my spiritual foundation was formed. No other institution has had the effect on my life and being as Mill Branch Missionary Baptist Church. I guess it was the first place that I saw faith in action although I was too young to fully comprehend what I was experiencing. That place didn't just make an impression on me; it is in me. It's in my DNA. I've heard that DNA has memory. Perhaps the ancestors of my parents left spiritual DNA in those church pews that was recognized by and connected to my soul. During my travels, I have been blessed to see the magnificent Notre Dame cathedral in Paris, The Sultan Ahmed (Blue) Mosque in Istanbul, The Sagrada Familia in Barcelona, Westminster Abby in London, mega churches, opulent temples, crystal cathedrals and awe inspiring houses of worship all over the world. None of them had the effect on me that a little country church in an enclave at the end of a sometimes muddy road has. Those beautiful and historic places of worship are not in my daily thoughts. Those places are not the frequent pleasant dreamscape that Mill Branch Missionary Baptist Church is. I guess they are just not in my DNA.

A FATHER'S WORK FROM SUN TO SUN

Throughout my childhood, the primary occupation for my father was tobacco farming. Like all of the farmers of color that I knew, he also held several other jobs because sharecropping on a tobacco farm never provided enough income to support a family year round. Farmers usually held other jobs to supplement their income. The first of these additional jobs that I can recall being held by my father was at Sledge's Saw Mill. The saw mill, and it's owner, Ferebee Sledge were very important contributors to the area's economy, and in addition to tobacco farming, the mill was the life blood of Whiteville's economy. Since Black people were never hired for any white collar and few blue collar jobs, Sledge's Lumber Company provided nearly all the non-agricultural jobs for Blacks in Whiteville. One of their full-time employees was my father's brother Henry. Uncle Henry was a lifetime employee of Sledge's or the companies that purchased and succeeded them. The lumber company also had rental properties in two housing sections called The First and Second Quarters which were located in the Borough of Brunswick, about two miles south of where we lived. Both sections had rows of small, fairly well maintained homes where many of the company's employees lived. My father's sister Ellen lived there long after her husband Cleveland died. Before Uncle Cleveland became ill, he had been a logging truck driver for The Sledge Lumber Company. In addition to our relatives, my family also knew everyone else who lived in The Quarters.

On the third Sunday of the month, my family would join the residents of the Quarters in worship at New Mount Zion Missionary Baptist Church, which stood at the entrance of the First Quarters. In addition to the First and Second Quarters, which housed relatives and other folks that I knew, Sledge also owned another section we referred to as The White Quarters. That area was for white employees of Sledge Lumber Company. I didn't know anyone who lived there. If you were just driving through the neighborhood, and didn't know its history, the beautiful spacious homes, with manicured lawns, on tree lined streets, would never have revealed the fact that they were Sledge rental properties. They certainly bore little resemblance to the quarters where Sledge's Black workers lived. When Sledge owned a lumber mill in the Brunswick community, he also owned a store on Highway 130 about two miles south of where we lived. The company store or commissary, as it once had been called, was the location where most employees of Sledge's mill did their shopping. Although the mill in Brunswick had been closed and the company store sold to a former Sledge business partner named E.L. Vinson long before I was born, the employees of the huge Sledge lumber mill in Whiteville still did their shopping at the company store in Brunswick. I don't think that many people knew the legal name of the store was The Brunswick Supply Company. We just referred to it as the company store. The company store not only provided credit for Sledge's employees, but they also provided the credit that was so crucial to area farmers until they took their crops to market. The building which housed the company store was a huge, one-room structure with a ceiling that must have exceeded twenty feet. They sold food, clothing, guns, and just about every other item you could possibly need or want. In true general store fashion, merchandise hung on every wall from the floor to the twenty-foot ceiling. The store clerks always knew exactly where everything was located and often had to scale a long ladder to retrieve a requested item. Think of it as a 1950s Super Wal-Mart.

The home next door to the company store was also owned by E. L. Vinson. It was a beautiful and tastefully done antebellum-style home that could have been used as a backdrop in scenes of the movie "Gone with the Wind." It was evidence of his success and the wealth that Sledge and his associates had achieved from their business enterprises in Whiteville.

Sledge's Lumber Company was the first enterprise I can recall that provided a non-farming job for my father. I don't know what job he performed at the mill, but I know the work was hard because my father would come home after a long day at the mill completed exhausted. In Whiteville, during those years, overtime was nonexistent. Black men were happy to get as many hours of work as they possibly could, for six days per week, at the regular low hourly rate. Through my mind's eye, I can still see my father coming home from work at Sledge's Saw Mill late on one Saturday afternoon. My father was a tough guy, but he looked as if the mill had whipped him on that day. He could barely make it up the walkway to our house. Although he was completely exhausted, his step quickened as he reached the middle of the walkway, cautiously glancing to his left and his right, trying to avoid the attack he usually suffered in our front yard on a near daily basis. Just before my father reached the house, his nemeses, my brother Bobby, who must have been about twelve or thirteen years old at that time, sprang from the hedge bushes where he had been hiding and dove for my father's feet. My brother made a tackle that any all-Pro safety would have been proud of. He had wrapped up both of my father's ankles sending him and his lunch box sprawling to the ground. By the time my father had regained his composure, and was set to take his revenge on his second son, Bobby, as quick as a cat, jumped up, evaded my father's attempt at catching him and was gone. When my mother and the rest of the family who witnessed one of Bobby's raids on his father, we would almost double over laughing whether my brother made a clean getaway or was caught and got a good head mauling by my father. During a head mauling, my father would grip your head under his arm and vigorously rub the top of your head with a clenched fist. Getting your head mauled was more embarrassing than painful. When Daddy caught Bobby and mauled his head, it was my father's time to do the laughing.

When Bobby escaped without being caught on that Saturday, my father's instruction to my mother was, "Lillie, you need to make those children behave!" My mother's reply through her laughter was, "They are your children. You make them behave!"

I don't think that my father ever wanted my brother to behave. We knew he enjoyed the matches of strength and wit with Bobby no matter how tired he was. Meanwhile my brother was somewhere around the house in hiding. He was probably plotting how he would spring Monday's surprise attack on our father. My father was to get one day's reprieve. My brother couldn't challenge my father the next day. The next day would be Sunday, and my father didn't stand for that kind of foolishness on the Lord's Day.

Another of my father's jobs during the tobacco off-season was at the Whiteville Pecan Market. Working during the winter pecan season represented a great opportunity for my father, as he could bring in additional income at a time when there was no work to be done on a tobacco farm. Every year, The T.B. Young Pecan Company from Florence, South Carolina would open a site for purchasing pecans at The Farmers Warehouse at the edge of downtown Whiteville. Each year, just like clockwork, the manager of the site would contact my father, and ask him to come in to work with him. I don't know when or how, but over the years, my father had become the preeminent pecan expert in Columbus County. His knowledge of pecans was nothing short of amazing in my eyes. He knew every variety of pecans grown in Southeastern North Carolina, and could access their value by the look and weight of one or two of them held in the palm of his hand.

In short, the pecan market could not run as it did without my father. The manager of the site never made that fact a secret to his employer T. B. Young or anyone else he encountered in the workplace. But this was North Carolina in the late 1950s or early 1960s, so no matter how skilled my father was, the job of management and the higher pay that accompanied it, went to the white man. Even after the manager made it clear that my father made the decisions on the class, quality and the prices they would pay, the white pecan sellers would still speak only to the white manager about those issues, turning to my father only for help with unloading the sacks of pecans to be sold. It was a comical site for me to see southern racial etiquette in action as the pecan sellers, the white manager and my father stood side by side and negotiated the buying and selling of pecans. The prices and pecan-related terms stated in my negotiation portrayal may not be accurate, but the tenor and tone of the sessions usually went as follows:

Seller to manager: "What will you give me for my crop of pecans?"

Manager turns to my father: "Wayland, how much should we pay for this batch?"

My father to manager: "$1.55 per pound."

Manager turns to seller: "$1.55 per pound."

Seller to manager: "That's a little low. I was expecting $2.00 per pound?"

Manager turns to my father: "Why so low Wayland? Can we pay him $2.00 per pound?"

My father to manager: "These are grade two Steward. We only pay $1.75 for grade one.

Manager turns to seller: "We don't even pay $2.00 for grade one Stewards. You have grade two."

My father to manager: "He has a large load, go ahead and give him $1.65."

Manager turns to seller: "Okay, I can give you $1.65."

Seller to manager: "Okay, It's a deal."

Manager turns to my father: Wayland, help him unload. I'll write him up.

This form of negotiation at the pecan market was sometimes frustrating to my father, the manager and even the sellers. Although my father was the one person at the market that could help them, sellers would never look him in the eyes or speak to him as an equal.

Even before the pecan market had closed in January, it was time for my father to begin his primary occupation: tobacco farming. The hundreds of acres of land once owned by the families of my parents were long gone by this time. The land that we owned at this time was sufficient for homes and large gardens, but we did not own the acreage required for tobacco farming. For the land necessary to grow tobacco, we turned to a farmer from the Mill Branch section named James

Earl Hill. He was the brother of Tom Hill, the owner of the house where I was born and the little store next to it where my brothers stole candy. Earl Hill had taken over the small family farm after he returned home from World War II. Because of his hard work and dedication to the land, he prospered as his farm grew with the post-war economy. He began to acquire additional farmland during that period and by the mid-1950s, he had purchased enough land for six sharecropping families to plant as much tobacco as they wished to plant.

The process of tobacco farming begins in abiding faith that you will have a prosperous year during the month of February with the planting of tiny seeds in a covered bed to grow the tobacco plants. It comes to a joyous end in late summer when the crop is sold in the warehouses. In the middle of the process, there are long hard days of toil in the unbearable Carolina heat. There are sleepless nights filled with worries that a draught, a flood, a hurricane, or a hailstorm might completely destroy the primary source of income for your entire family. It was a difficult way to make a living, but for some folks who farmed tobacco, it was all that they knew. Some people, however, just love tobacco farming. I think that my father was one of those people.

Although my father was the one who liked tobacco farming, it was the entire family who had to participate in it. There were no child labor laws on a farm. As a matter of fact, children were expected to do farm labor. When America was primarily an agrarian society, school hours and school seasons were set to make children available for farm work. The school day ended at two or three in the afternoon because there was still sufficient light for us to do farm chores. The school year ends in May or June, making children available for work during the growing season on a farm. School would begin again in the fall when the harvest is complete. If your family was involved in tobacco farming, even before the school year ended in May or after it began in September, there was work for children to do on the farm. After-school activities and sporting events had to be either scheduled around your work or they were replaced by your work on the farm. From the beginning of the great North Carolina tobacco boom in the 1880s, to the early 1950s, 900 man hours of labor was required to cultivate one acre of tobacco. It was a labor intense occupation, and the labor demands of tobacco farming sometimes required school-aged children to work on the farm during school hours. While education was always valued in our family, my education, and the education of every child of tobacco farmers that I knew, was compromised by the demands of the farm. That's just the way it was. That was just one of the things you dealt with when you made your living on a tobacco farm.

Tobacco beds must be prepared for planting in January. The planting beds themselves must have been about twenty feet long and about ten feet wide. There was usually about four to six beds grouped together in an open field, but near the edge of the forest to help shield the tiny new plants from the cold north wind. Each bed would have rich fertilized soil devoid of any weeds, and they were framed by logs that were ten to twelve inches in diameter. Early February would be the time to sow the tobacco seeds in the bed that had been prepared the prior month. Once the expensive tiny tobacco seeds were broadcast into the carefully prepared tobacco beds, they were watered and covered with large linen or cheesecloth-type material attached to the logs framing the bed. The cloth material was to protect the valuable young plants from the cold and frost. All of the sharecroppers on Earl Hill's farm would work together as somewhat of a communal manner, while preparing and planting the tobacco beds as the plants would be used for all of them. The families on the farm worked well together, and all of them except the family of Ben Robinson were related to us. Although we were not related to the Robinsons, we worked with them for many years and had a close relationship with them that was just like the rest of our family. The Robinsons were also members of Mill Branch Baptist Church as well.

Early in the month of April, when the tobacco plants were about six to eight inches high, it was time for the real work of tobacco farming to begin. After the fields were deep-plowed and fertilized, the rows prepared, and the Farmers Almanac consulted to make sure we had the proper moon for planting, the plants were carefully gathered from the tobacco beds and transplanted in the fields. As with almost everything else associated with tobacco farming, planting tobacco was also very labor intensive. In the early days, planting was done by digging a hole in the earth with a wooden peg, placing a tobacco plant into the hole, adding a piece of fish or *some other* natural fertilizer with water, and closing the hole. During my youth, we were a little more advanced than they were in the early days, but the process was still hard work. Because our entire tobacco field of several acres of land had to be planted in one or two days, four or five two-person teams of workers had to be employed to complete the task. An ingenious gadget we called a transplanter was used for placing the tobacco plants in the freshly prepared rows. A transplanter was a device made of lightweight metal, most likely tin, and it stood about three feet tall. It had a cone shaped cylinder that held water, and yet another for dropping in the tobacco plants. Both cylinders narrowed at the bottom into a smaller cone used to burrow a hole into the plowed ground. The male team member's strength was required to carry the cylinder full of water, and operate the spring release on the handle, while the female team member walked backwards as they dropped a single plant into transplanter cone provided for that purpose. As each plant was dropped, the operator of the transplanter thrust the device into the ground and pulled the spring release, dispensing the plant, and the correct amount of water, followed by a tap of his foot to close the hole. This whole operation was done with such precise rhythm that the operator of the gadget was able to set each tobacco plant about two feet apart while working at a regular walking pace. The water supply was carried in two huge four-foot high barrels drawn on a wooden sleigh by a big Belgium farm horse named Emma. When the water reached a low point in a transplanter, the operator would yell "water boy!" That was my signal to spring into action. As a water boy, it was my job to fill a bucket with water from one of the barrels and hurry to fill the transplanter of the operator who was running low. I would then drive the horse and sleigh a few feet in the field to keep pace with the workers.

From the time the tobacco plants are in the ground, until the time the final product is sold, there is always work to be done on the farm. Quite a bit of work needed to be done in early spring, before the end of the school year. During this time of year, school activity was usually more intense, and end of the year testing was also being done. These school days were far too important to miss for work on the farm. Although we didn't stay home from school to work on the farm during this time of the year, my brothers and I sometimes worked a couple of hours before school, and we worked after school on a regular basis. When the school day was over and our friends who were not children of farmers bounded off of the school bus to hit the basketball court or just to hang out with their buddies, quite often my father was standing by his car, waiting for us to change from school clothes to work clothes to join him on the farm. My brothers and I all hated tobacco farming, but none of us hated it more than Bobby.

If Daddy was not waiting for him when he got home from school, Bobby would hide out until my father could waste no more time looking for him. He would not come out of hiding until Daddy had left for the farm. When we got home in the evening, Bobby usually had to suffer the consequences of his actions. Bobby knew there would be hell to pay if he didn't go to the farm after school, but he hated the farm so much, he would rather take a whipping that go to the farm after school. My father did cut me some slack or made allowances for my after school activities. I played varsity baseball and I also played drums in the school band. When I had practice or games after school, my father never kept me from participating even though there was work to be done.

If you were able to control the insects and disease that could destroy your entire tobacco crop, and you had prayed your way through the natural disasters of spring, your reward would be even harder work during the summer. Most kids were happy to see summer come. To most farm kids, the end of the school year means full-time work on the farm. Even at an early age, I preferred the history and English I learned at Central High School to the tobacco field and the hot sun waiting on Earl Hill's farm. The summer months of June, July and August were the most important to tobacco farmers as everything done during these months was to prepare for the harvest, then perform the harvest, and sell the harvest. Of the three tasks, preparing for the harvest was the hardest work. Fields had to be plowed to turn under some of the weeds and to push the soil close to the roots of the tobacco plants. Whether the plowing was done with the big horse named Emma, one of the mules, or in later years, a tractor, that job was always reserved for my father. You had to be skilled to plow a tobacco field. If my father had trusted that task to one of his careless sons, we would have most likely plowed under half of his tobacco plants. However, there was still plenty of work for us to do during this period. I remember using a handmade curved stick to gently pull from the soil the tips of the tobacco leaves covered by the plowing. We also did a lot of weeding with hand-held hoes and rakes to prevent the weeds from overtaking the crop.

During this time of intense growth, tobacco plants had to be "topped and suckered." Like most other plants, tobacco plants grow flowers before coming into maturity. When this flower grows at the top of each plant, the farmer must manually snap off the flower by hand. In addition to the flower buds at the top of the plant, parasite buds called suckers grow between the leaves of tobacco plants. The flower buds and "suckers" had to be removed because they sucked the nutrients from the plant, stunting the growth of the all-important tobacco leaf. Suckering, or removing the little buds from between the leaves, was a never-ending process. As soon as you completed suckering your entire field, a new crop of the "little suckers" had grown in their place, and the process had to start all over again. The laborious task of suckering tobacco and many of the other jobs we performed as children on the farm are no longer necessary. Farmers discovered that uncovering tobacco leaves after plowing was a waste of time, and they now apply a chemical to the tobacco plants to prevent them from growing suckers. The hundreds, or maybe even thousands of hours we spent before and after school working at just those two jobs alone would not even be required on today's tobacco farm. I guess I was just born too soon. (Damn.)

Before your crop could be harvested, threats to its survival seemed to come on a daily basis. There was the threat of not enough water. There was the threat of too much water. There was the threat of too much hot weather. There was the threat of too much cold weather. There was the threat of hurricanes, hailstorms, and the dreaded tobacco worm. The nicotine in tobacco plants makes it toxic to most insects, so they won't eat it. (Yes, we are willing to put into our lungs, the smoke of something that most insects will not eat, but that's another story.) The horned tobacco worm however, can eat the plant and suffer just one effect. It makes them fat! Unchecked, the worm will slowly destroy an entire field of tobacco. In fact, the appetite of this insect is so veracious, its Latin scientific name Manduca describes it perfectly. The Latin name Manduca's English translation means glutton. When the tobacco plants were small, we would fight the tobacco worm with powdered pesticides applied manually. We used a coffee can nailed to a stick with small holes in the bottom of the can to dispense the poison onto the plants. This poison worked best very early in the morning because it would stick to the freshly fallen dew on the plants. This meant that quite often on school days, my entire family would be in the fields shaking insecticides on tobacco plants before sunrise. We would then return home, wash the poison off of our bodies as best as we could, eat a full breakfast and be ready for school by the time the school bus arrived. When the plants were taller, my father would use a horse-drawn, or in later years, a tractor drawn sprayer to battle the tobacco worms.

Also in those early years, the pesticides were a lot more potent. Before DDT was banned, it was the pesticide of choice for killing tobacco worms. Now just think about that for a minute; here you have a plant that most insects will not eat, sprayed with DDT, then the cigarette manufactures add more nicotine and additional chemicals, and we are crazy enough to pay those cigarette makers to allow us to ingest the smoke from that product into our lungs. As I said before, that's another story, but the DDT my father freely handled year after year is part of my family's story. My father told me that even before DDT and some of the other strong pesticides were banned, he had concerns about using them. What he saw in the fields following a spray treatment gave him cause to be concerned. When he worked in the fields a few days after they had been sprayed, he would see rabbits, snakes and birds lying dead between the rows of tobacco. The pesticides that they used were targeted for insects. If they were strong enough to kill small animals, it could not be safe for humans. These poisons were being used in the 1950s, and we did not have all of the information on their effect on humans as we have today, so my father continued to use them until they were banned. I am convinced that it was the use of those poisons that caused his death. Although my father died in 1979, he suffered occasional seizures for several years before his death occurred. He believed that his illness and the brain tumor that would eventually take his life was a direct result of working with those powerful pesticides. On this point, I am in total agreement with him.

Early in July was finally the time to begin the harvest. I use the term harvest as not to confuse, but had I used that term when I was young, most of the tobacco farmers and workers would have thought I was very strange. You don't harvest, pick or even gather tobacco. You *crop* tobacco. The word crop here is used as a verb, meaning to harvest of gather. The people who gathered the tobacco were called *croppers*, so July was time for the croppers to crop the tobacco. Tobacco plants in New England and some other areas of the country are used for cigars, rappers for cigars, and other tobacco products. Some are harvested by cutting down the entire plant, and harvesting the entire field at one time. During my youth, the variety of tobacco grown in North Carolina and Virginia was used primarily for the manufacture of cigarettes. It was also harvested differently. The leaves on the plant ripened from the bottom to the top, and were gathered each week as they ripened. The first leaves to be gathered were called sand lugs as they hung just above or sometimes on the dirt or sand in the field. Because they were so low to the ground, they were covered with sand and were difficult to gather, or to crop. Gathering sand lugs was the most arduous task that had to be done during this period. Since the tobacco was cropped from the bottom, the croppers had to bend low to the ground to remove the two or three ripe leaves on the bottom of the plant. The croppers would then place the leaves that they just removed from the plant, under their free arm. The croppers would repeat this process, while bent low to the ground until they could no longer carry the bundle of leaves. Only then would they stand and place the armload of tobacco into the horse or mule-drawn sleigh designed to transport the tobacco leaves to the barn. The croppers would work in this manner sometimes from sun up until sun down. In addition to the back breaking work, cropping sand lugs also had another risk. Since the leaves were only an inch or so from the ground, the area under the leaf was a perfect place for snakes to rest or hide. Tobacco is cropped at a very rapid pace. The cropper had no time to see where he was placing his hand as they gathered it. Although danger could be lurking under every tobacco plant, to maintain their pace of work, most croppers threw caution to the wind as they rhythmically snatched the two or three ripe leaves from the bottom of the plant.

Seeing a snake in a field was a common occurrence. Picking one up accidentally was not something that happened often, but I had heard of people doing it, and I have actually witnessed it more than once, although it was not something that most croppers overly concerned themselves with. Most croppers that is, except my brother, Bobby. A fear of snakes is a healthy thing, and my brother had a little more than just a healthy fear of snakes. He was like Indiana Jones; he hated snakes! He didn't want to be anywhere around them or even see them. When he saw a snake on television, he would turn away because he said he would dream about them. Why is it that the person who hated snakes the most would be the person to see or find them more often than anyone else? I have no idea, but if there was a snake anywhere in Columbus County, either Bobby would find the snake or the snake would find Bobby. He would see more snakes that anyone I have ever known. Bobby even managed to pick up a snake while cropping tobacco, not once, but TWICE! The first time it happened, Bobby was working on someone else's farm, so I don't know the details first-hand, but on the second occasion, Bobby was working in my father's field, so I remember it well.

While cropping the dreaded sand lugs, Bobby was always careful to look where he placed his cropping hand. Although the work is done at a very rapid pace, Bobby would take the time to move the bottom leaves to make sure that there were no surprises lying beneath them. Being that cautious had to slow the process considerably, and he must have endured a lot of complaints and ribbing from his fellow workers. I don't know what happened on this particular day to avert his attention. Bobby may have gotten caught up in the pace of the work, or the bantering that always went back and forth between the croppers, but somehow he was cropping the lugs without his usual caution.

He was moving along with his coworkers, rhythmically snatching the bottom leaves from the tobacco stalk with his right hand and then with a slapping motion, holding them under the opposite left arm. At the point when his arm was almost full, he thought he felt movement in the bundle of tobacco under his left arm. After a fraction of the second it took him to confirmed his worst fears, Bobby had dropped the bundle of tobacco where a snake was squirming, and before the bundle had even hit the ground, Bobby was completely out of sight, tearing through the tobacco field like a wild man. Why he was running and where he was going, no one knew. My father thought that the snake had bitten him, and the last thing a person should do when bitten is to increase his heartbeat and get poisoned blood moving faster through your body by running. My father took off after my brother and only caught him when my brother was completely out of breath. My father then began to frantically search Bobby's side and under his arm yelling, "Where did it bite you?!!"

To my father's surprise, Bobby replied, "It didn't bite me."

To that, my father said, "You mean to tell me that you tore up all of my tobacco running through the field and you weren't even bitten!"

I told you that my father loved his tobacco.

Once tobacco is gathered, or cropped, it is placed into a horse or mule drawn sleigh that was about six or seven feet long, about four feet wide and about four feet high. The sides of the sleigh were constructed of burlap to gently hold the gathered or cropped tobacco without breaking the leaves. This sleigh was called a drag, and when it was used to move the cropped tobacco leaves from the field to the barn, the process was not called moving or transporting. It was called dragging. When I was too young to crop tobacco, my job was to drag tobacco, meaning to drive the sleigh that held the tobacco, from the field to the barn. Since the entire weeks tobacco crop had to be *"put in,"* meaning that it had to be gathered, tied to sticks, and carefully placed in the barn for curing, all in one day, everything had to move like clockwork. Although dragging the tobacco was done by young boys, it was an integral part of entire workflow. The croppers in the field could not be kept waiting for the drag, and the women who tied or strung the tobacco on the sticks could not be kept waiting for the tobacco from the fields. So just like clockwork, when I was dragging tobacco, I had to deliver the empty drag to the field, and take full one to the barn at such precise intervals that it kept everyone working. Just like most of the other jobs on the tobacco farm, my job as a drag boy was replaced by the much more efficient tractor and wagons designed for transporting tobacco from the field to the barn. Even greater automation replaced the tractor with a device that is just driven through the field with the croppers sitting in the shade for heaven sakes, while they cropped the tobacco that is also strung by the women riding on the unit. Again, I was just born too soon.

Because of the labor demands of harvesting tobacco, July was also the time when we became acquainted and reacquainted with the migrant farm workers that came into the area to work. Some of them were from Hamlet, North Carolina, the hometown of jazz legend John Coltrane. Most of them, however, were from the area around Georgetown, South Carolina. They actually lived in an old house near the tobacco fields we tended. We called them Geeches. They were Gullah people and spoke in a dialect that both confounded and amused us. For example, instead of saying something like "Please turn off the light," they might say "Out de lite."

Another worker that came each year was my cousin Bobby. Not to be confused with my brother, my cousin Bobby was the son of my Uncle Rob who lived in Wilmington, North Carolina. He would leave Wilmington at the end of each school year and come to live with us in Whiteville. He wanted to earn money to pay for high school expenses and clothes for the coming school year. Wanting to earn your own money as a young person is an admirable thing, but earning it in tobacco fields when you are unaccustomed to the hard work and hot sun is a difficult chore. Country boys, toughened by farm labor, would laugh and poke fun at city kids who had "monkeyed" while trying to work along with them in the fields. When someone felt faint from the heat and pace of work in the field, we would say that the person feeling faint was carrying the additional weight of a monkey on his back. If the person collapsed, we would say that the monkey got him, or that he had monkeyed. The country boys would always set a fast pace of work in the hot noon day sun just to test the stamina of a city kid unaccustomed to that kind of work. More often than not, they were unable to withstand the heat and pace of work, and when the monkey got them, we counted it a victory. My cousin Bobby was one of those city kids, and the first summer he came to live with us, my mother was concerned about his welfare. His rail thin appearance only heightened my mother's concern for the brother's child left in her care for the summer. Bobby very quickly proved that my mother had no reason to be concerned. Although he was slight and looked like a strong wind might blow him over, Cousin Bobby was tough as nails. He did everything that we did on the farm and when we finished a task in my father's fields, he would make even more money by going to work for someone else. I discovered early on that my cousin not only had the ability to make money, he also had the ability to keep his money. He was, shall we say, very thrifty. He watched every penny that he spent. When Bobby worked on our farm, my father kept a ledger of every day's work that was done and the amount of money owed to my cousin. When Bobby worked for someone else, he would bring his money home and give most, if not all of it to my mother for safe keeping. When the summer ended and it was time for him to return to Wilmington, my mother not only gave him what she was holding for him, but my father paid him for his work for the entire summer. He would return home to Wilmington, with what seemed to us at the time, like a boatload of money.

Bobby's money management skills, his toughness and his fortitude would again be exhibited later in his life. After Bobby graduated from Williston High School in Wilmington, like so many other young Black men, he decided to join the Army. He wanted to go to college, but he knew his family could not afford to send him, so he devised a plan to serve in the military and use the G. I. Bill to get college education. He chose the Army because he would only be required to serve three years instead of the four required by the Navy and Air Force. While he served in the Army, he managed to send his family enough money to build their first and only home. Although the Army pays you just enough to keep you poor, Bobby was determined to get his family out of The Taylor Homes Projects he had lived in all of his life in Wilmington. He sent home enough money during his three-year service to make it happen. Bobby's fortitude was again tested when a machine gun he was operating on an Army firing range exploded in this face, causing him to lose sight in one eye. He did not let the accident stop or even slow him down. After he was discharged from the Army, he entered A & T College, now A & T University in Greensboro, North Carolina. Persevering through his challenges, he graduated from A & T and became a successful architect. He is now happily retired and living in Chesapeake, Virginia. Once while we were reminiscing about the hard work on the farm, Bobby said that suckering tobacco, and cropping sand lugs in that hot sun, formed his attitude toward work for the rest of his life. He said that whenever he came upon the most difficult of assignments, the assignments that no one else wanted, the ones that seemed impossible, he would just pause and say to himself, "I've done something harder than this." I'm not at all surprised that my skinny cousin had a successful career. Remembering how careful he was with money, I also wouldn't be at all surprised if he had a few pennies stashed away somewhere.

Once we had *put in* a barn or sometimes two barns of tobacco, my father's work schedule only increased. The ripe but still pale green tobacco leaves had to be cured for three to four days before it could be prepared for market, so in addition to the work that farming demanded of him during the day, he also had to babysit the tobacco at night as it was curing in the barn. Curing tobacco is a tedious process. The kerosene fueled heating system had to regulated to burn at a precise temperature for a certain period of time, perhaps one day. Then the temperature would be increased for another period of time. This would go on for several days and nights, under the nearly constant watchful eye of my father. If he worked during the day, and was up all night curing tobacco. When did he sleep, you may ask? For that question, I have no answer.

Finally, during the month of August, it was time to sell the crop and see some of the financial reward for all of those months of hard work. Before tobacco was taken to market, however, there was yet another stage to go through. Once the tobacco is cured, the doors and windows of the barn used for curing are left open so that the moisture in the morning air can cool the cured tobacco and make it supple and easily handled. My father believed that the moist air also added a little weight, and more weight meant more dollars at market. The cooled tobacco was then moved from the barn to yet another barn we called a pack house. If there was a pleasant time for tobacco farming, I guess this would be the period. The work of removing the tobacco that had been strung on sticks, grading it by the quality of the leaf and tying it into small bundles to prepare for market was done during this time. Most of this work was done indoors, sitting down, and it was done at a pretty leisurely pace. That's one of the reasons it was a little more pleasant than the months of work that had preceded it.

A second reason this time may have seemed pleasant was the amity shared among the other families gathered in the three pack houses behind Earl Hill's residence in the Mill Branch section of Whiteville. My family worked in the smaller pack house immediately behind the residence. Working in the second and largest pack house was my Uncle Willie Johnson and his wife Aunt Emma, who was my mother's oldest sister. They were the parents of nine girls, and several of them would work with their parents at that time. The Johnson family shared that space with my father's cousin Bertha Bellamy and her family, and Cousin Bertha's brother, Pete Bellamy along with his family. The third pack house was occupied by Ben Roberson, his wife Katie and several of their children. Of all the folks that worked on that farm and in those pack houses, the Roberson family was the only ones who were not in some manner, related to us.

My job in the pack house was to *take off* tobacco, meaning to untie the small bundles of leaves tied to sticks that were earlier hung in the barn for curing. When I had taken off, or provided enough tobacco for the adults to grade and retie, I could play with Earl Hill's son Jimmy or Ben Robinson's son Joe, who everyone referred to as Joe Boy. Working in the pack house wasn't as much fun as romping through the nearby woods with Jimmy Hill or Joe Boy Robinson, but it was certainly more interesting and educational. Since the work was done inside and at a different pace than other farm work, my parents and the folks that worked for my father in the pack house would spin many tall yarns and even divulge some family secrets. I would go about my work, pretending to pay no attention, but with an ear always inclined for conversation I was not meant to hear. One story that my father told while we worked in the pack house concerned an event that occurred while he worked on the farm some years earlier. This story was unforgettable because it was so improbable, but this is my father's story.

As the legend goes, many years earlier, my father farmed three plots of land that were accessed by a road directly across Highway 130 from the house of my birth and Tom Hill's house and store. The access road ran through the forest to a clearing on the right that would be the first field, and then back through dense forest again to the second and finally the third clearing. The distance from Highway 130 and some form of civilization to the third clearing could not have been more than a mile, but a dense forest and a youthful imagination made it seem like a hundred miles. It was while plowing this third clearing my father said he had his very unusual experience. While working the field as he had done many times in the past, the mule pulling the plow became very agitated. The mule stopped in her tracks. My father noticed the mule's flared nostrils, the hair standing up on her back and the mule's ears pointing forward. My father was an experienced farmer and recognized these signs as fear in the animal.

The mule then tried to run with the harness and plow attached to her. My father regained control of the mule by taking the bridle and stroking the mule on the head to calm her down. He then began to look around to try to determine what was causing this panic in the animal. After standing there with a firm grip on the mule for several seconds, he spotted a large catlike creature walking across the end of the field. The cat was over three feet high and very large. It was obviously an adult. What was it? The eastern panther common to this area during colonial days was long gone. One or two had been spotted when they reentered the area, but these sightings were extremely rare. This was no panther my father watched walk across the end of the field. He had seen a panther in the past and this was no panther. My father, being an avid hunter and outdoorsman was accustomed to animals, even bears scurrying off into the woods when they came in contact with humans. This thing had no fear at all. It was calmly strolling across the plowed field and at one point it stopped, turned and looked at my father and the mule before walking off into the thicket. He had not seen this kind of cat before, but he knew exactly what it was. He had seen pictures of it many times. He had seen pictures of it in newspapers and magazines. He had also seen its picture in the religious paintings of the Bible. He had seen paintings in his picture Bible of David slaying this animal before he slew the giant. Yes, what my father swore he saw was a fully grown African loin with the unmistakably fully grown mane associated with the male lion. How could an African loin get to the Mill Branch section of Columbus County, North Carolina? I have no idea, but if my father said that he saw it, he saw it! We can only speculate that it must have escaped from captivity somewhere and made its way to the area undetected. You would think that my father would give up farming that field after seeing that creature. Not a chance. My father always found a way to do what he needed to do, and he needed to farm that land to support his growing family. He continued to work all three of those fields, even the one where he and the mule had been startled by the creature. However, after that sighting, he did tie his rifle to the plow when he worked that field alone. He never had to use his rifle against the creature that he saw. Thank God, the lion never made another appearance. He must have had the faith of David to think that he could stop a lion with a 22 caliber single shot rifle.

Although listening to tales and playing with the other children at the pack houses was fun, one aspect of this period was not. The school year would start before this part of the tobacco season had ended. My brother and I would always go to school every day for the first week. We would register, get assigned to a homeroom, and get our school books. After that, we would stay out of school to work on the farm for the next one or two weeks. At the beginning of each school year, I would have to study like crazy to catch up with the other kids who were in class every day. I was a solid B student, so it was not really difficult to read the material that I had missed and soon be on par with most of the class. The one subject which I could never catch up on, though, was math. At the beginning of each school year, I would miss the fundamentals of math for that year. Since there was no tutoring for students who were behind, I would just struggle all year with the subject. Since each subsequent year's math subject was built on what was learned the prior year, I struggled with math throughout my high school years. I was failing calculus so badly during my senior year that I just dropped it. Calculus was not a required subject, and I already had enough credits to graduate after my junior year, so dropping calculus had no effect other than contributing to my poor math education.

Thank God, the active period of tobacco farming ended in late August or early September with carefully packing up the graded, tied, pampered and pressed tobacco, and taking it to the warehouses in Whiteville to be sold. The buyers for R J Reynolds, American, and all of the other cigarette manufactures would descend on Whiteville to purchase the main ingredient for their Marlboro, Camel, Lucky Strike and other cigarette brands manufactured in Richmond, Virginia. Earl Hill made it a point to know all of the buyers, and even entertained some of them at his vacation home on nearby Lake Waccamaw to insure that his farmers not only got a fair price, but that they got the best price available for their crop. With the infusion of the much needed capital in the economy of Columbus County, the streets of its county seat Whiteville would bustle with activity that conveyed a message to everyone that *we just got paid!* It was also a time of celebration and thanksgiving in the Jones household. Perhaps even time to buy that expensive freezer we needed to store my mother's vegetables. Maybe even time for my father to buy that nice used car that he had been eyeing. One thing that I was sure it was time for when the tobacco season was over; it was time for my brothers and I to go to school every day, and it was time for my father to begin working at one of his other jobs.

A Mother's Work
Was Never Done

My mother was a cook. It wasn't just her job; it was her vocation. She was good at it and she enjoyed doing it. She especially enjoyed cooking for her family. Cooking for her family was never a task; it was an act of love, it was a way of giving, it was one of her contributions and a source of immense pride. I always assumed that she also enjoyed cooking on the series of jobs that she held, but I'm really not sure whether she did or not. I know that she never grumbled. Perhaps she dealt with her situation in manner the apostle Paul expressed in Philippians 4:11: "I have learned to be content in whatever circumstances I am."

My mother was born just nineteen years after the turn of the twentieth century in Lees Lake, North Carolina. She would have been old enough to work outside of her own home in the 1920s, so I guess that the only work available for a "colored girl" during that time was farm labor and some kind of domestic work that included cooking. My mother's first job was shucking oysters and cooking at a local restaurant in Lees Lake. My father was farming tobacco on the nearby Watt's farm at that time, so I imagine that she worked on the farm during the day and at the restaurant by night.

Each night my mother worked at that restaurant, my father and his friends would wait anxiously for her to return home because they knew that she would be loaded down with more seafood, including oysters, than they could eat, and certainly more that they could ever afford to buy. I guess it was my mother's first job that was at least partially responsible for my family's love of seafood, especially oysters. All of us loved oysters, especially my father. While engaging in his favorite pastime, slurping down a bushel of the oysters with his sons, he would jokingly express his love for the little mollusks by saying "fish make you live long, oysters make you love long." Dad seemed to have almost as much fun joking about oysters as he did eating them. Then again who knows? Maybe he wasn't joking!

The first job that I recall my mother holding was in the home of Charles McNeil and his wife Francis. Charles McNeil worked in the pharmacy business with his brother John who owned McNeil's Drugstore on Madison Street in downtown Whiteville. Charles and Francis McNeil lived in one of Whiteville's upscale segregated neighborhoods. The house was in close proximity to his brother John and his wife Carrie Margaret where my mother's sister Violet worked. I imagine that my mother did the same kind of household chores for the McNeils that she did for her own family. Cooking, cleaning, doing the laundry and taking care of the children. As Black-white, employee-employer relationships go, I guess this one was as good as any other. At least my mother never complained about them. But then again, my mother never complained about work. She did, however, make a comment about Francis McNeil *testing* her on one occasion, and she did not like that. When domestics found a small amount of money, or a small piece of jewelry lying around their employer's house, they believed that it was placed there to test the honesty of the employee. In the estimation of the employer, the amount of test money would have been just large enough to temp the employee, but small enough to convince the employee that it would not be missed if stolen. White homeowners wanted to know if the colored girl working for them would steal, so my mother and many workers like her believed that the employers would occasionally test them. I don't think that my mother would have stolen anything from anyone for any reason, so to put it mildly, she did not like to be tested.

My mother's next domestic job of note was with the Marks family in Whiteville. The farm equipment company owned by Mr. Marks appeared to afford the family a life of true southern comfort. The family was thoroughly entrenched in the circles of the community's elite. The large, stately family home was located on Whiteville's main thoroughfare, Madison Street, just north of the downtown business district. The Marks home made a bold statement about the family's class and status in the neighborhood where wealth, class and status was most evident. Four people were often required to maintain the Marks family home. Two men often worked outside of the house, while two women worked inside. Reverend Curtis Leach, a local minister that lived two houses from our home was one of the outside workers, and my mother worked with another lady on the inside. Mom's primary responsibility was cooking the meals, while the other woman's responsibility was cleaning the house. Sometimes however, my mother would assist with the housekeeping.

When my mother worked for the Marks, she always seemed to bring home household items given to her by Mrs. Marks. These items were prized by my mother, but I considered them junk. The only items I did not consider junk and was always glad to see were the magazines and periodicals my mother would bring home. Magazine subscriptions were a luxury the Jones family would not even have considered. Although the magazines Momma brought home were neither *Jet* nor *Ebony*, I still read them cover to cover. In addition to the household items, Mrs. Marks would often send us hand-me-down clothes that her sons outgrew or no longer wanted. There were four boys in the Marks family, three of which were about the same age as my brother Bobby, Larry and me. I'm sure Mrs. Marks meant well when she sent us the clothes, but my brothers and I refused to wear them. We had to work for white people to provide food and shelter for our families, but our pride would not allow us to wear the clothes they discarded. When my mother brought them home, we would just give them to someone else. There was no way that my mother would tell Mrs. Marks that we were too proud to wear her children's clothes. Black people would never want their employers to know that they were too prosperous or too proud. If you were too uppity or had too many material possessions that were the least bit appealing, you couldn't work for white folks. Whites had a place in that society and Blacks had another place. If Blacks appeared not to be staying in their place, many white employers simply would not hire them. If you appeared to be just getting by or living a day-to-day, hand-to-mouth existence, you were employable. Show too much pride or prosperity and white folks didn't want you working for them. To make sure white employers did not think their Black employees were too affluent, those workers would sometimes resort to using something called poor mouth or "po mouf" as it was called by the older generations. Poor mouth meant always speaking of one's self as being poor or in need. This may also have meant not wearing expensive clothes on your job, or not flaunting your new car in front of your boss.

You never wanted your employer to be aware of everything you owned. Prideful, prosperous Black folk would upset the social order, and I guess those employers didn't want to contribute to changing the system that they enjoyed. I simply loathed the practice of speaking po mouf, and detested even more the racism that made it necessary. Mrs. Marks continued to show her generosity by sending us hand-me-down clothes as long as my mother worked for her. So we would not appear to be too prosperous, my mother continued to show her appreciation by making a big fuss over the clothes, but my brothers and I continued to give them away.

My mother continued to work for the Marks family during my high school years and for several years after I left home. She somehow managed to work for the Marks until tobacco planting season began. She would them work with my father on the farm and work in the Marks home sparingly during the summer. She would then return to the Marks after the tobacco season had ended.

Mrs. Marks was pleasant enough, and I remember the occasional brief greetings from her when dropping my mother off or picking her up at the rear door of the Mark's home. However, it was a very short conversation that I had with Mrs. Marks after I finished high school and joined the Air Force that is most memorable. In fact, I will never forget it. It changed my thinking about race and class. It changed my life. Before that conversation,

I was a firm believer that I was obligated to defend my country. I was a history buff, you see, and had bought into to history of America that I had learned until that point in my beloved Central High School. I had studied the American history the North Carolina Department of Education wanted me to know, and admired the heroes of that history such as Benjamin Franklin, Thomas Jefferson, Patrick Henry and Thomas Paine. I knew little to nothing about the amazing history of ancient Africa or African people, nor did I know much about the real heroes of Black Americans. We didn't talk about them during regular history classes or even during our studies of famous *safe Negroes* during Negro History Week. I just knew the American history I was taught at Central, so when I joined the Air Force, I was proud to be counted as a defender of "American liberty."

Anyway, while I was home on leave following Basic Training, I drove to the Marks home as I had done many times, to pick up my mother after work. I was parked in the circle at the rear door when Mrs. Marks came out of the house and leaned over to speak to me through the passenger side window. She said, "Hello Billy!" using my family nickname. "I hear you have joined the Army."

"Yes ma'am, I joined the Air Force," I responded.

As Mrs. Marks stepped aside to allow my beaming mother to get into the car, she again bent down and said, "Well don't let the Russians get us."

I assured her that I would not and drove off with my very proud mother. All along the drive home, all that evening as I sat on the front porch, during that night, and for several days afterwards, I could not get Mrs. Marks and her comment, out of my mind. How could such a pleasant exchange haunt me so? How could such an innocuous comment have such an effect on me? How could those few words start me on the path of questioning my values and changing my life? When Mrs. Marks said, "Don't let the Russians get us," I began to go over in my mind her family situation and my family situation. I couldn't help it. I just kept going over it again and again. The Marks family seemed to have all of the good things America had to offer. I'm sure Mr. Marks took a risk going into business and worked hard to get what they had, but they also had every advantage. Meanwhile, my family worked extremely hard just to keep the wolf from the door. I did not begrudge the Marks of their wealth; as a matter of fact, I admired it. What bothered me so was her comment: "Don't let the Russians get us." They were living the American Dream; they had everything to defend, yet she was asking me to defend it for her. At that time, everyone was afraid of the communist, and southerners, whites, as well as Blacks had a fear and loathing of communist that bordered on paranoia. Mrs. Marks had four sons just like my mother, and I couldn't help but think if they want to preserve their way of life, why weren't her sons keeping the Russians from getting them? Why were my brothers and I expected to protect and defend their way of life? I couldn't imagine her sons ever worrying about tuition payments at the fine, southern universities they attended. When my brother Jaye attended A & T College in Greensboro, he lived with the constant fear that our parents would not be able to scrape together the required tuition for him to continue the next semester. Mrs. Marks' sons came back home from college to gainful employment and the beautiful homes, and lifestyles that their employment afforded them. They spent their weekends playing golf at the Whiteville Country Club, water skiing on Lake Waccamaw or frolicking in the waves at Myrtle Beach. Neither the employment nor the lifestyle that they enjoyed so much was available to us, even if we were qualified for the jobs or even if we could afford the lifestyle. With the exception of teaching in the Negro School System, educated Black folk had to leave Whiteville to obtain meaningful employment and the advantages attached to it.

From the day of that conversation with Mrs. Marks, my ideas about military service began to change. While I took pride in my military service, that service was no longer altruistic. The Air Force provided me with the opportunity to further my education, and the chance to meet new people and see different and exotic places. The military offered life possibilities that I probably would not have had otherwise, and for those opportunities, I served my country and put my life in harm's way. No longer did I count Patrick Henry, Thomas Paine, George Washington, Thomas Jefferson or even Abraham Lincoln as early American heroes. I then started on the path that led to new heroes like Crispus Attucks, Joseph Cinqué, Nat Turner, Toussaint Louverture, Denmark Vesey, David Walker and John Brown.

Even with the inequities of my early life, I still believe that America is worth protecting. I just don't believe that it's only the responsibility of those at the very bottom of the economic scale to do so. No, I'm not even a little bit of a socialist. I am a dyed-in-the-wool capitalist. I just believe that men and women of every economic class should stand shoulder to shoulder in defense of our core beliefs. I challenge anyone to question those right wing individuals with hawkish pro-war sentiments. Challenge the people who make comments like, "We should go over there and kick their asses." Ask them if they ever served or have intentions to serve in the military. What I have found when I asked – and believe me I've asked – is that they have never put their lives in danger for their principles, nor do they have any intentions of doing so. This is especially true among upper middle class or well-heeled right wingers that I have experienced. Right wing hawks are always in favor of war, they are just not in favor of fighting in a war. Since the day of that short comment from Mrs. Marks, I have tried to discourage my young family members from being used as human cannon fodder in American wars as long as those with the most to lose here at home, are willing to just sit back and enjoy life, while we are shipped off to foreign jungles and deserts to defend their liberty.

Just a few short years after my encounter with Mrs. Marks, Mr. Marks died and their American Dream became a nightmare. I was told that the farm equipment business he owned was apparently heavily leveraged, so shortly after Mr. Marks' death, his creditors foreclosed on the business and the family lost all of their property, including the beautiful house on Madison Street where my mother worked. Now Mrs. Marks's sons would be faced with a life that they had never known. They would go from being the cream of Whiteville's high society, to becoming ordinary working stiffs. There were rumors all over town of suicide attempts by family members unable to deal with the sudden and drastic class change. Some family members left town, unable to deal with the embarrassment of being suddenly reduced to the middle class. Mrs. Marks moved into a small apartment above a store in downtown Whiteville. After several years of having my mother and others work for her, and after being out of the workplace for decades, she took a job teaching at one of the local schools. Following my mother's work on the farm after tobacco season that year, she would have to find another job.

The next position held by my mother was that of a cafeteria cook with the Whiteville School System. She worked for several years, in several different schools, but she never worked at Central, the school that I attended. During those years, the school system was segregated. Central was a Black school, and my mother worked for the white Whiteville School System. My mother's habit of bringing food home from her job started when she worked at that seafood restaurant in Lees Lake, and it continued with every job she had, including her job with the school system. I don't think that the cafeteria food she brought home at that time was anywhere near as tasty as the seafood she brought home when she worked at the restaurant in Lees Lake. We devoured it anyway. Teenage boys will eat anything.

I believe that my mother enjoyed the job in the Whiteville School System more than any other. This was the first job that she held where she did more than just manual labor. Occasionally, workplace meetings were held on this job to review practices and procedures. She also traveled to Charlotte or Raleigh for three-day conferences on health, hygiene, sanitation, and other practices related to preparing and serving food safely. As inconsequential as these meetings and conferences may seem to you and I, they were a big deal for my mother. For the first time in her life, she was being paid to sit down and discuss her work. Staying in a fancy hotel when she went away on a conference was also a new and exciting experience. She enjoyed the daily interaction with the school children, and she made lifelong friends of some of the school's teachers. The cafeteria job in the Whiteville School System also provided another benefit not available from working on the farm or in the homes of the McNeil and Marks families. This was the first job where social security payments were made, entitling her to a social security pension. The job also came under the North Carolina State Pension System, so she was also entitled to a small monthly pension and health insurance after she retired. Without that health insurance, I'm sure that she would have never lived to the age of ninety-two.

AUNTS AND UNCLES,
OFTEN CALLED BY OTHER NAMES

Although there were dozens of relatives in my family who lived varied, and interesting lives, it would be next to impossible for me to chronicle, or even to mention them all. However, the siblings of both of my parents were very special to me. I am, to a degree, who they were. I knew them by my interaction with them on a regular basis, and by the family stories told of them. Now, I would love for you to know them.

Carl Lester Hill was my mother's oldest brother. He and his family had lived elsewhere in Columbus County until the mid to late 1950's, when he built his house on his inherited lot, situated between our house and Grandma Bert's house. On May 12, 1930, Uncle Les married Rosa Belle McCray. Her family was originally from Marion County South Carolina, but they had been living in Whiteville for several years by that time. Ironically, Uncle Les and Aunt Rosie had ten children, the same number of children born to his parents and his grandparents. Since his father died at an early age, he must have had to take on the responsibility of the man in the family when he was just twenty years old. Just like all of the Hill men, he carried a stern and serious countenance. In addition to his stern disposition, his six foot five frame also conveyed a no-nonsense message.

Once, upon hearing that his daughter Pauline, who we called Polly, had been in a physical altercation with her husband, Uncle Les never spoke a word, he just calmly went outside, opened the trunk of his car, took out a tire iron and proceeded to walk across the field that separated his house from the house that his brother Willie rented to Polly and her husband Wesley Flower. Uncle Les had a short waist and legs that seemed to go on forever. It was those very long legs that earned him the appropriate nickname of High Pockets. Those long legs seemed to gobble up real estate when he headed somewhere with serious determination, and today, High Pockets was definitely serious.

As he approached his daughter's house, her husband Wes came out, demonstratively waving his hands in what appeared to be an attempt to explain what had happened between him and his wife. Totally ignoring Wes' explanation, and without saying a word, uncle Les calmly walked up to Wes and whacked him on the side of the head with the tire iron. Wes of course dropped like he had been shot. Everyone who saw or heard that awful blow thought that Wes was dead. Uncle Les then turned, walked back across the field to his car, put the tire iron back in the trunk, then went into his house without a word. Thank God when Wes was revived, he was fine and didn't even go to visit a doctor, although I'm sure he had a headache for several days.

My father told me a funny story about Uncle Les. It happened when Uncle Les was a young man and had decided that he no longer wanted to be under the authority of his father. One day my grandfather had to make a *correction* to Uncle Les's behavior, and he no longer was going to stand for that. He must have been about sixteen or seventeen years old at the time. He was a man and he was not going to be disciplined like a boy. He was already taller than most men in the family and he no longer was going to follow the strict house rules of The Right Reverend Robert Luther Hill. He was leaving home.

Without packing anything, Uncle Les left his father's house on foot and he carried nothing with him except a bad attitude. The serious determined look on his brow and the strides he was able to take with those long legs was a signal to anyone who might be a witness to this act of defiance that he was a man; no one was going to tell him what to do. It was about two miles from the family home where the attitude changed, a calm came over his face and his strides shorten as my grandfather drove along beside him in the family car. No words were exchanged. His father just reached over and opened the passenger door of the car, Uncle Les got in, and they returned to the home where Reverend Hill's authority was still in effect and never challenged again by Uncle Les.

When the family had gatherings at Grandma Bert's house, Uncle Les was the person responsible for keeping the peace. Every child that played at Grandma Bert's house, whether they were family of not, knew that when uncle Les spoke, you had better listen! Everyone knew that he didn't stand for any nonsense. That is, except when he had a drink or two. When he was drinking, the stern exterior would disappear and he would become a totally different person. Not only did he laugh, but he had this funny high pitched *heh,heh,heh* cackle that made all of us kids laugh with him. It was a somewhat of a strange sight for me to see this tall man with the stern disposition, exhibit such a totally different personality when he drank. Some in the family said that his serious demeanor and size caused them to fear uncle Les. That was not true for me. I had a healthy respect for him. I admired his position of leadership in the Hill family and his position of authority during the Sunday gatherings at Grandma's house.

On every first Sunday of the month, Uncle Les could be seen dressed in his grey double-breasted suit, towering over all of the women as he stood on the front row of the choir loft in Cherry Grove Baptist Church. He was always positioned in the front row although every other man on the choir was in the rear, because he was the churches one and only tenor. When I was about ten or eleven, Uncle Les left the church and its choir. I was disheartened and thought it shameful when Cherry Grove Church finally "put him out" for drinking. I am not one of those people who believe that drinking is not even close to being a sin or even a character flaw, but most Baptist churches in the Bible Belt south would disagree with me. With the loss of that stern disposition after a few drinks, some folks thought that he became easier to engage but a little more difficult to respect. That was never the case for me.

Emma Johnson was my mother's oldest sister. Before she married Willie Johnson, her only husband that I knew, she was married to Harvey Cato. She and Harvey Cato were divorced and he had left Whiteville long before I was born. I had heard that he had left North Carolina because he was wanted by the FBI. Legend claimed that the FBI always got their man, but Harvey Cato was wanted by them for over thirty years, and they never got him. The locals in Whiteville commonly referred to him as the smartest Negro in the area because he had a reputation of cleverly evading the law. One of his daughters, told me that when she lived in Baltimore, her house was under constant surveillance by the FBI. She said that her father had once come to visit her and left without being discovered while the FBI was watching the house. He *must* have been very smart – or invisible. Although I never saw Harvey Cato, I remember seeing a picture of him once. Early one morning,

Aunt Emma walked down the hill from her house to ours with a copy of *True Detective* magazine in her hand. She opened the magazine that someone had given to her, pointed to a picture of a Black man in the magazine and informed us that the man in the picture had been her first husband and the father of her two oldest daughters. Beneath the picture was a written description of the man in the picture. Between the picture and the physical description was a line written in bold print: **"Wanted by the FBI."**

Throughout my young life and even into adulthood, Aunt Emma would often say to me, "I helped to get you here, and I carried you around the house." When I was young, that was her way of reminding me that I should show her special respect. After I had left Whiteville, it was a reminder that I should make a special effort to visit her when I was in the area. She did indeed help to get me here. When my mother was pregnant with me, she was being attended by a doctor who made house calls. On one of his visits, he examined my mother and assured her that I was not going to make my appearance for another week or so. He then got into his car and continued his rounds. At some point later that day, my mother went into labor. Someone, perhaps my father got to a phone somewhere in our Mill Branch neighborhood and called the doctor's house in Whiteville. He was still out making his round of house calls. Since none of the doctor's patients had telephones in their homes, a search was instituted to try to find him. The doctor was eventually found in the Camp Ground section of Whiteville. He was at the home of the Lacewell's, visiting their baby Christine, who, by the way, would grow up be my senior prom date some seventeen years later. We also dated a couple of years after we both finished high school. Meanwhile, back at the Jones household, I was not waiting for the doctor to be found, and I guess there was not enough time to secure the services of the legendary midwife Miss Millie Ann. Aunt Emma was summoned, and she delivered me, a beautiful baby boy! That's how Aunt Emma helped to get me here. Carrying me around the house is a separate issue.

I asked for help from The African American Studies Departments of Temple University and University of North Carolina in my research about the tradition of carrying someone around the house. Neither university had any information on the practice. During countless Internet searches I could find nothing about the tradition. My daughter's father-in-law, Dr. Adalekan Oyejide, was born and raised in Ikire, Nigeria. Although he is a pathologist and not an anthropologist, he is well versed on African traditions, so I asked him about it. He said that he had not heard of it, but it had to come from somewhere, so it probably did come from Africa. I don't know if it's related to Mother Africa or just the Black south, but during my early life, the practice was widespread. During those years, when a child was born, the mother and child remained in the house for about twenty or thirty days. I also seem to remember that there may have been limited access to the baby by individuals not very closely related to the family. After the period of isolation was over, someone other than the parents would take the newborn outside of the house for the first time. They would walk completely around the house with the child in their arms. I imagine that the person carrying the baby around the house was introducing them to the outside world. That same person would also take on the responsibility similar to that of a Godparent. Traditional folklore also claimed that the baby would *take after*, meaning the baby would have the same traits as the person who took them around the house. My sister-in-law, Judy Wilson, is from the southern town of Jeffersonville, Georgia. I asked her if she knew anything about the tradition. She said that she did not remember the tradition herself but two of her aunts from Georgia confirmed that the practice was indeed a part of Black family tradition there. Her aunts even told her about a part of the tradition of which I was unaware. Judy's aunts told her that the person carrying the baby around the house would place a coin in the baby's diaper. The symbolism was part of a wish, hope or prayer that the child would always have financial resources available to them. Most family members thought my mother's youngest brother, Joseph Nathaniel Hill, was the person who carried me around the house. Everyone called him Nate, but my mother named me Joseph after him. My Aunt Emma said that although I was named after my Uncle Nate, it was she who took me around the house. In addition to giving my Aunt Emma the respect for being my mother's oldest sister, I had to also honor her for "getting me here, and taking me around the house," if she put a coin in my diaper, I'm not so sure that it worked!

Robert James Hill was the second of my mother's brothers. We didn't see as much of Uncle Rob as we did my mother's other siblings as he and his family lived about fifty miles away in Wilmington, North Carolina. There were good paying jobs for Black people in the shipyards of Wilmington, so I imagine that was one of the reasons he went there. Another reason for being there was his beautiful wife, Irene Baldwin, who hailed from nearby Leland. His aunt Bertha and her husband, Uncle Obadiah also had a large farm and lived comfortably there. Those three factors may have been the reason he chose to live in Wilmington.

Uncle Rob was a quiet and unassuming man who carried the stern and serious look of all of the Hill men. Also like the other Hill men, he was tall and slender. I don't think that I have ever seen him when he was not neat and well-dressed. Then again, I only saw him on special occasions where he would not have been wearing work clothes. He had a gentle manner, and only spoke in soft tones as if speaking loudly would be offensive to your ear. Uncle Rob would never want to be offensive. There was never a problems with the appearance of his teeth, but he always covered his mouth when he laughed. He had the perfect demeanor for his senior usher position at Mt. Calvary Baptist Church in Wilmington.

Before Uncle Rob moved to Wilmington, he worked for The Whiteville Tobacco Company. His oldest son, my cousin Bobby who used to come work my family's farm during the summer time, told me that he even worked for that company after he moved to Wilmington. He helped the tobacco company determine the best quality of tobacco to purchase and also helped with loading the purchases for shipping to the cigarette manufacture's warehouses.

Uncle Rob also worked at the naval shipyard in Wilmington before the shipyard and the jobs that it provided moved to Newport News, Virginia. After the shipyard closed, Uncle Rob worked for City Dixie Cleaners until his death. During the years he worked for the shipyard in Wilmington, he and his family lived in a complex where many other shipyard workers lived. I think the complex was called Delgado Mills Village, but I'm not really sure. The only location I remember Uncle Rob and his family living was a housing project called Taylor Homes, but the family had always dreamed of having their own home. Using money his son Bobby sent home while he was in the Army, the family built their very own home on 31st street in East Wilmington.

My oldest brother Jaye W had a closer relationship with my Uncle Rob and seemed to know him better than I did. Jaye W said that despite the serious appearance, there was another side to Uncle Rob. Jaye W said that he really had quite a bubbly personality that none of us ever saw and that he loved to tell stories and jokes and that he had a million of them. Of course he would cover his mouth if one of his jokes made him laugh. During my entire life, I have never heard a negative comment about Uncle Rob. I also have never met anyone who didn't like him.

Violet Jones was the sister that was closest in age to my mother. She also looked more like my mother than her other three sisters. Most of Aunt Violet's acquaintances called her Vi. When we did refer to her by her full name, our southern accents overtook our speech, and we dropped the "o" from her name. Her name then changed from Violet, the beautiful flower, or radiant color, to the non-descript Vi-Let. Just as my mother had done before her, Aunt Violet also married a Jones. Aunt Violet's husband was Daniel Jones. He was of course Uncle Dan to his nieces and nephews, but because of his size, most adults called him "Big Dan." His family was originally from the Lumberton, North Carolina area. Most Joneses in and around the area of Whiteville are related to my family, but I could find no connection of his family to ours. My schoolmates, who didn't know my aunt and uncle personally, naturally thought that since Aunt Violet's children were Joneses, I was related to them through the Jones side of my father's family, and not the Hills of my mother's side.

Big Dan did not work the tobacco farms like most of the other African American men in the area. He worked for a water well drilling company. He drilled many of the backyard water pumps in Columbus County, including ours. In addition to his job as a well driller, Uncle Dan supplemented his income with several other hustles. To Aunt Vi's dismay, he once built a jook joint with a pool table in their yard next to their house. Aunt Violet was a preacher's daughter so you know she and the other members of nearby Cherry Grove Baptist Church did not like that. I don't think that disapproval mattered much to Big Dan. He pretty much did what he wanted to do without too much regard for public sentiment. Uncle Dan also gambled for money and he didn't apologize to anyone for that either. I never really saw him gamble, but he did once demonstrate to me how card dealers cheat using a method called palming. He concealed a card under his enormous palm while he dealt an entire deck of cards.

As I stated earlier, Aunt Violet and my mother worked for the McNeil sisters-in-law. My mother worked for Francis, and Aunt Violet worked for Carrie Margaret. Carrie Margaret's was a daughter from the powerful and prominent Powell family in Whiteville. One of Carrie Margaret's daughters, actress Jane McNeil, was featured in the hit television series, *The Walking Dead*. Aunt Violet had worked for the Powells when she and Carrie Margaret were no more than children themselves and she continued to work for Carrie Margaret after she and my aunt had grown up, married, and established her own households. Carrie Margaret McNeil and my aunt had a long-term work relationship, but I don't think that Uncle Dan appreciated the relationship or wanted her to work for the McNeils. Each morning, Carrie Margaret would pick up Aunt Violet for work, and then drive her home in the afternoon when her workday was complete. On one memorable morning, for some unknown reason, Uncle Dan decided the he did not want Aunt Violet to go to work for Carrie Margaret McNeil. After Aunt Violet got into the passenger seat of the car as usual, Uncle Dan came out to the car and demanded that she get out. When she refused, Uncle Dan opened the door, lifted her out and carried her into their house kicking and screaming. When Uncle Dan put Aunt Violet down in the house, she just calmly returned to the car. He then rushed to the car before Carrie Margaret could drive away and carried Aunt Violet back into the house. Again, Aunt Vi returned to the car, and following her third sojourn back to the house in the arms of her husband, she must have told her employer that she could not come to work that day. Now, Carrie Margaret was, shall we say, a very high-strung person. Upon hearing the news that my aunt would not be coming to work, she became frantic. She began to pull her own hair, and paced back and forth on the front porch as she yelled through the windows and closed door, "Violet, you have to come with me! What I am going to do? I can't do without you today!" She undoubtedly had some event planned for that day where my aunt's help was crucial, but that held no sway with Big Dan! Mrs. McNeil was obviously in distress, but none of that mattered to Big Dan or the neighborhood kids who witnessed the spectacle. We almost doubled over with laughter. First, we laughed because the scene was so comical, and secondly we laughed because it was one of those few times we got to see defiance of white authority.

I loved that Aunt Vi's house was directly behind ours and I got to spend a lot of time there. I was sandwiched in age between two of Aunt Vi's six boys, so I was always able to join them in boyhood activities and mischief. After playing all day in the wooded areas, yards or fields of a relative or neighbor's home, when mealtime came, usually you just sat at the table with the other family members and ate. Like my mother, Aunt Vi was a good cook, and I ate many meals at her house. My aunt had nine children of her own. Six of them were living at home for most of the time when I was growing up. None of us were wealthy people, yet Aunt Vi and our other relatives always seem to have more than enough food for their families and for us uninvited guest. How they accomplished that feat remains a mystery to me even until this day.

My mother said that she and Aunt Violet were next to each other all of their lives. They slept next to each other as little children. They were always together growing up. As a young woman, Aunt Violet traveled with my mother and father to South Carolina to witness their marriage ceremony. They built their homes within shouting distance of each other, and that came in handy for my mother. When my mother wanted to summon her sister, she would just stand in the back yard any yell "Yoo-hoo, Vi-Let!" Once when I heard her doing this, I said, "Ma, why don't you just go into the house and call her on the phone?" She replied, "Yes, I could do that but it just wouldn't be the same. This is better."

I was at home just days before Aunt Violet made her transition. Her passing was not one of trouble or concern. While in the hospital, and then during her short stay in the nursing home owned by her former employer, the McNeil family, she just thanked God for her life, her children and for her salvation, and she went peacefully. I miss more than Aunt Violet's good food and hospitality. I miss her serene and gentle nature. She always spoke to me in a quiet and gentle manner and never raised her voice at me from my earliest recollections of her until her death. Every time I return home, the first thing I do is look through the kitchen window of our house and imagine her sitting quietly and peacefully on her front porch. Aunt Violet taught me a lot about living and a lot about dying. She did not approach her impending death pleading for more time. She just thanked God for her children and the life that God had given her. I sincerely hope and pray that my transition is just like Aunt Vi's. Just as Aunt Violet thanked God for her life, I too thanked God for her life.

Willie Hill, was my mother's third brother. His wife, Gertrude Freeman was from the same area we called "Across the Marsh" as my father's relatives. Of all of my mother's brothers, Uncle Willie was the one closest to my father. My father probably had more social and work-related interaction with Uncle Willie than he did with any of my mother's other brothers. Before my father's first trip to Philadelphia, he and Uncle Willie spent so much time discussing the logistics, one might have thought they were about to make pilgrimage through the desert to Mecca. I can still remember them sitting around the dining room table and carefully plotting their course from Whiteville to Philadelphia on Highway 301, timing their trips to avoid rush hour in Richmond and Washington. This was the 1950s and they also needed to determine the best time and best path through some of the small southern towns to avoid being hassled by racist police.

Uncle Willie was a hustler, and he would try any legitimate angle to make a buck. He, my father, and the husband of one of my mother's cousin named Cicero Richardson, even tried running a pulpwood logging business, but it did not last very long. To make a few bucks, Uncle Willie once rented out his house and moved to a house on Earl Hill's farm where he and my father were sharecroppers. He had made the decision to move his wife, Aunt Gertrude, his two sons and three daughters to a totally isolated property some two miles down an unpaved road, presumably because the house was rent free. After a year of stars for streetlights and nothing but wild animals for neighbors, I think Aunt Gertrude and his daughters convinced him of the error of his ways and they moved back to their house in the Cherry Grove neighborhood.

Most of Uncle Willie's relatives, neighbors and friends called him Rabbit. Our generation had respect for their elders, especially older relatives, so we would never use his nickname in his presence. Behind his back however, even his nieces and nephews called him Rabbit or Uncle Willie Rabbit, so it was common to hear him referred to by that name all of my life. I was curious about the name's origin, so I asked my father how Uncle Willie got the name. My father said that as a boy, Uncle Willie was the fastest runner in the area. No one else was even close. One of the quips my father enjoyed making about Uncle Willie's speed was that he was so fast that the wind would pin his

ears back when he ran. Another was, he was so fast
that he could turn a corner while running and lean
so low to the ground that he would scoop up dirt
in his pants pocket without ever breaking stride.
Now that's fast. I guess name was appropriate!

Catherine Smith is the sister of my mother with
which I had the least personal interaction during
my youth. I only saw Aunt Cassie during those
years when she would travel from her home in
Philadelphia to Whiteville, usually to attend a
funeral of a member of the family. Aunt Cassie
was the first of her generation to migrate to
Philadelphia. Her uncle Roland and her aunt
Mary had been a part of the great migration
from the primarily agrarian societies in southern
states to industrialized northeastern cities such as
Baltimore, Philadelphia, and New York. Although
our Hill and Jones family trees have branches in all
of the major cities of the northeast and elsewhere,
more of us reside in Philadelphia than in any of
those other city outside of the south. The migration
of our family to Philadelphia was typical of the
migration patterns seen in most families who left
the south for reasons ranging from financial to
personal security. Usually a pathfinder such as
Uncle Roland would leave a familiar environment
such as Lees Lake, North Carolina, to seek
employment or just a modicum of dignity in a
northern city. Once they were established, they
would make room for other family members such

as Uncle Roland did for his sibling Mary and later for his niece Cassie.

Prior to Aunt Cassie's move to Philadelphia, she met and married John Smith from nearby Wilmington, North Carolina. John had the light skin and straight hair that was preferred in men by many African American women of that day, so he was very popular with the ladies in Columbus and surrounding counties. Neither his popularity nor his indiscretions ended after he said his marriage vows. Aunt Cassie intimated that his philandering was legendary. In addition to being unfaithful, Aunt Cassie's husband had other issues that made the marriage untenable. Her husband John was a violent and extremely jealous man, and that is a very dangerous combination. After suffering abuse at the hands of her husband and totally believing his threat to kill her, Aunt Cassie escaped from Whiteville and John, secretly fleeing to Philadelphia. She lived with her Uncle Roland when she first arrived in Philadelphia. Uncle Roland also secured employment for her at the laundry where he was employed on Mervine Street, a short distance from their home. Eventually, John tracked Aunt Cassie down at her uncle's home in Philadelphia and convinced her to give him and their marriage another chance. Her decision to try to salvage the marriage would have a devastating effect not only on her life, but on the lives of her family as well.

Soon after Aunt Cassie agreed to return to her husband, he joined her in Philadelphia, quickly found work and they both began adjusting to their new life there. They were both young and living in a new and exciting environment. These should have been happy times, but old habits die hard and old demons even harder. Before long, John was up to his old womanizing habits while still remaining insanely jealous of his wife. While he would tolerate no constraints on his way of life, he wanted total control over Aunt Cassie's life. He viewed every moment they were not together with suspicion, and when he was caught red-handed in a compromising position, he would turn the tables on his wife, demanding to know why she was away from home in a position to catch him. When the abuse continued, Cassie threatened to leave him and go back home; he again threatened to kill her, except now he was issuing an additional threat. He now began to tell Aunt Cassie that if she returned to Whiteville, that he would not only kill her but he would kill her entire family. She believed him. She was terrified. She had to leave.

Aunt Cassie said that the last thing that she remembers saying to her husband was "its 6:45." She said that they always arose at 7:00 AM to prepare for work, so that was her answer when he asked her what time it was. They never spoke again. The two of them got out bed, dressed, had their breakfast, and left for work just as had been their daily routine in the past. She said that she had gone to great lengths to make that day appear as any other, but she had long planned that it would be the day of her liberation. Once she was sure that her husband was on his job, she doubled back to the house, packed whatever she could carry and left Philadelphia. When John came home from work and discovered that his wife had left, he was furious. In a rage, he burned the remainder of Aunt Cassie's possessions, packed a bag, his pistol, and set out to make good on his promise to his wife.

Aunt Cassie was sure if John found her that he would kill her. She was also sure that if he found her in her family's home in Whiteville, he would fulfill his promise to kill them. She could not go back home. Aunt Cassie went to Washington, D.C. instead. A childhood friend, Virginia Gore, who had lived near the family in Whiteville, was now living in Washington, D.C., so she secretly arranged to go there to escape the wrath of her husband, and to keep her family out of danger.

When John arrived at my grandmother's house in Whiteville, he never mentioned to them what they already knew – that his wife had left him and that he was searching for her. His greeting to the family was one of excitement and warmth, their response was cordial. He told Grandma Bert that he was just on a few days' vacation and asked if he could spend the night before going on to Wilmington for a visit with his mother. Fearing for the life of her family, Grandma Bert was terrified of saying no. She was also terrified when she said yes. Grandma said that it was the worst night of her life. No one slept. She prayed all night, while her son-in-law was in the middle bedroom that separated her bedroom from the bedroom of her children, where she said that John spent the night carrying on irrational conversations with himself. When John found no sign of his wife in Whiteville, the next morning he left for his mother's house in Wilmington. Sometime during the next day, John's inescapable demons returned. He locked the door to a bedroom in his mother's house, placed the muzzle of his pistol directly against his heart and pulled the trigger.

Aunt Cassie was sure that the news of her husband's death was nothing more than a ruse by her husband to lure her to him. Only after she was assured by trustworthy sources that her husband was indeed dead did she agree to return to North Carolina to attend his funeral. Because she had not left Washington, D.C. immediately upon hearing of John's death, she missed the funeral service at the church all together, arriving in Wilmington just in time to witness him being buried. She was in no position to provide much consolation to his family. There was not even an attempt from John's family to provide any for her because they held her responsible for his demise. Following his burial, there was immediate tension between Aunt Cassie and John's family, so Aunt Cassie gathered herself, her adolescent son James who had been living with Grandma Bert at that time, and returned to Philadelphia.

Once Aunt Cassie was back in Philadelphia, she set about the business of carving out a life for her son James and herself. She continued to work at the laundry and she also did domestic work. During the summer of 1981, when she came to a celebration at my house in Wyncote, Pennsylvania following the baby blessing of my daughter Kaya, she commented to me that she had done domestic work in my neighborhood many years earlier when no Black people lived there. Aunt Cassie was also employed for several years at a children clothing manufacturer, but the house that she would later purchase on 18th Street in the Tioga section of Philadelphia supplemented her income and later may have been her primary source of income.

When I first arrived in Philadelphia in the mid-1960s, the 3300 block of North 18th street was tree lined, well maintained and beautiful. Most of the block's residents took pride in the large, stately homes there. The open-air verandas and stoops that looked out onto 18th street were inviting respites from the city's summer heat. The homeowners counted these homes as their little piece of the American dream. Aunt Cassie's house at 3345 was just a few paces from the point where 18th Street intersected with Ontario. It was a large, three-story brownstone type of building that my aunt had purchased in 1956. When any of her relatives relocated to Philadelphia, or were just there for a quick visit, they always made their way to 3345 North 18th Street. It was a Philadelphia family landmark. Just as Uncle Roland had done for Aunt Cassie, she provided a comfortable place to live for her brothers, sisters, and later her nieces and nephews when they migrated to Philadelphia. While she was willing to help her relatives to establish themselves when they came, her efforts were not altogether altruistic. Make no mistake about it; she ran a business, and if you did not find work and start paying rent by a certain period of time, she would threaten to buy you a ticket and put you on a Greyhound bus heading back to Whiteville. For all of our family transplants to Philadelphia, failure was not an option, so Aunt Cassie never had to make good on her threat.

During the busiest period of Aunt Cassie's boarding house business, the Blue Laws that prohibited the sale of alcohol on Sunday were still in effect in the state of Pennsylvania. The bars and nightclubs also closed at 2:00 AM, leaving a throng of partygoers wanting a place to drink after 2:00 AM on Friday and Saturday nights as well as all day on Sundays. Those laws provided a perfect opportunity for my industrious aunt to fill a need in the Tioga section of the city. In addition to her boarding house business, she also ran a speakeasy out of her basement. To accommodate her (after-hours) business, she renovated the large basement of her home. When it was completed, with a bar and mood lighting, it looked just like a nightclub. The relatives and other boarders who lived in the five or six bedrooms in Aunt Cassie's house must have had the same regard for the basement as they did for a classy nightspot. They would sometimes dress in a suit and tie just to go downstairs in the house where they were living. The basement was not only the location for locals to party when the bars were closed, but friends and relatives from as far away as New Jersey and Maryland also descended on Aunt Cassie's house and that basement to party on weekends.

Before I relocated to Florida in 2010, Aunt Cassie once commented to me that I should visit her more often since I had lived with her when I first came to Philadelphia. I agreed that I should see her more often without correcting her about living in the big house on 18th Street. My brother Bobby was married and owned a house in the Germantown section when I came to Philadelphia. I lived with him before I purchased my own house in the Mt. Airy section of Philadelphia. I didn't correct Aunt Cassie because I'm sure she just assumed that all of her nieces and nephews in Philadelphia lived with her at one time or another over the past sixty or so years. In almost every case, she would be correct in her assumption.

Aunt Cassie died on July 20, 2013, two months before her ninety third birthday. She had survived all of her siblings and even her only child, James who had died in her house less than two months prior to his mother's passing. Aunt Cassie's death not only closed the book on a generation of our family, it also closes the book on the house on 18th Street. Since her son James preceded her in death, I suppose that the house on 18th Street that has seen so much of this family's history, will fall to James' only son; a cousin that I have I have never met.

Joseph Nathaniel Hill was the youngest of my mother's brothers, and it was his name that my mother chose for me when I was born. Nate was tall and lanky like his older brothers Les and Rob, and he loved to dress in the zoot suits and Stacey Adams knob toe shoes that were the stylish rage of the period when he was a young man. Nate was the name most often used by family when they referred to him, but he was also known as "Gone." Although most of his friends and relatives remember calling him Gone, none of us can remember why.

During the early 1950s before he migrated to Philadelphia, he was unmarried and living at Grandma Bert's house. I remember a very funny exchange between Nate and Grandma Bert that occurred one evening when I was at Grandma's house. I wasn't there for any particular reason, but just as with most of the grandkids, I was just hanging out at Grandma's house. Nate was getting dressed to go out. As he dressed, he walked around the house singing that period's rhythm and blues hit: *"Annie had a baby, can't work no more, every time she start to work, she had to stop and walk the baby cross the floor, yea, yea, yea."*

When Grandma Bert heard him singing, she adorned her face with one of her infamous frowns of distress, and she gave Nate a disapproving look from the corner of her eye, then shouted, "You hush-up singing that reel in this house!" The older members of my family referred to jazz, rhythm and blues, and rock and roll music as reels. I never really understood why they called them reels. I can only assume that the name came from the circular shaped LP's that held the music. Nate was already laughing at his mother's agitation when he asked her, "Ma, what's wrong with that song?"

He knew what was wrong. This was the early 1950s when decent folk didn't even say the word pregnant, and he was singing a reel about a girl having a baby. That song's lyric may have been gentile by today's rap music standards, but it was highly controversial when the Hank Ballard song hit the airways in the 1950s.

In addition to the baby reference, the "work" that Annie could no longer do because of the baby was a coded sexual message that all of the hip youngsters of that period clearly understood. I don't know if the censors understood the message when they tried and failed to get the song banned from the radio. I don't know whether Grandma Bert understood the lyrics or not, but I do know that she successfully banned that song from her house.

On January 5, 1943 Nate was inducted into the United States Army. He was drafted to help stop the Germans who had sunk our ships, bombed European cities, overrun our allies, slaughtered thousands of our soldiers, and murdered millions of Jews. The country that refused to show him simple human dignity, now called on him for its defense. Nate answered the call. He completed basic training at Fort Bragg in Fayetteville, North Carolina, just about forty miles north of Whiteville. Once he had completed basic training, he was shipped off to Europe. Nate said that as soon as he and his fellow Black troops arrived in the war zone, they were repeatedly assigned to the most dangerous positions. They were *always* on the front lines. On one occasion, a mission had to be completed that was considered so dangerous, that no one was expected to return from it. Nate said that the white officer in charge chose only Black soldiers for the mission. By the grace of God, Nate was one of the Black soldiers who returned alive. It turned out to be the last battle Nate was to fight against the German Army. For the rest of his military career, he was at war with the American Army.

Uncle Nate was willing to be inducted into the army and fight for his country, but he now faced the dilemma of fighting against a German Army and for an American Army that he felt were both trying to kill him. Although I was a very young boy when he made that comment to me, I remember it very clearly. I never forgot that conversation. The next time he was asked to risk his life, he said "HELL NO." Nate told me he had no intention of dyeing for a country that gave him nothing but a hard time. He refused to fight for the *great liberator* in her effort to free people on distant shores when he was kept in a prison of oppression in his own hometown. An irony not lost on Nate was that German prisoners of war held in Columbus County, had far more rights than he had, although he was born and had lived his whole life there. The prisoners from the country that had committed so many atrocities and crimes against humanity, could eat in the white mess hall and be treated in the white section of Columbus County hospital, while my uncle Nate could do neither. Most importantly, although they were prisoners from the murderous Nazi regime, they were respected as men. Joseph Nathaniel Hill had committed no crime, yet he was not respected by white people at all, and they were now trying to get him killed.

Following a declaration from the Black soldiers, that they were not willing to be used as cannon fodder, the army promptly placed the group that included Nate, in the stockade. The guards, who had a special distain for Black prisoners, handed out the harshest punishment for Nate and his fellow soldiers. Nate told me that he believed the inhumane living conditions in that stockade was an effort by the army to rid itself of the problems he and his fellow soldiers had caused. He said that he and his fellow prisoners were forced to live in an outdoor stockade during the middle of the cold European winter without so much as tent. They were exposed to that winter's cold, rain and snow. Their only shelter was foxholes the prisoners were allowed to dig in the stockade yard. Whether the army was trying to use the environment to rid themselves of these problem soldiers we may never know, but Nate did say that several of his fellow prisoners died as a result of that treatment.

During the World War II years, more than 1.7 million court martial cases were tried for various reasons. Of these court martial cases, 21,000 Americans soldiers received some kind of sentence for refusing to fight or desertion. Forty-nine of those American soldiers received the death penalty. One was actually executed. Nate said that he witnessed that execution. On one of those cold days in January of 1945, all of the soldiers from the outdoor stockade where he was held were loaded into the one of those military troop carrier trucks. They were not told where they going, they were just ordered to get into the back of the trucks. After traveling for some distance, they arrived at a location that I now realized was Saint-Marie-aux-Mines, France. They were ushered off of the trucks and ordered to assemble. The entire assembly of prisoners was then ordered to watch the execution of Eddie Slovik, the only soldier executed for desertion during World War II. Uncle Nate said that the message the army attempted to communicate to them was very clear. The message was *fight or this will happen to you!* Uncle Nate said that even after he witnessed the execution, he still refused to fight.

Before Nate was discharged from the army, he was transferred to the stockade at Fort Bragg, where the inhumane treatment continued. When a box containing a cake, fried chicken, and other treats from Grandma Bert's kitchen, made its way to the stockade, the guards refused to give the package to him. According to my cousin Marvin Hill, the guards open the package, rummaged through the contents of the box and rendered them uneatable, by dumping them on the ground at Nate's feet.

I could not find any evidence that he was ever court martialed, so I don't know how Nate's case was adjudicated. I made a formal request to the Veterans Administration National Archives for all of his military records. Most of my information about his service came from conversations with him or other relatives, and I wanted to know what the military said about his service before I wrote about it. I got nothing from the Veterans Administration. They informed me that his records were destroyed in a massive fire at their facility in St. Louis, MO on July 12, 1973. Considering Nate's issues with the military, I don't believe anything that I was told by the VA.

Uncle Nate was discharged on December 14, 1945. When he emerged from the taxi that had delivered him to Grandma Bert front yard, he was mobbed by family and friends. The longest greeting, however, was reserved for his mother. Grandma Bert's tears of joy and praises to God for bringing her son home safely, wash away all the agony she had suffered during his absence.

After his return from the military, Uncle Nate lived in Whiteville until the mid-1950s. He then relocated to Philadelphia as so many of his relatives had done before him. He later married Deloris Nokes, who was born and grew up in Philadelphia. Nate lived out the remainder of his life there and died in 1991. He is buried in Northwood Cemetery located in the East Oak Lane section of Philadelphia.

Eva Lee Nance was the fourth of my mother's five sisters. She was nine years younger than my mother, and for a short period during my very early life, she and her family lived next door to us in the rented house that stood on the site where my Brother Jerry's house now sits. Aunt Eva's husband was William McKeithan Nance. To me, he was Uncle WM. Most of his family members lived in the nearby Quarters section that I mentioned earlier, where many of the employees of Sledge's Mill also lived. The most vivid recollections that I have of Aunt Eva are when she and her family lived just off of Harrelson Road in the Brunswick section of the county. They lived in a small, wooden, unpainted house situated just a few hundred yards behind the large, white, antebellum-styled home with the large white columns common to that style of home. The big beautiful house belonged to one the area's most successful white farmers, Garland Anderson. I believe that Garland Anderson was their landlord.

I spent many days and nights at Aunt Eva and Uncle WM's house because their son Ralph was about my age. We were as close as brothers when we were growing up. Although I had three brothers myself, my brothers and I did not do all of the things kids do together because of the difference in our ages. My oldest brother Jaye is ten years older, Bobby is four years older and Larry was four years younger than I am. The difference in years mean nothing as adults, but most kids don't relate to other kids with a four year age difference. Since Ralph and I were about the same age, we did everything together. Aunt Eva not only had to manage our activity, but she also had to manage our mischief. Just as any nine or ten year-old kids would do, we go into a lot of mischief. We also go into a fight about once a day. When we were caught fighting, the punishment would be so severe that neither of us could barely endure it. Our punishment for fighting would be separation from each other. Before handing down our sentence, Aunt Eva would always say, "If the two you can't get along, you will just have to stay away from each other." After a day or two of punishment, we would beg and plead with our parents to let us play together again. We would promise *never* to fight again. Those promises were usually kept for about one or two days.

Another reason I loved staying at Aunt Eva's was because of her husband, Uncle WM. He kept the kids entertained with his ghost stories and his kidding around. He always got a big kick out of telling us that we were eating frog legs from the previous night's catch in the local swamps, when I believe that we were only eating chicken. (Maybe they were real frog's legs.) Another form of entertainment provided by Uncle WM was the drive-in movie. My parents didn't go to the movies, but they would allow Uncle WM to take me, so he would pile about ten kids into his car and head for the local drive-in. Since the cost of admission was based on the number of people in the car, Uncle WM would stop about one half of a mile from the drive-in gate. He would then put about six or seven of us into the trunk of the car. Once we were safely through the gates and had paid the greatly reduced rate, parked and had the movie speakers placed in the car, Uncle WM would open the trunk and we would all scurry out and make a mad dash for a good seat in his car. Uncle WM also introduced me to scouting. He was not a scout leader himself, but I clearly remember the evening he took his son Ralph and I into town to sign up with the Cub Scouts.

Uncle WM's friend Harry Simmons was the Cub Scout leader, and a couple of years later, when we graduated to the Boy Scouts, Isaac Jones was our leader. Because of the relationship with scouting that began with Uncle WM, I have been a lifelong admirer and financial supporter of the Boy Scouts of America.

By the time Uncle WM introduced me to the Cub Scouts, he, Aunt Eva and Ralph had moved from the house off of Harrelson Road to a house his family had constructed nearby in the Cherry Grove section where we lived. After they moved there, I probably spent even more nights at their home. Every time there was an issue where my mother had to farm us out, I always stayed with Aunt Eva. Although I didn't even know that my mother was expecting a baby, I spent the night at Aunt Eva's house when my brother Larry was born. Aunt Eva and my mother also worked together in the cafeteria for the Whiteville City School System, so I also saw a lot of her when they rode together. On March 22, 1991, Aunt Eva died from complications of amyotrophic lateral sclerosis (ALS), commonly referred to as Lou Gehrig's disease. She was 65 years old.

The thought of those days and nights spent at their home, the drive in movies, the Boy Scouts, even the fights with my cousin Ralph brings back some pleasant memories. Then again, all of my memories of Aunt Eva are pleasant ones.

Mazie Bell McDaniels was the youngest of my mother's siblings. It is unlikely that she remembered the Lees Lake area where she was born or her father, as she was just twenty months old when he died.

According to my mother, Aunt Mazie was carried in one of her sister's arms as the family marched behind the mule drawn wagon carrying her father to the Hill family Cemetery. The family moved to the Cherry Grove section of Whiteville when Mazie was about three or four years old.

Almost everyone in the community and several members of my own family had nicknames; "*High Pockets*" for Uncle Les, "*Rabbit*" for Uncle Willie, "*Gone*" for Uncle Nate, "*Steer*" for my cousin Marvin, and "*Blue*" for my brother Bobby. Aunt Mazie's nickname was "*Cricket*." I have no clue of the origins of some of the names like Gone, Steer and Blue, but Aunt Mazie probably got her name because she was the youngest member of her family and as a youngster, she was also diminutive in stature.

Aunt Mazie married Curtis McDaniel from the nearby town of Chadbourn, North Carolina. During the mid-1950s, the couple relocated to Hempstead, New York, where her husband had relatives. After a few short years in New York, the marriage ended and Aunt Mazie relocated to Philadelphia. With her daughter Annie, and her son Rudy, who would became the internationally acclaimed jazz bassist Jamaaladeen Tacuma, Aunt Mazie moved into her sister Cassie's big house on 18th Street.

When I discussed Aunt Cassie's house earlier, I said that Aunt Cassie ran a business out of her home. Just as in most businesses, Aunt Cassie had a least one employee. That was Aunt Mazie. In addition to the after-hours business Aunt Cassie ran in the basement, her residence was home for many boarders. At any given time, she would have several unrelated boarders in addition to family members living there. With all of that activity, the house had to be kept clean, and many meals had to be prepared. I don't know what the financial arrangement was between Aunt Mazie and her sister, but Aunt Mazie worked in that house while she lived there, the house was always beautifully maintained, and the food was always delicious.

After Aunt Mazie left the home of her sister, she and her family lived at 15th & Venango Streets in the Tioga section of Philadelphia before moving to 10th & Norris Streets in North Philadelphia. For the last twenty years of her life, Aunt Mazie lived in the Interfaith House for senior citizens in the Germantown section of Philadelphia. While she was living in that area, I had a business appointment at an elementary school that was near her home. As I was walking down the hall of the school with the principal, I spotted a large picture of Aunt Mazie on the bulletin board. I asked the principal why she had a picture of my aunt in her hallway. She informed me that my aunt was a reading buddy for the children in her school. Aunt Mazie would visit the school, tell the children her life story and read with them. The principal could tell by the smile on my face that I was really proud of my Aunt Cricket. I took that opportunity to inform the principal that my Aunt Mazie's family had started a school on her family's land, with no other financial assistance other than what her Hill family could provide. Aunt Mazie died on August 14, 2012, and is buried in Bala Cynwyd, Pennsylvania.

Henry Daniel Jones was my father's only brother when their mother died in 1918. Although two additional brothers, Walter and Rudolph were born to their father's second wife, Uncle Henry was his only brother born to their mother Maggie. Uncle Henry was just five years old when his mother died. My father, his older brother, was about nine; his sisters Ellen and Adell were nearly three and one years old, respectively. Shortly after the birth of Walter, my grandfather and his new family relocated to Philadelphia, so Uncle Henry was the only brother with which my father had any kind of relationship. The years of their late teens and early twenties were consumed with, shall we say, "youthful exuberance." That time period has been described as The Roaring Twenties, and the description of the period is also a good characterization of some of their activities during that time. They roared through Columbus County drinking, fighting, and partying. That was the Uncle Henry of family lore, not the one that I knew.

The Henry Jones that I knew was the father of twelve children and the husband of Estelle Ford, whom he had married around 1935. For several years he was a deacon and active member of The Cherry Grove Baptist Church located near our home. Unlike my father, he had joined the church in his community and the not the Mill Branch Baptist Church that was a part of our families history. He was called to the ministry in 1971. Beginning a ministry at 58 years old must have been a daunting task. My guess is that the calling to ministry was something he had struggled with and delayed acceptance of for several years. Despite his late start, he went on to pastor Pleasant View Baptist Church in Shallotte, North Carolina for 17 years, Roseville Baptist Church in Willard, North Carolina for seven years, and First Baptist Church of Chadbourn, North Carolina for seven years. A common practice for churches in the rural south during those years was to hold services only once a month, so a minister could typically pastor more than one church at a time. I'm almost certain that Uncle Henry pastured those three churches concurrently. Another reality of rural southern churches is the fact that their congregations were seldom able to provide total financial support for a minister who preached only once per month. To support their families, most ministers were required to have a regular job. Uncle Henry worked for The Sledge Lumber Company for all the years I was growing up in North Carolina. I don't remember him ever working anywhere else.

Uncle Henry also had a love of singing. I will never forget the excitement I felt when I first heard Uncle Henry on the radio. During the years when he was a fairly young man, he always seemed to be associated with a singing group. Uncle Henry, Aunt Ellen's husband Uncle Cleveland, and a neighbor named Dock Lewis had formed a singing group. I imagine they would sing gospel songs a cappella at local church events. Early on Sunday mornings, before church services of course, the group would sing live on WENC, the local radio station in Whiteville. I was just a kid at the time, but I have a vivid memory of the family gathering around the radio to hear Uncle Henry and Uncle Cleve sing. That may not seem like an earth-shattering event today, but in the early 1950s, Black people weren't on any broadcast media in Columbus County, North Carolina, so hearing my uncles on the radio was a big deal! Apparently Uncle Henry and Uncle Cleveland passed their love of singing on to their children. Both Uncle Cleveland's and Uncle Henry's children and grandchildren have a love and talent for music and singing. Uncle Henry died on November 26, 1991. He was 78 years old.

Ellen Bell was the older of my father's two sisters but still just a very young child of about three years of age when her mother died and her father left Columbus County. Since she and her siblings were without either of their parents, her older brothers, Henry and my father were very protective of her and their baby sister, Adell. Her brothers may have felt the need to protect her, but my father claims that when he and his brother Henry got into the mischief that was all too common for young country boys, Aunt Ellen would never protect them. Dad said that Aunt Ellen was always willing to participate in their bad acts, such as stealing a neighbor's watermelons or some grapes, and she would also agree that they were all in it together and swear not to tell. My father said that as soon as the children sat down at the dinner table with their Grandpa Peter, Aunt Ellen would always give them up. She would begin the conversation with a comment such as "guess what we did today?" In an effort to silence Aunt Ellen, Dad and Uncle Henry would begin kicking her under the table because they knew what was coming next. No matter how hard they tried, they could never prevent their sister from spilling the beans. She would even admonish her brothers by saying, "Stop kicking me. If you didn't want me to tell it, you shouldn't have done it!" She would then detail the day's action that was sure to result in a whipping for both of her brothers, and most likely gain admiration for her from Grandpa Peter for giving up her brothers. No matter how many times Aunt Ellen testified at the dinner table against her brothers, they continued to be protective of her from her childhood to the early years of her adult life.

Aunt Ellen married a handsome young man named Cleveland Bell, from the small town of Fairmount, North Carolina. Fairmount is in Robeson County about thirty miles west of Whiteville. The Sledge Lumber Company that was so important to the economy of Columbus County was also significant in the lives of Uncle Cleveland, Aunt Ellen, and their family. Uncle Cleveland drove a logging truck for the company, the family shopped at the company store, and they lived in an area called The Quarters, where most of the homes were owned by The Sledge Lumber Company. They simply lived the life that was typical for Sledge employees. On June 16, 1949, life for the Bell family changed forever. Uncle Cleveland died at the age of thirty, leaving my aunt widowed at the age of thirty-two with eight children. This tragedy thrust upon yet another member of our family one of those monumental obstacles that on the surface would seem almost impossible to overcome. Economic safety nets like welfare payments or food stamps did not exist for disadvantaged Black families in Columbus County, North Carolina. Although some poor whites received public assistance, it was unavailable for Black people. What was a poor widow with eight children supposed to do? Aunt Ellen did what our family has always done. When our family faced those challenges in the past, by the grace of God we always found a way to move forward. Just as our ancestors had done throughout their history,

Aunt Ellen and her eight children had to make a way out of no way.

Aunt Ellen's oldest son Rodney was about seventeen years of age when Uncle Cleveland died. He had already left school and by this time he was working a full-time job to help support his mother and seven siblings. When Aunt Ellen's two oldest daughters, Shirley and Ann Marie (Pancake) were of working age, they joined their mother as employees on the night shift at the re-drying plant in Whiteville. The Re-drying plant was the location of the final step in the processing of cured tobacco before it is shipped to the cigarette manufactures. The plant located just east of the center of downtown Whiteville provided employment for dozens of area locals, including my father, but that work was only available from late summer to early fall.

For the rest of the year, Aunt Ellen and her children took whatever jobs they could get to hold their family together. I imagine life must have been extremely difficult for Aunt Ellen and the children after the death of Uncle Cleveland, but that difficulty was only compounded when Aunt Ellen's oldest son Rodney died in a suspicious house fire in that infamous section of Whiteville called the Hole. Aunt Ellen continued to live in The Quarters for several years after Rodney's death before moving to the Camp Ground section of Columbus County. She died there on May 5, 1992. She was 76 years old. I have always been so very proud of Aunt Ellen and all of my relatives who showed amazing strength and perseverance in the face of adversity so our family would not only survive but would thrive.

Maggie Adell Frink was my father's younger sister and just an infant when her mother died. All of her parenting was done by her grandfather Peter and her step-grandmother Sena Jones. Of course, her brothers were very protective of her just as they had been with her sister Ellen. My father played the big brother role all of Aunt Adell's life, even during her married life. Aunt Adell was married to Leroy Frink from the community of Shallotte, North Carolina, and when she and her husband had one of their serious disagreements, she would always call her big brother. My father would go to retrieve his sister, who would then take up residence in our house. My brothers and I were always thrilled when Aunt Adell came to live with us whether the visit lasted for a few days or for several weeks. When the time came for her to pack her belongings and go back to her own house, we were always sad to see her leave. I felt as if she was going far, far away. She actually lived less than three miles from our house when I was about five or six years of age, and even closer when she and Uncle Roy built their house less than a mile from our house.

Aunt Adell had no children of her own so she doted on all of her nieces and nephews. When we were little kids, she kissed us, hugged us, and conversed with us in the *"baby talk"* language that parents concerned about speech development would not allow today. She gave us nickels, dimes, quarters, and loving pats on the head when were older. I simply adored her. I will never forget the special gift that she once gave to me that meant more to me than the change she always put in my pocket. She gave me my fortune. Aunt Adell often played a game with children where she would use the Bible to assist her in telling your fortune. She would close her eyes, open the Bible and place her finger on a random page. She would then read the verse on the page in which her finger had landed, and interpret it as your prophetic fate. If her finger landed on I Samuel 17:49, the chapter and verse referring to the slaying of Goliath by David for example, she might have proclaimed that you were destined to experience some great obstacle or trouble in your life, but that you would overcome it and win in the end. The destiny that she would proclaim for you would never be anything scary, or something that would fill you with dread. Her fortunes were always meant to encourage. During one of Aunt Adell's extended stays at our house, she was playing the game with some of the neighborhood kids and me as we waited out a summer afternoon rainstorm. When it was my turn to have my fortune read by Scripture, Aunt Adell closed her eyes, opened the Bible, and let her finger rest on a random spot in the book. Her finger landed on Ecclesiastes chapter 11, verse 1.

Aunt Adell read; "Cast thy bread upon the water: for thou shall find it after many days." I was really confused! What did that mean? Should I throw some bread in the stream that ran behind the house of the old widow Miss Annie Smith?

No, that's not what it means, Aunt Adell said to me. She then went on to explain my fate in the very simple terms that could be processed by my young mind. She told me that it meant that when I saw someone who was hungry or someone who needed something, I should always try to help them or give them some of what I had. She said that if I did it, later in life, I would always get back more than I gave to the person that was in need. It has been over six decades since Aunt Adell explained my fortune through that Bible game. Her simple explanation of the verse has had a profound influence on the way I have lived my life. The tremendous blessings that I have received and the state of grace in which I live is a testament to the undisputed truth of what Aunt Adell interpreted for me that afternoon.

It was a mild January day in Philadelphia when I left to attend the funeral of Aunt Adell, but when I arrived in Whiteville on the same day it was absolutely freezing. I guess it was one of those unusual quirks in the east coast weather pattern that caused the temperature to be much colder four hundred miles south of Philadelphia where it should have been warmer. The weather may have also been symbolic of the dread I felt on my mission of paying respect to an aunt that I loved so much that was gone to soon. Near the end of her life when she realized that she had little time left, she went about the business of putting her life in order with her friends and relatives. She wanted to assure herself that she would leave no unresolved issues that could possibly impede her transitions into her new life. She also asked my father to tell me that she had waited as long as she could for me to come home. She could wait no longer; she had to go. On January 20, 1968, Aunt Adell succumbed to multiple sclerosis. She was only 49 years old. I have always felt that it was a shame that someone who loved children so much, left no children of her own to mourn her passing. Maybe God's gift to us was to have her affection spread over far more children than could possibly have been her own. Maybe God's gift to her was to have more children love and remember her than she could have possibly borne.

Carl Lester Hill *"High Pockets"* and wife Rosa Belle McCray Hill Photo source: Gene Hill

Emma Hill Johnson with her husband Willie Johnson Photo source: Emma Johnson Walker

Robert James Hill and his wife Irene Baldwin Hill
This picture was taken at the wedding of their son
Robert Jr. Photo source: Robert Hill Jr.

Violet Hill Jones and her husband Daniel Jones
"Big Dan" Photo source: Peggy Jones

275

Willie Hill *"Rabbit"* photographed taken at his 78th birthday party in 1996. His wife Gertrude Freeman Hill photographed during the late 1950's.
Photo source: Nancy Hill & Peggy Jones

Catherine Hill Smith with her husband John Smith
circa late 1940's or early 1950's.
Photo source: Jamaaladeen Tacuma

Joseph Nathaniel Hill *"Gone"* circa 1943.
Photo source: Deloris Nokes Hill

Eva Lee Hill Nance and her husband William McKeithan Nance *"Doubem"*.
Photo source: Linda Nance Simpson

Mazie Belle Hill McDaniels *"Cricket"* circa mid 1950's Photo source: Robert Jones

Rev. Henry D, Jones and his wife Estelle Ford
Jones circa mid 1940's.
Photo source: Rev. Henry D. Jones Jr.

Ellen Jones Bell and her husband Cleveland
Bell. Ellen was photographed in 1968, Cleveland
Photographed in 1948.
Photo source: Cleveland Bell Jr

Adelle Jones Frink and her husband Leroy Frink.
Adell circa 1960, Leroy circa 1943.
Photo Source: Sarah Jones Shipman and Joe Jones

WHERE IS MY TOWN?

I wrote an article for my hometown newspaper, *The Whiteville News Reporter* that was published on October 8, 2009. The essay titled "Where Is My Town" was my attempt at describing the dramatic difference between present-day Whiteville and the Whiteville of my youth. I have included the article in this project as well as some background on the location where so much of our family history occurred.

The town of Whiteville is located in southeastern North Carolina, about forty-five miles west of Wilmington, one hundred sixty five miles east of Charlotte, and about fifty miles north of Myrtle Beach, South Carolina. The name Whiteville, when pronounced by most locals in their southeastern North Carolina accents, comes out sounding something like Wyat-ville or in some cases, Wah-vul. The area now known as Whiteville was settled in the early 1600s. Although the town was chartered in 1873, historical records mentioning Whiteville date back as far as 1733. When settlers came to the area, The Native American Siouan Tribe was already living there between what is now the Columbus

County courthouse and Lake Waccamaw. The official birthplace of the great Native American warrior Chief Osceola is Tallassee, Alabama, however some historians claim that his mother Polly Coppinger actually gave birth to him in the vicinity of Whiteville, before being relocated to the Georgia or Alabama area.

The town is named in honor of John B. White, who donated the land to the county where The Columbus County Courthouse now sits. The area was originally called White's Crossing, but later renamed Whiteville. John B. White was perhaps the area's most prominent citizen, as he was the owner of a huge area plantation called Marsh Castle. He likely also owned scores if not hundreds of slaves as his holdings included over two thousand acres of land and he certainly didn't work all of that land himself. White was not only rewarded with a town named for him, but he also became the area's first state senator.

The location of the railroad depot and what is now "Downtown Whiteville" was once a totally different town called Vineland. The two towns merged in 1926 under the name of Whiteville. My relatives who left the area before Vineland was merged referred to their hometown as Vineland. As you saw earlier, Shaw University listed Vineland as the hometown for my grandfather Luther Hill when he attended the school from 1921 to 1926. My grandfather, Seymore Jones, left the area for Philadelphia in the early 1920s. He called his hometown Vineland until he died in 1973.

I would have never considered the possibility that anything of historic significance happening in the sleepy hamlet of Whiteville before I began to research its past, but Whiteville played several small roles on the stage of American history. A. R. Ammons, widely considered one of the most important poets of the twentieth century is a Whiteville native. The famous McCoy conjoined twins who I covered earlier, were born there, performed all over the world and died there. During the Revolutionary War, neighborhood Tories, who supported England, and Whigs, who favored independence, fought several battles in Whiteville. One of those battles took place on the plantation of James Baldwin. I believe some of my ancestors were slaves on that same Baldwin plantation. Although I have no proof that they were slaves there, my great, great grandmother Rebecca Baldwin was born in the same area where the Baldwin plantation was located, and I still have Baldwin relatives that live near that location. Where else would they have gotten the name? They certainly didn't bring the name with them from Africa. The famous Revolutionary War hero General Francis Marion, the Swamp Fox, and his army came to the area now known as Whiteville on August 28, 1780 after being driven out of Charleston, South Carolina by the British.

Whiteville was even a footnote in the history of one of the most notorious outlaws in American history, Henry Berry Lowrie. Henry Lowrie lived in neighboring Robeson County during the 1860s, and was the most famous outlaw still unknown to the majority of Americans. Oppression by local authorities because of his Native American heritage, and his refusal to become a slave to the confederacy, forced him to live outside of the law. He and his band of Native American and African American outlaws lived primarily in the swamps near Lumberton, North Carolina. So famous (or infamous) were his exploits that the state of North Carolina placed a twenty-five thousand dollar reward on his head. That would be well over six hundred thousand dollars in today's money. By comparison, the highest reward ever offered for the legendary Jesse James was ten thousand dollars yet everybody knows the name of Jesse James, and few have ever heard of Lowrie.

Around 1864, while Lowrie was being held by local authorities, he was moved from the jail in Lumberton, North Carolina, where authorities were afraid he might escape, to the jail in Whiteville where he did promptly escape. By the way, once free, Lowrie broke into a Lumberton bank and stole the twenty-five thousand dollars being held there as a reward for his capture. Take that Jesse James!

Soldiers from Whiteville and the surrounding area played a part in the death of one of the most famous and commanding figures of the Civil War: Lt. General Thomas J. "Stonewall" Jackson. During the battle of Chancellorsville, Stonewall Jackson, and General A. P. Hill, led a group of soldiers on a scouting mission between union and confederate battle lines. Imagine that, two generals on a scouting mission. Upon their return, Jackson's party could not be identified so they were challenged by the sentries from the 18th Regiment. The commander of the 18th Regiment was unaware that Jackson and his party were between enemy and confederate lines, so when the Jackson's party advanced toward confederate lines under the cover of darkness, he assumed they were the enemy and ordered his troops to fire. On May 5, 1863, the 18th North Carolina Infantry Regiment, comprised of men from Columbus and surrounding Counties, fired on their own soldiers, critically wounding the brilliant tactician, white supremist, and one of the most beloved generals of the confederacy, Stonewall Jackson. He would die eight days later.

The Civil War was also reported to have brought General William Tecumseh Sherman and his Union Army through Whiteville. Stories have long been passed down about locals hiding or burying their money and other valuables to prevent the looting soldiers of Sherman's army from taking them. I even heard a rumor that my great-uncle Jim Cato had found money that had been buried during the Civil War. Uncle Jim and Aunt Annie lived in a large white home with a long beautiful front lawn. Their stately home and large yard was situated next to The Cherry Grove Baptist Church on Highway 130. When one spoke of that house, they would usually say that it was the nicest house in the area owned by a colored or *white* person. The local whites must have thought that since he was a Black man with the largest and most beautiful house in the Cherry Grove area, he could not have worked hard on his own farm, and earned the money to build it. They also never considered the possibility that he may have saved the money he earned as a soldier fighting in Europe during World War I, where he claimed to have crawled through trenches with blood two inches deep. The prevailing consensus among some of our local residents was that he must have come upon his money by some other means like stealing or finding it!

Prior to the Civil War, Whiteville had a thriving wine industry. I guess my father's relatives from Across the Marsh in Welches Creek maintained their expertise in wine making from that bygone era. I have never seen any evidence of that industry being in Whiteville other than perhaps the name Vineland, or the great homemade wine turned out by some of its local citizens. From its earliest history, timber and its processing into lumber, turpentine and tar was important to Whiteville. However, the primary economic engine that drove Whiteville's economy was agriculture. Sweet potatoes, strawberries and peanuts were important crops, but tobacco was king. It was once said that one out of every three people in Whiteville earned their living directly or indirectly from tobacco. When tobacco thrived, Whiteville thrived. With the decline of tobacco farming in the area, the closing of lumber mills, and the shipping of textile jobs out of the country, Whiteville has experienced a downturn in its economy that has made Columbus County one of the poorest counties in all of North Carolina. The contrast between the town with a booming agricultural economy and the town I saw in 2009 inspired me to set down my musing in the following article for *The Whiteville News Reporter*.

The News Reporter, Thursday 8. 2009
Where's my town?
by Joseph Jones

My wife and I were in Whiteville recently to celebrate and participate in the fourth annual Lillie Mae Jones Day. We try to visit my hometown once or twice a year, but we make it a point to be there on September 20th to celebrate the day designated by Columbus County commissioners to honor my mother. On this visit to Whiteville, I was determined to show my wife the Whiteville of my nineteen sixties memories. We had all day Saturday September 19th to explore Whiteville and the surrounding area. Before we began our tour, I explained the significance of tobacco to the region's economy. For years I had been telling my wife how I had labored in tobacco. I did everything from the planting of the seedling beds to preparing tobacco for shipment to the cigarette manufacturing plants. Now it was time to show her how tobacco was grown, gathered (cropped) and cured. I drove to areas where I had worked the fields but could not find tobacco growing in any of them. The only tobacco barns I could find were dilapidated and by appearance, had not been used for years. Oh well, let's move on to the next stop on the tour. Next, I would show my wife where we took the tobacco to be sold. Her interest was piqued when I spoke of the excitement generated at the warehouse listening to the syncopated calls of the tobacco auctioneer soliciting the best price for the product of the farmer's hard labor. My father often sold tobacco at a warehouse in downtown Whiteville. I think that it was called The Farmers Warehouse. I know it was torn down several years ago. I drove my wife to see the warehouse near the Whiteville exit for Highway 74 although I knew there would be no tobacco sold there. It is now a furniture store. I was a little disappointed because what I was able to show my wife about tobacco farming had little resemblance to the tobacco industry in Whiteville during my youth. After trying to explain planting, cropping, dragging (transporting tobacco from the field on a sled) and stringing of tobacco, I could tell she just did not "get it." She said maybe instead of a forestry museum, you should have a tobacco museum in Whiteville. Is this Whiteville, I thought to myself? Where is "King Tobacco"? Where is my town?

Next on the tour was downtown Whiteville. While my wife Carol and I drove around the streets of Whiteville, I tried to convey to her a sense of what downtown Whiteville was like when I was young. It was Saturday afternoon. On Saturdays, the town of my youth was vibrant, bustling and busy. It seemed that everyone from the surrounding communities came to town on Saturday. Although the public transportation bus system had gone out of business, even people without cars found their way to town. They walked, came in the backs of pickup trucks and hitched rides with friends. My family also found it necessary to go to town every Saturday. Even before my father could park the car, you could hear street vendors yelling "ball (boiled) peanuts! Ten cents a bag, three for a quarter, seven for fifty cents!" They always seemed to do a brisk business as Whiteville streets were packed with shoppers. As wives shopped, husbands sat in waiting on a large wooden plank near the railroad tracks opposite the Whiteville train station. My mother always disapproved of my father sitting there and talking with the other men. The plank where the men sat was a gathering point for unemployed men during the week, thus earning the name "the lazy bench." My mother did not want her husband associated with anything referenced as lazy. While my father sat on the lazy bench discussing the issues of the day, my mother shopped at Leder Brothers or one of the other stores in town. I always liked shopping at Leder Brothers because Doc Curry worked there. He was the only Black salesperson in Whiteville at that time. If Mr. Curry was busy when we went to Leder's, we would wait until he was available. There was a store for every need downtown. When we were young, our parents took us to Moscow's to get our school clothes. Kramer's had a nice selection, but if I wanted something sharp and hip for the times, I went to J.S. Mann. This was a time before credit cards provided us with instant gratification and prolonged heartache, so we could not say "charge it." If you did not have enough money to purchase that item you just had to have, you put it in *layaway*. On your Saturday visits to town you would pay down your item on layaway until it was all yours.

As we continued to drive around, I pointed out the food markets, fish markets, drug stores, jewelry stores, sporting goods stores and any other kind of store one needed in a small town.

When the tour had ended, when the flood of memories had run its course and I had run out of things to say, my wife asked, "Joey, where are all the people? Where is your town?"

Good question, I replied. WHERE *IS* MY TOWN? All of the stores were closed. There was no one hawking boiled peanuts on the streets. Ward's Grill was closed. I couldn't even get an "all the way" hotdog for lunch. There were only one or two cars parked on the street. Whiteville looked like a ghost town.

Just as we had driven around earlier looking for signs of the tobacco industry, we then set out to find the shoppers of Whiteville. With just a quick drive down Highway 701 to the WalMart complex, we found the people we were looking for. The crowded parking lot indicated that they were all inside WalMart shopping.

I left Whiteville as a teenager over forty years ago. Although I have a sense, I really don't know the full impact the declining tobacco and clothing industry had on the downtown area. I don't know if WalMart is financially good or bad for the region. I do wonder if WalMart's gain of retailing dominance is too much of a loss of community and small town character. The WalMart complex in South Whiteville is very impressive. Hopefully, they are providing the jobs necessary for a stable and healthy community. While sitting in the car watching the shoppers go in and out of the complex, I could not see or feel any sense of community. Gone were the Moscows, Kramers, Leders and Manns, the storeowners your parents knew personally. Gone were the sights, sounds and smells of downtown Whiteville. Gone were the places men waited as women shopped. Gone were the vendors shouting "ball peanuts!"

I guess that when a town with character is being replaced by a strip mall with no character, it is considered progress. There is always a price to be paid for progress. In this case, I wonder if the price is too high.

After sitting in the parking lot for a while, we decided not to go shopping in WalMart that Saturday afternoon. We decided to go home. We had enough of looking for my town without being able to find it.

Just as Thomas Wolfe stated in the title of his famous novel *You Can't Go Home Again*, I know I can never go back home to the Whiteville I wrote about in the *News Reporter* article no matter how much I might be nostalgic for it. There was also a Whiteville many of us would never want to go home to. It's the Whiteville that so many of us hurried to escape from as soon as we were able. That's the Whiteville where every facet of life was dominated by racial prejudice. It was a place where the way of life was predicated on the assumption by most whites that Black people were inferior, thus relegating them to the status of second-class citizens was indeed the proper thing to do.

In my mind, the laws, rules and traditions relating to race were needed by whites to convince themselves that they were the superior race, as much as they were needed to convince us that we were inferior. The purpose of racial segregation in Whiteville, as it was everywhere else, was not only to control your actions, but to control your mind. If one can be convinced to think of himself as inferior, you won't need to control his actions to keep him oppressed; he will do that himself. This phenomenon is best explained in a quote from Carter G. Woodson's book *The Mis-Education of the Negro*:

> "If you can control a man's thinking you do not have to worry about his actions. When you determine what a man shall think you do not have to concern yourself about what he will do. If you make a man feel that he is inferior, you do not have to compel him to accept an inferior status, for he will seek it himself. If you make a man think that he is justly an outcast, you do not have to order him to the back door. He will go without being told; and if there is no back door, his very nature will demand one."

Those mind controlling laws, rules and traditions governed everything that we did. They dictated where we went to school, where we worshiped, where we could work, where we socialized, who we could socialize with, and where we could live.

While African Americans in Whiteville didn't live in predominantly white neighborhoods, whites sometimes lived in African American neighborhoods. Although I was born in the rented house next door to my families white landlord Tom Hill, it was in a rural area on a property where he also lived. In Whiteville, Blacks did not typically live in white neighborhoods.

The section of Cherry Grove where my family and relatives lived was inhabited by Black people who almost always owned their homes. The few properties that were rented were usually owned by a relative of the renter. There were very few rental properties or houses owned by folks who did not live in the neighborhood. One of those exceptions was the house that stood next door to us on the land where my brother, Jerry's house now sits. My father told me that the house next door was owned by a white family who had lived there for several years before our Black neighbors and our family moved into the area. When the father of the family died, he willed the house to his son. Fearing that his alcoholic son would immediately sell the property and drink up the proceeds from it, the father put a stipulation in the will forbidding his son from selling the property for twenty-five years after his death. It was the father's hope that his twenty-something year older son would have kicked his alcohol problem by that time. Since the son could not sell the property, he rented it to anyone who needed and could pay for a place to live. The first occupant I can recall being in the house was my Aunt Eva and Uncle WM. I also remember my cousin Juanita and husband Edward Burns living there. Other than those two families, I remember mostly a succession of misfits, drunkards and very poor white families living there.

Our family was not rich by any stretch of the imagination, but we certainly fared much better than most of the white folks that rented the house next door to us. The white families that often lived next to us were contradictions to the idea of Whiteville's perceived social order. They were white, they were poor and they always needed help. My mother was Black and she always provided it.

I have a vivid recollection of one of the white families that lived next door to us and I also remember the issues the family had that would sometimes cause disharmony in our small neighborhood. There were three children in the family. A girl between the ages of two and three, a young boy about five years old, and another boy named Robbie who was about my age of ten or eleven at that time. The mother was a plump woman with a round face and ruddy checks. For the life of me, I can't remember what the father looked like. I do remember, however, that he had a serious drinking problem that manifested itself almost every weekend. I also remember the screaming, crying and noises that came from that house when he was on one of his rampages. I don't know if he beat his wife because of his drinking or because he was just an abusive and miserable human being; but beat his wife, he did. The abuse that he would rain down on her was not just of a verbal nature, nor was it just an occasional slap or a blackened eye. The beatings his wife endured sometimes left her bloodied, and in at least in one case, a beating left her with a badly broken arm.

During one of the beatings, the wife swooped up the two small children and ran to our back door. Standing in the rear door of his house, the husband was spewing obscenities at his wife and continued to do so even as my mother ushered the woman and her two small children through our kitchen door. Robbie remained in his house with his drunken father. After the beaten, crying mother and her hysterical children were consoled, my mother did what all southern Black hosts did at that time. She asked if they would like something to eat. The woman told my mother that she would appreciate something for the children because they had not had anything to eat since the prior day's breakfast. Complaints to her husband about their hungry children had enraged her husband and had precipitated the fight. I was shocked. As I have said before, we were not rich, but we always had plenty of food. I knew a lot of people that I would consider poor, but I didn't know anyone who went hungry. My mother fed the woman and her children, then gave her food to take home after our white neighbor deemed it was safe for her to return to her house. My mother continued to supply the woman with cooked food from her kitchen and fresh vegetables from her gardens until the family moved away some two years later.

I never mentioned the altercation that happened at his house the next day as Robbie and I played together in the fields and woods near our houses. Even at that early age everyone knew where to draw the line when it came to conversation. You just didn't talk about what went on between grown folks in their homes. Robbie didn't mention it either. It was more than likely something in which he had become accustomed.

Robbie was the only white kid in our neighborhood but we quickly integrated him into the group of my cousins and friends who played cowboys and Indians, explored the stream just past the house of the old widow, Miss Annie Smith, and played baseball in one of the many open fields in our area. We treated him just as we did every other kid in the neighborhood. Although we were not allowed inside his house, he came into our houses. He was no different from the rest of my friends, yet he was different. Robbie was white and society said that he was different. On school days, he was just one of the many neighborhood kids playing games on the shoulders of the Highway 130 while we waited for the school bus. Ronald Leach, who had lived just two houses from us, next door to my grandmother, had been struck by a car and killed in the same area where we played. Although he had been killed several years earlier, we still carried the parental admonishment in the back of our minds to be careful and look both ways before we darted back and forth from one side of the road to the other. Our parents always feared we might suffer the same fate that befell Ronald Leach.

When the buses pulled up to the stop located across the street from my house, Robbie would waive goodbye as he boarded the school bus designated for white kids headed for the white elementary school, and we would board the bus headed for Central High School.

I have no idea what Robbie's life was like at his school. I don't know if he had friends there or not, but I do know that we were his only friends and his only world outside of school. He was not better educated, he was no wiser, he was no stronger, nor was he a better person than any of the other kids in our neighborhood, but society told this child that he was better than us. Even though his family depended on the charity of Black neighbors for their survival, social order and tradition dictated that his whiteness made him superior to us, and that we were not worthy to sit in a classroom with him.

My brother Bobby had a quote about race that fit the Whiteville of my childhood and was most certainly applicable to the town's earlier years. The quote was "race trumps everything." It is a tragedy of the human spirit that we could not just live their lives and interact on just a human level without having this race thing permeating every phase of our daily lives.

My brother Bobby tells a story of being surprised by a comment made by Crowell Black, one of Columbus County's most prominent and wealthiest citizens. He told my brother, "You know that I'm really close to your father. I would do anything for him."

Now isn't that ironic? He was really close to my father, but other than some business transactions for a couple cars, I had never known them to have any interaction with each other. They never appeared to be friends. Apparently they had lived their entire lives as close friends without Crowell Black ever sitting foot inside our house or my father setting foot in his. They never did the thing friends do. There were no friendly conversations in each other's living room over a glass of cool lemonade, nor did they have one Sunday dinner together, yet he counted my father as a friend for which he would do anything. Crowell Black was a white man and my father Black, so those kind of social interactions of people of different races just were not done. That was the state of racial separation in Whiteville, and I suppose every other southern town like it. How did Crowell Black and my father become friends, and how did he come to tell my brother Bobby about the friendship? Since the story has a little of my family history in it, I think that it's a story worth telling.

By the time Crowell Black made the statement to my brother about my father, he owned an automobile tire sales and service company with multiple locations in southeastern North Carolina. In addition to owning several other businesses, he also had extensive real estate holdings in the area. He was by all standards, a wealthy man. My brother Bobby had been in Whiteville to explore a business opportunity involving a property owned by Crowell Black. Although Black was enthusiastic about my brother getting the property, the business project my brother was exploring did not come to fruition, but my brother also had been speaking with Crowell Black about financing a car through a bank in Whiteville. He wanted the car but it was too late to complete the paperwork before the bank closed on Friday afternoon. The bank would be closed on Saturday, and he was leaving town on Sunday. When Crowell Black heard of my brother's dilemma, he met with Bobby and told him that if he wanted the car, he should go to the bank that Friday evening at 7:00 PM, and ring the bell at the side door. Even though the bank was closed, someone would meet him there and complete the paperwork in time for his to pick-up the car on Saturday. Surprised that one of the richest men in Columbus County would have the bank opened for him, my brother wanted to know how he could do it, and more importantly, why he would do it. Crowell Black then explained to my brother that he *could* have the bank opened because he was one of the principle owners of the bank. The reason why he *would* do it was because of his relationship with my father. He would do anything for my father, Black exclaimed. Crowell Black then went on to explain how the relationship between him and my father had evolved.

It is well known that The Great Depression left millions of people without income and homeless, but the impact of the depression and the homelessness it caused was focused more on large metropolitan areas that it was on small rural areas like Lees Township, North Carolina. Just as there were homeless people in the big cities, the depression left people homeless in rural areas. According to my father, Crowell Black's family had been one of those homeless families. My father had told me many times about how Crowell Black went from being homeless to being one of the wealthiest men in Columbus County. My father said that Crowell Black and his father Sam Black had come to Lees Lake during the height of the depression. Seeking something better over the next horizon, poor people by thousands hopped trains, hitched rides and even walked to some other location that might hold out a greater chance of survival than the place they had been. Crowell Black and his father arrived in Lees Lake Township during those depression era years on foot. My father never spoke of a mother, just the boy and his father. Having no place to live, they camped in a wooded area near my great grandfather's farm. By this time my father's mother was dead and his father had moved from the area, so my father and his siblings were living with his grandfather, Peter Jones. Crowell Black's father either had enough money or obtained enough money to purchase a calf. He then slaughtered the calf, hung it from a tree near their campsite and butchered it. He then went around the neighborhood selling the beef from the calf he had butchered in the woods.

He used the proceeds from the first butchered calf to purchase another, and from those humble beginnings, the Black family grew into one whose wealth, power and influence was on par with the business elite in Columbus County who had bloodlines running back to colonial times.

I don't know if Crowell Black related to my brother the story of his humble beginnings, but he did tell him what caused his admiration for my father. This part of the story I had never heard from my father. Crowell Black told my brother that when they first came to the area of Lees Lake and camped in the woods near my grandfather's farm, they were hungry and had no food. Even during the depression, food was plentiful for my father's family because they grew it on their own farm. Crowell Black said that my father's family always fed them food during those very difficult times and he said that for the rest of his life, he would never forget those acts of kindness.

I suppose that my father and Crowell Black's friendship manifested itself the only way it could in a segregated society. Who knows what this and so many other relationships would have been like in a color blind Whiteville. Perhaps they would have been good fishing and hunting buddies and their wives and children would have been friends. Maybe they would have not really liked each other and not socialized at all. Isn't it a shame we will never know because simply put *race trumps everything*, even friendships?

The friendship between my father and Crowell Black, however tentative it was, did serve my brother well on that occasion. All it took was one call from Crowell Black to have the bank opened on a Friday night to accommodate my brother. Amazingly, the person that met my brother at the side door of the bank was none other than the bank's president.

Whiteville and Columbus County was typical of the southern segregated societies we have all read about in novels and watched depicted in movies. Political power was in the hands of its white citizens. The decent jobs, even the blue collar ones were held by whites. The schools were segregated. Medical facilities were segregated. While white owned restaurants such as our neighborhood's Joe's Barbeque, were happy to take our money and pass food orders through a window or quickly through a back door held only slightly ajar, they would have never considered offering us the hospitality that southerners made famous at one of their tables inside. Although every facets of life was segregated in Whiteville, the most segregated time and place in Columbus County was at 11:00 AM on every Sunday morning at every church in Columbus County. It would have been unthinkable for Blacks and whites to sit next to each other and worship the God who bled, suffered, and died for the redemption of us all.

In every sense, the area where I grew up was racially segregated, but one act common to those southern period novels and movies that I never witnessed in Whiteville was the act of white violence. I know that there had been racial violence there at one point. It was visited upon my own family. As I discussed earlier, I am certain that my great-Uncle Alexander Lewis was killed by a mob of local white men in Lees Lake Township during the early thirties. The Ku Klux Klan was also very active in Columbus County during the early fifties. Horace Carter, the young editor of *The Tabor City Tribune* newspaper, and Willard Cole, editor of *The Whiteville News Reporter*, both won Pulitzer Prizes for meritorious public service in 1953, for their articles decrying Klan violence in Columbus County. The two editors endured hundreds of death threats on their own lives, as well as threats on the lives of their wives and children. The Klan also instituted a campaign to stop businesses from advertising in the newspaper, thus attempting to force the newspapers into financial ruin. They even threatened to kill Horace Carter's dog. Now, when you threaten to kill a man's dog in North Carolina, that's a serious threat! Because *The Whiteville News Reporter* was much larger and had more influence than *The Tabor City Tribune,* the Klan hated its editor, Willard Cole, even more than they hated Carter. Willard Cole was forced to carry a gun everywhere he went. It was largely due to the uncompromised truth that Horace Carter and Willard Cole printed in their newspapers about Klan violence that led to The Federal Bureau of Investigation, and The

State Bureau of Investigation collecting enough evidence to charge, convict and imprison nearly 100 Klan members in Columbus County.

Although Whiteville had this history of racial intolerance and even racial violence, it was something that I never saw much of when I was a growing up there. Perhaps during those years Black people were content with the status quo and didn't make enough demands for racial equality to draw the ire of local whites. Maybe we didn't agitate for change enough to cause our white citizens any concerns. By the time the Blacks in Whiteville started to advocate for racial equality during the Civil Rights Movement of the 1960s, I had already left the area.

There was one incident, or series of incidents, I can recall that did have the potential to cause racial problems. During the late 1950s or early 1960s, a group of white youths decided that it might be fun to terrorize the Black residents of the neighborhood called the Quarters. The presumed teenagers would go on late-night drives and fire their guns into the yards and homes of the people living there. If this situation had existed in one of those novels or movies about the segregated south, the result would have been Black people hiding, and whimpering in their homes until they were saved by the white hero. That is not how the problem faced by the Black folks living in The Quarters was solved. The young men who lived there got their guns, (everyone in Whiteville had a gun) and laid in wait for another midnight ride by the young whites. When the white kids drove through the neighborhood firing their guns wildly, the young Black residents emerged for hiding and let loose with a surprise volley of gunfire into car in which the kids were riding. The screaming heard coming from inside the car was almost drowned out by the screeching tires made by the shot up automobile beating a hasty retreat from The Quarters. Although I'm sure the young men from The Quarters felt very proud about what they had done, they never boasted about it. They were sure that when they fired into the car they heard someone cry out ("The niggers shot me!") The young men of the Quarters tried to keep their exploits secret as they did not want repercussions from the local law authorities. Even though the residents of The Quarters kept the incidence a secret, the white kids got the message and never again made night rides there.

The races were, of course, separate in other forms of entertainment that did not include shooting at each other. I have no idea where the white kids in Whiteville went to dance and party, but I knew several places where the Black kids went to dance and have fun. In the area of Whiteville near Central High School, The Sherwood, Stewart's Place and Smith's were "hangout" locations for Black kids to gather, talk and dance. There were also jook joints called Punk's Place and the Black and Tan located in the Black section of town called the Hole. It was not a place that you wanted to go if you were faint of heart. My brothers and I were strictly forbidden to go there. Of course that meant we went there every chance that we got. My parents were justified in not allowing us to go to the area called the Hole, and especially not to Punk's Place or the Black and Tan because there were stabbings and shootings there on a regular basis. There were also jook joints in the area south of Whiteville where we lived. One of our neighbors named Matthew Hawkins ran one such joint right down the street from our house, and my cousin Ed Davis ran another called The Hop in an area close to The Quarters. Both joints were a thorn in the side of churches and Baptist neighbors who lived within earshot of the sounds of Chuck Berry or Lloyd Price emanating from those clubs. Local teenagers who were members of the nearby Cherry Grove Baptist Church had to be very careful not to allow my great uncle, Stedman Lewis or one of the other deacons from the church, see them entering either of those spots. I don't know what penalty the church imposed on a young member found guilty of cutting or shooting someone in one of those places, but they would put you out of the church if you were seen dancing there.

Black people who were looking for more of a wholesome form of entertainment than you could find at the local nightspots could go for picnics and fish fries at nearby lakes and beaches. They had access to local lakes and beaches only if they were designated as one where Black folks were allowed to go. Whites enjoyed picnicking, camping, boating, swimming and other activities at the nearby Lake Waccamaw, and another place called, of all thing White Lake. (I'm not kidding) We could go to neither. Blacks swam and picnicked at a place called Jones Lake near Elizabethtown, North Carolina. Whites went to Myrtle Beach for seaside entertainment, water sports and for swimming in the ocean. We were not allowed in Myrtle Beach. Although I lived some forty miles from Myrtle Beach, South Carolina, I had never seen it until years after I had left North Carolina and returned as an adult to vacation in the Myrtle Beach area during the early 1970s. To white folks, going to the beach could have meant going to Topsail, Wrightsville, Carolina, Sunset, Surfside, or Myrtle Beaches. We went to none of them. We had our own beach. It was called Atlantic Beach. When a Black person said, "I'm going to the beach" everyone knew for sure where the person was headed. They were going to Atlantic Beach, South Carolina.

Atlantic Beach is a city that encompasses 29th through 32nd streets with a western border just a short distance beyond Highway 17, and an eastern border of the ocean. The shoreline for Atlantic Beach was contiguous with Myrtle Beach and North Myrtle Beach, but what it offered Black revelers were experiences that could not have been found by visiting either of its neighbors even if we had been allowed to go there. In the early thirties, Gullah or Geechee people established hotels, restaurants, gift shops and nightclubs in those four blocks. Called The Black Pearl during its early years, Atlantic Beach was the only oceanfront location from Virginia to Georgia where Black people could gather or vacation in comfort without fear of embarrassment or rejection. It was a jewel to the Black community. I went there once on a high school class outing to enjoy the beach, have lunch and dance with classmates, but school outings were not the kind of functions that made Atlantic Beach famous. Atlantic Beach's fame and the reason we wanted to go there was for the festivities that occurred on Saturday and Sunday nights. On weekends, the Black elite, hip teenagers, hard drinking adults and tobacco field workers all descended on Atlantic Beach. As soon as you turned off of Highway 17 onto the main drag in Atlantic Beach, what you encountered was a sight that I have never seen duplicated anywhere other than the confines of that four block area. There would be a countless number of Black people everywhere. You were forced to drive very slowly and carefully as you navigated your way through the throngs of people that often walked in the middle of the street. Sometimes they would even jubilantly hop on the hood or trunk of your car and ride through the crowds with you to your destination. It was a party, and you were well into a partying mood even before you found a place to park your car. The pulsating rhythm of Little Richard merged with those of Ray Charles, Ruth Brown, Sam Cooke, and Etta James as you strolled past the open doors of one club after another. If you walked past a club or a tent packed primarily with men, it was a sure sign that one of those "hoochie coochie" shows was going on inside. The scantily clad girls in the show might be doing anything from stripping to smoking a cigar with unmentionable parts of their bodies. It was a show for adult men, but if you had the price of admission, you were considered an adult.

The place where everyone from Whiteville had to make an appearance was Punk's Patio, the open air or patio deck styled club located directly on the beach. The club was owned by a man from the Whiteville area named Punk Daniels. I never knew his proper given name because everyone referred to him as Punk. He was well known to Whiteville residents because he also owned the club called Punk's Place there. The drinks flowed like water and so did the sweat on the dancers who danced the slop, twist and the shag or swing on the floor of Punk's Patio during those hot summer nights. When you needed a break from the crowd, or the heat and the sweat of the dance floor, you could cool off in the refreshing night sea breeze by simply stepping off of the deck and taking a stroll with your girlfriend or the one you were hoping would become your girlfriend, onto the beach that was next to the patio. Punk's Patio was the place to be and we all wanted to be there whenever we were in Atlantic Beach.

Whenever a large number of people and a large quantity of alcohol meet at the same location, there are bound to be problems, and Atlantic Beach had its share. Liquor and testosterone-fueled bravado occasionally disrupted the party atmosphere with a fist or even a knife fight. When a fight did break out, the Atlantic Beach police department was promptly on the scene. The police force consisted of one car and one very tough, no-nonsense police officer by the name of Henry "Pork Chop" Hemmingway. Of the fights that I witnessed at Atlantic Beach, I never saw Pork Chop Hemmingway's authority challenged. He usually restored order posthaste.

Just as there were restrictions on me going to places like the Black and Tan in Whiteville, there were also restrictions on me going to Atlantic Beach. I was not to go there on Saturday because of the large drunken crowds, and I was not to go there on Sunday because it was the Sabbath... and there were large drunken crowds. Just as we violated Jones family rules about going to places in Whiteville, we violated the rules on going to Atlantic Beach. If you wanted to truly experience Atlantic Beach, or The Black Pearl, you had to be there on the weekend. The weekends were the time everything happened at the beach, so other than the one class trip that I took there on a school day, the countless other times that I navigated the crowds to dance and party in Atlantic Beach was on Friday, Saturday and Sunday nights.

I had some time to kill one day during a visit to the Whiteville area in the fall of 2004, so I decided to take a ride down to Atlantic Beach. When I arrived in the area where I thought it was located, I drove up and down the streets trying to find it. Finally, a gentleman came out of one of the buildings and flagged down my car. He said that he had seen me driving around so he decided to stop me and ask if I needed help. I told him that I was looking for Atlantic Beach. He told me that I was in it!

"No, it can't be," I told him. I said that I was looking for the place where all of the Black restaurants, hotels and shops were located. There was only a few run down building with some residential homes nearby.

Again, he said, "this is it."

"What happened to all of the clubs and restaurants? Where was Punk's Patio?"

The gentleman pointed to a few planks of wood that had once been painted blue and looked as if it might have been part of a deck at one time. That was Punk's Patio, the man said. He could see my disappointment, so before he started to explain what had happened to The Black Pearl, he introduced himself and confirmed his identify with a business card imprinted with the seal and the business name: Town of Atlantic Beach. He was John Sketers, Mayor Pro tem. Mr. Sketers then explained to me that since segregation laws were struck down in the state of South Carolina, the Black people who had once patronized businesses in Atlantic Beach took their business and their dollars to the white establishments where they had been denied access during Atlantic Beach's heyday. Unable to compete with the businesses in Myrtle Beach, Atlantic Beach went into and continues into decline. It has not seen the same kind of development as the area surrounding it because the property owners refused to sell to developers who were trying to steal their property by offering its owners a fraction of what their beachfront property was really worth. I guess until developers decide to pay property owners what their land is worth, the glory that was Atlantic Beach will be just a pleasant memory. Even if Atlantic Beach is redeveloped, it will never again be the Black Pearl. That was a time and place that no amount of redevelopment dollars can get back. Until the property owners and developers decide what Atlantic Beach is to become, the countless numbers of us who witnessed its heyday will have Black Pearl Saturday night memories, but Atlantic Beach will probably remain a rundown Black beachfront town located in the middle of the prosperous Myrtle Beach Grand Strand.

African American citizens of Whiteville no longer have their food orders passed through a windows or back doors of restaurants. The beaches, lakes and campsites no longer have race restrictions and the resorts of Myrtle Beach not only accept

Black dollars, but campaign for them. There are no segregated public schools, and any vestiges of segregated housing appear to be based on economics conditions rather that race. My cousin Harold Troy is a city council member and mayor pro tem of Whiteville. There is additional Black representation in city and county government as well as the school board. During a visit with my mother to her African American physician, I was surprised to see that his crowded waiting room had more white patients awaiting his services than Blacks. That was a scene I did not expect and never would have witnessed while growing up there. That same doctor also lives in the beautiful, white, antebellum-style house with giant columns that once belonged to my Aunt Eva's and Uncle WM's landlord Garland Anderson. A Black man owning such a beautiful house with a corral of fine horses out back was also something that would have been inconceivable to me when I was young child. By any measure, the area has experienced dramatic improvements in race relations.

I was not a part of the push for racial equality in Whiteville that facilitated those improvements. I had relocated by that time. On the surface, Whiteville appears to have progressed with the rest of the country towards putting an end to the three hundred year-old tradition of social segregation without experiencing the violence and bloodshed that took place in many southern cities, and even some northern cities. Those changes are ones that

I like going home to, but Whiteville has also had some quality-of-life setbacks since the 1950s and 1960s that are not so nice to come home to. The tobacco, lumber and textile industries that had pumped dollars into the local economy have been greatly reduced or have disappeared altogether. This has left Columbus County struggling with an unemployment rate that, at one point, hovered over 14%. Anytime you hear of a high unemployment percentage in any area, the rate of unemployment for people of color is sometimes double the overall number. This presents a challenge for the entire area. With the loss of those jobs came all of the social problems associated with economic decline. The once vibrant downtown area of Whiteville now looks like a ghost town. There are no more teenage hangouts like The Sherwood, Stewarts or the forbidden jook joints like The Hop, Punk's Place or The Black and Tan. Going to the beach now means really going to the ocean. The term no longer means going to the clubs of Atlantic Beach.

There is no more Central High School and some of the activities that take place within a stone's throw of what is now Central Middle School discredits the awesome legacy of Central. Finally, when I go to Whiteville, I sometimes feel like a stranger. Other than the few classmates still living there and some of my relatives, I now know few people in a place where I once knew every Black person I encountered. Still, with all of the changes that have taken place since I left Whiteville, I feel the need to be there occasionally. I need to see what has changed and what is familiar. My longing for ripe juicy scuppernog grapes, picked and eaten directly from the orchards in the back yard of my family home, can't be satisfied by grapes from the supermarket. The cuisine from finest restaurants in the world pale in comparison to Whiteville's blue speckled butterbeans and okra cooked with enough fatback to be just slightly unhealthy. I need to pat my feet and wave my hand to the syncopated rhythms of the music and message that warms my soul when I visit the churches that molded me. Just once in a while, I need to be near the school that honed, sharpened and launched me into the world. I need a hug from the people that still carry the blood of Maggie Yeoman, Peter Jones, Dolly Baldwin, Squire Lewis, Fanny Parker and Henry Hill. Maybe Thomas Wolfe was wrong after all; perhaps you can go home again.

WE HONOR AND REVERE YOUR NAME

In 2004, *The Philadelphia Inquirer* requested an essay related to the landmark Supreme Court ruling in the case of *Brown v. Board of Education*. The essay was requested for the celebration of the fiftieth anniversary of the court's ruling that made school segregation illegal everywhere in the United States. I wrote an article titled "No More Beloved Community" about the special place my high school was before the enforcement of Brown v. Board of Education, and what was lost in our communities after schools integration occurred. The Inquirer editors loved the article and printed it in their weekend edition with a large picture of yours truly. Just as I included the piece about my hometown of Whiteville written for *The News Reporter* in the prior chapter, I am including the article about the school I attended, Central High School in this section. Before the article, let me give you some background on the school that when alumni sing the school song, they proudly proclaim that "We honor and revere your name."

From the very beginning of our history in America, Black people have always had a thirst for learning. Slave and slave master alike realized that education would surely aid in our liberation, so even when whites criminalized education for Black folks, we suffered severe retributions as a consequence for simply trying to obtain knowledge. After emancipation, Black folks drive to educate themselves and to provide an education for their children was nothing less than phenomenal. After emancipation, community schools like my familie's Mill Branch School, sprang up in churches and private homes all over the country. Just after the turn of the twentieth century, wealthy philanthropist, and part owner of Sears, Roebuck Company, Julius Rosenwal, made huge contributions to aid in the building of schools to educate Black children all over the south. His contribution to Black education should be applauded, but Rosenwal provided matching funds to Black communities who had the desire to seek education for their children, and the fortitude to raise the money to build those schools in areas where they were clearly not valued or even wanted by the white majority community. Both Rosenwal *and* the civic minded people from our communities are true American heroes.

Whiteville Colored School was established in 1880 to provide a basic elementary education for Negro children. The extraordinary support for education from the Black community only increased after this school was established. Black people from the community donated land for buildings, and in many cases, only obtained funds for needed educational projects if they matched funds allocated to them by the county. Our people were so committed to the success of Black education, that they even imposed a special tax on themselves to insure that our school would remain functional. While the taxes collected from the Black community helped to provide sufficient support for the white schools, the county would not provide enough of the revenue partially generated by our own tax dollars to operate our school. For that reason, our community took the phenomenally unselfish act of placing a special tax assessment on themselves to provide revenue directly to the school. Thus they were double taxed to education their children.

In 1928, W. M. Rheinhart, the former principal of The Mt. Olive School, was sent to Whiteville by the board of education to organize the high school which became Whiteville Negro High School. By 1930, the school had become a combination elementary, middle and high school. During the late 1940s, a new brick building was added to the school's campus to accommodate students from outline areas surrounding Whiteville. The school started by our Hill family ancestors as a part of Mill Branch Church had long been closed by that time, but The Diamond Branch School located south of Whiteville in the area locals called Cut

Tail, the Camp Ground School north of the city, which had been destroyed by fire in the 1940s, and The Spring Hill School located in an area west of the city, provided elementary education for Black children in their communities. The new building at Whiteville Negro High School facilitated the consolidation of students from Diamond Branch, Camp Ground and Spring Hill Elementary Schools onto one campus. Based on a recommendation by John A. Campbell, the principal when the consolidation took place, the name of the school that would educate all Negro children in Whiteville and surrounding areas was changed to Central High School.

During my twelve years at Central High School, and even until this day, I have never seen the inside of any of the buildings at the white Whiteville High School. As a matter of fact, I have never even set foot on the campus although for several of the years I was at Central, my mother worked there. I imagined that the classrooms in the buildings there were much nicer than the ones in our small wooden buildings at Central. I imagined that the books and all of the facilities were better than those provided for us in that separate but very unequal segregated school system, but would I have attended Whiteville High School if it had been an option? Not a chance! Central was special. Even though I played hooky from school on occasions and caused my teachers grief by my attraction to the same mischief as other school-aged boys,

I loved Central and loved being there. I believe most of my fellow students felt the same way. We lived in an age before graffiti found its way on schoolhouse walls, but I can't even conceive of the possibility of any of us wanting to deface our school in that manner. Trash or paper, even a tiny bit was not allowed to rest on our classroom or hall floors for very long before someone in authority either picked it up or ordered you to do so. I remember a campus, though small and unassuming, was kept in pristine condition. We did not walk on our grass; we used the paved sidewalks. We raised, lowered and properly folded the American flag on our campus each day. We would always run to the flagpole, hastily lower and remove the flag during inclement weather. Once the threat of stormy weather had passed, we would raise the flag again. We followed the proud tradition of not flying the flag in the rain because we were a proud school.

When a new gymnasium was finally built on our campus, we were so enamored with the beautiful hardwood court that we would remove our street shoes and only walk on the floor in our socks. The only shoes you wore on our gym's hardwood floor were proper athletic shoes. Even though the Central campus was far less impressive than the larger Whiteville High School campus, Central was ours, and we were proud of it. Whiteville High had a football program, Central didn't, and I had always wanted to play high school football. Whiteville had a better baseball program than Central, and although I played on Central's baseball team, I would love to have played in a larger program such as Whiteville High's program. The Whiteville High baseball statistics and scores were posted in the local newspaper. Such a thing would have never been considered for Central. Even after I consider all of the obvious advantages students had at Whiteville High School, I still count myself blessed to have attended Central before the local school board stopped ignoring the Supreme Court's order and finally integrated the schools in Whiteville. Hopefully, the essay that I wrote for the Philadelphia Inquirer will convey my true sentiments about my years at Central.

The Philadelphia Inquirer Sunday May 16, 2004
No more 'beloved community'
Joe Jones
Lives in Wyncote

Image my surprise during a visit to my hometown of Whiteville, N.C., when a relative and former teacher stated that he wished school integration had never happened.

Like me he had suffered the injustices of a very separate and a very unequal school system. Surly, he remembered some of the old decrepit buildings with coal-burning stoves on our campus. Did he forget the hand-me-down books and supplies that we received only after the all-white Whiteville High School considered them no longer usable? Had he forgotten what it was like? He couldn't have. He was on the front lines of the war for racial equality during those turbulent and troubled '60s.

Unlike so many of us, he did not leave Whiteville for the false promises of big cities such as New York, Philadelphia or Baltimore. He returned and fought for the change that has little resemblance to the segregated school system I remember before or even for several years after *Brown v. Board of Education*. He is now a local community and political leader highly respected by black and white residents.

I now travel more frequently to my hometown because of my aging mother. Visits to Whiteville, the place of my formative years, and visits to Central High School, the place of my early formal education, have become more important to me. I have become far more appreciative of and I have a greater need to know more about the family, the church, and the schools that were the life blood of our segregated community. Some of us who lived the experience refer to it as the beloved community.

The segregated Central High School of my youth was an integral part of our beloved community; after the church, perhaps the most important part. When there are few other institutions that care about you, your school becomes even more important to your development and self-esteem. I remember a school where I was valued. The principal and teachers understood me. They knew who I was. They were part of my community, and they knew my parents.

I remember a long-standing tradition at the beginning of each school year of inviting your teacher to Sunday dinner. Not only were some of us faced with the terror of having our teachers break bread with the family, but we were forced to deliver the invitation. Imagine how difficult it was to disrespect a teacher or misbehave in class after the teacher had spent a Sunday afternoon as an honored guest in your house. There were no disputes among teacher, student and family. How could I convince my parents that I was right and the teacher wrong if my parents knew and respected the teacher? They believed that the teacher had only my best interest at heart.

When our 5-foor-7 Mr. Singleton threatened as he often did, to throw one of our 6-foot-5 basketball players out of the window, we knew he was only trying to mold us into the men he knew we should be. When our principal, Mr. Powell, said that you did something, as far as our parents were concerned, you did it! The principals, and teachers at Central pushed, prodded, encouraged, cajoled, and, yes, even threatened us, so we could be as successful as our intellect and hard work would take us. In our segregated school, we were expected to excel and highly praised when we did.

I contrast my experience with the stories of relatives and friends who had teachers after *Brown V. Board of Education*. Who were not part of their community. Many complain that their teachers never expected very much of them. They say they were not expected to succeed. Despite very good grades, they claim that counselors suggested careers such as cooks and hairdressers. I have never heard of anyone at the segregated school in my beloved community being advised to become a cook or hairdresser even if they had less-than-stellar grade-point averages.

The experience at Central High School prior to the effects of *Brown* was one of those very pleasant and foundation-building events in the lives of most of us who attended. Although parts of the old building and the used books and equipment fell far short of what we were entitled to, and short of what we needed, Central remains a special place in our hearts and minds. The reverence for this place in this time before *Brown* is the reason Central has alumni chapters in most major cities on the East Coast.

I recognize the advantages gained and advancement made in education since *Brown.* I have seen educational opportunities in my own family that would have been next to impossible in a segregated environment. Do I want to go back to the years before *Brown v. Board of Education?* Do I wish that school integration had never happened? Certainly not! Do I long for the beloved community before *Brown?* You bet!

R. Grayer Powell was the principal of a still segregated Central High School when I graduated in 1962. Mr. Powell, a long-time Whiteville resident and local leader in the field of education, had been appointed principal in 1958. During Mr. Powell's tenure at Central, he was the highest paid principal in the Columbus County School District. During those years, principals were compensated according to the number of teachers directly under their supervision.

Because the district's white elementary, middle, and high schools each had individual principals, and Central was a school comprised of grades one through twelve, with one principal, Mr. Powell supported far more teachers than the principals of any of the white schools. As a result of a racially segregated school system, Mr. Powell, the district's only Black principal, was its highest paid.

Mr. Powell had a passion for all things relating to Central, and he had no problem displaying that passion on any given day as he went about his duties on the campus. He was a no-nonsense leader and he got things done. The students and teachers at Central all had a healthy respect for Mr. Powell. Central was his school and his authority was not challenged.

I recall one day when I was allowed to drive the family car to school, four of my friends and I decided to sneak off campus after the first period to visit the girls at a school near Lake Waccamaw. My girlfriend, Anita Hassell went to that school, and my buddies, Isaac Shipman, Gene Mosley, and Robert Coleman also had girlfriends at the school, so convincing everyone to cut class was an easy sell. As my friends and I were cruising down the street heading for Highway 74 toward Lake Waccamaw, who do we encounter in the lane right next to us? It was the last man on earth that we wanted to see; none other than our principal, R. Grayer Powell. Everyone knew that if Mr. Powell caught us, it would have meant the death penalty or worse! As soon as my cohorts saw

Mr. Powell, every one of them immediately dropped to the floor of the car. Being the driver of my father's precious 1953 Buick Roadmaster, I had to be careful about making any sudden moves, so I just pretended to look straight ahead while occasionally glancing at Mr. Powell as he rode alone in his car next to me. Mr. Powell had a serious look on his face. He seemed to be deep in thought just before he turned and looked right at me. Whew, he didn't recognize me! I knew he did not realize who I was because had Mr. Powell recognized me as being from his school, he would have run down our car and stopped it. He was not the kind of man to let things go until later, so when we turned toward Highway 74, headed for Lake Waccamaw, and Mr. Powell continued in the circle around Columbus County courthouse, we knew we were in the clear.

During Mr. Powell's tenure at Central, the academic standards were raised, the requirements for graduation were increased, and a greater level of community involvement was achieved. In addition to the academic prominence, Central also fully displayed its athletic prowess during those years. The school's basketball team went undefeated, winning 55 straight games during the 1967 and 1968 basketball seasons. The team averaged a phenomenal 115.6 points per game, while holding opponents to only 60.4 points per game, winning consecutive state championships. On May 20, 1967, Mr. Powell died after a brief illness. There was a tremendous outpouring of grief and sense of loss in the community after his death. Central had lost its greatest leader.

After the Whiteville schools were finally integrated in 1969, the school that had educated Black children from grade one through grade twelve became Central Middle School. My former high school history teacher, Lloyd Best was appointed principal of the integrated district's middle school. Although Central High School no longer exists, it will always be special to me and I believe to everyone who was a part of the Central High School experience. It was more than just an impersonal institution where we were required by state law to attend until we were sixteen years old. Together with our churches and our families, Central served as one of those cornerstones necessary for the building of strong character in oppressed children that not only helps them to survive, but helps them to succeed in spite of their circumstance.

In addition to the "We honor and revere your name" line in the school song, the next to last line "Your history, we know is ever yet untold" is an even more important reference to our feelings about that school. Of course we know the institutional history of Central, but is human history *is* ever yet untold, because it continues to unfold. Its history continues to evolve in the lives of alumni who had seeds of success implanted in them during the years they spent there. They have gone on from a place where the white majority community considered them second-class citizens, to the lofty heights of which their families and teachers had dreamed and prayed.

Everything has its season. Perhaps the season for a segregated Central has passed and is no longer needed. Maybe our children's children will know little to nothing of its importance even if they live in the area. I can't predict if future generation will hold our old school in such high esteem, but those of us who had the Central High School experience, will always honor and revere the name.

BLACK SCHOOLS

BLACK SCHOOLS OF THE WHITEVILLE AREA

Whiteville #1	Whiteville Colored School
	(later Whiteville Negro High School)
Whiteville #2	Camp Ground School
Whiteville #3	Rose Hill School
Whiteville #4	Spring Hill School
Whiteville #5	Cherry Grove School
Whiteville #6 & 7	Diamond Branch School and
	New Brunswick School
Western Prong # 1a	Flag Pond School
1b	Brown's Chapel School
Pleasant Plains #1	Mill Branch School

This wooden building once served as classroom space for the Whiteville Colored School, which later became Whiteville Negro High School, then Central High School.
Photo source: Franklin George

Whiteville Negro High School's basketball team in 1947. Although the school won two state championships in the 1940's, it is unlikely that those championships were won by this team. Photo source: Franklin George

The Central High School campus circa 1955. Photo source: Franklin George

High school friends: (L-R, first row) Norman Rouse, David Lewis, Walter Boone- Bellamy (L-R, second row) Neil Kirk, Elmer Johnson, Gene Mosley, Isaac Shipman, Harold Tucker

Central students: (L-R) Franklin George, Edward Stewart, (unidentified) Preston Page, Isaac Shipman

Socializing at a local jook joint called The Hop: Willie Teacher, my girlfriend's sister, (I don't remember her name) me and my girlfriend at the time, Anita Hassell

James Daniel Debeuneure, who was known as James Daniel Toon when we were classmates and members of a Do-Wop singing group at Central. He perished aboard American Airlines flight 77, which crashed into the Pentagon during the 911 terror attacks.

Central High School's basketball team averaged 116 points per game while holding opponents to 60. They won 55 consecutive games plus state championships in 1967 and 1968.
Photo source: Franklin George

R. Grayer Powell served as principal from 1957 until his death in 1967. He was widely regarded as Central's greatest leader.
Photo source: Franklin George

Neighbors
Montgomery County

The Philadelphia Inquirer • WWW.PHILLY.COM • L

Community Voices *Fifty Years Since "Brown v. Board" Ruling*

No more 'beloved community'

Joe Jones
lives in Wyncote

Last Call for 'Brown' Essays

This is the second of three weeks in which Voices is publishing essays related to tomorrow's 50th anniversary of the U.S. Supreme Court's *Brown v. Board of Education* ruling. We're looking for essays that recall the times in which the ruling was handed down, and the aftermath, including reflections on how life has or hasn't changed.

If you'd like your story included in next week's Voices, send an essay of 200 or 300 words to Inquirer/Voices, 120 N. High St., West Chester, Pa. 19380 by Tuesday. Send e-mail to pavoices@phillynews.com or fax to 610-701-7630.

If you have questions, or want to talk over a story idea, call Kevin Ferris, Pa. Voices editor, at 610-701-7944.

Joe Jones often returns to his hometown. "I have become far more appreciative of and I have a greater need to know more about the family, the church, and the schools that were the life blood of our segregated community. Some of us who lived the experience refer to it as the beloved community," he says.

The article that I wrote for The Philadelphia Inquirer about life at Central High School before the Supreme Court decision on *Brown v. Board of Education* integrated schools in Whiteville.

GRANDMA BERT AND
HER HOUSE

W hen I was a young boy, the mother of my mother was the only grandparent that I had known. I only got to know my paternal grandfather many years later after I had moved to Philadelphia, so consequently Grandma Bert was the first person that I knew of her generation on either side of the family. During the years that I remember her, she was in her late fifties or early sixties, but during those years I thought of her as an old woman. Since I'm now much older than she was at that time, I realize that she was *very, very, young.* I have never seen any pictures of her as a young woman, and I can't quite imagine what she might have looked like then. I only knew her during the time of her life when all young children most likely consider their grandparents old folks. Although she did not appear to be a physically strong person in her later years, I believe that she had been so at an earlier time in her life. She had to have been a strong woman to give birth to ten children, and then to raise those children as a single parent after she was widowed at thirty-nine years of age. Her countenance exhibited that strength of character necessary to overcome her life's struggles. Even though her face would sometimes express frustration through the frown lines on her brow, she also carried this serene look on her face that indicated she was at peace even through her storms. Aunt Violet and my mother inherited that very same expression.

While doing genealogy research on my grandmother, I could find nothing about her in the census records from Lees Lake that I have relied on so heavily. I found information on her parents and her siblings, but nothing on Bertha, Lilly Bertha, or Lillie Bertha. I tried to rationalize her absence from the data by the possibility of mistakes in one year's census and by the time the next census was taken ten years later, she could have married and left the Lewis home. I was stumped! Once again, my cousin Carrie Kemp set me on the right track. While I was speaking to her one day about another issue of family history, I mention that I couldn't find any variation of Bertha Lewis living in her father, Esquire Lewis's house. Carrie then asked if had looked for her real name. "You know her real name was Beulah, everybody just called her Bert."

I could not believe what I was hearing. I have lived nearly seven decades and I have always had a keen interest in family history, yet I didn't ever know my own grandmother's name. I knew that my mother's name of Lillie was my grandmother's first name, and since I had only heard my grandmother referred to as Bert, I assumed that her name was Lily or Lillie Bertha. Grandma lived right next to us and as a child I had heard this pillar of our community addressed as Grandma Bert, Aunt Bert, Cousin Bert, and Mrs. Bert, but never in my life had she been addressed as Beulah. I remembered my grandmother so well and thought I knew something about her; her it turns out I didn't even know her name.

After I was over the shock of not knowing my grandmother's *real* name, I started to search for historical data on Beulah Lewis. In the records that I searched, I often found her name spelled as Lily, Lillie, Bula, Bulah and Beulah, but the information was there. Her young life started to fall into place for me. Armed with the new information I now had, as I periodically spoke with my brothers and cousins, I asked them if they knew the name of their maternal grandmother. To date, I must have asked at least ten people who grew up as close to her as I did. They all gave me the same answer; Bertha or Lillie Bertha. Now I don't feel so badly about not knowing my grandmother's name since none of them knew it either.

Grandma Bert's house sat by the side of the road just like our house, and when I was very young, one of my mother's many gardens separated our house from hers. Some years later, my mother had to give up that garden on her brother Lester's property when he decided to build a house there. When you are a small child, everything seems so much larger than it actually is, so Grandma's house seemed to be huge. When I now see the empty lot on which the house once stood, I realize that it could not have been very large at all. In fact it was probably quite small. It was an unpainted clapboard house with a front porch that stretched across the entire front of the house. Beyond the grassless back yard was the vegetable garden that was common to every home and almost a necessity for the survival of every family in the neighborhood. The house was a utilitarian, simply built house, but somehow elegant in its simplicity. When anyone entered the house from the front, they usually went straight through the small living room to the larger dining room where the family congregated. In the traditional, southern homes of Blacks, no one actually lived in the living room. It was reserved for very special guest like the preacher, the insurance man, a teacher and respectful white folk. If the dining room became over crowded during one of our family gatherings, some grown folk might venture into the living room, but we didn't usually sit there unless there was a special occasion or we were with special people. Grandma's kitchen had a large wood-burning stove that I remember as being quite beautiful, or maybe it was just beautiful in my mind's eye when I recall all of the wonderful meals that I ate after they were cooked on it. Although the stove had only one area for burning the wood, somehow the heat could be controlled in the different compartments of the unit such as the oven for baking, the stovetop for cooking and even a compartment for keeping food warm. The house also had a feature that I had not seen before or have seen since in any other home. There was a large fireplace with one opening in the dining room and another opening in the master or front bedroom, thus the one fireplace could be used from both rooms. Hanging over that fireplace in the dining room was a large grey oval shaped picture of my grandfather standing with three other men. The resemblance to his son, my uncle Willie was striking. The look of the four men in the picture could not be described as anything less than regal as they stood erect in their finest Sunday suits. When I looked at the picture, I just knew that my grandfather, The Reverend Robert Luther Hill must have been someone important, so gazing at that picture made me feel important.

I have done some limited research to the identity of the other men in the picture, but as of yet I have not been successful in determining who they were. One possible identity of the other men in the picture came from members of our family. They said that they had been told that the other men in the photograph were fellow seminary students at Shaw University in Raleigh, North Carolina. My mother claimed that they were local ministers from the Columbus County area who my grandfather would tutor between his semesters at Shaw. Every image the family has of our grandfather was copied from that picture. It was my generation's only connection to him. Sadly, the original picture that hung over that fireplace no longer exists. Before Grandma's house was torn down, the picture was passed around the family, neglected and eventually destroyed. When I was told that the picture had been destroyed, I was heartbroken. What a shame; the source of so much fascination and family pride is gone.

The picture that seemed to mesmerize me was not the only reason I loved being in Grandma Bert's house. I loved the warmth that I felt on my face when I sat on the floor in front of the fireplace, and the warmth from the love and sense of belonging I felt each time I entered the house. It was not my house, nor did it belong to any of my numerous cousins who always seem to be there. All of the kids in the family and unrelated neighborhood kids spent so much time there that we all felt as if we belonged.

During the early to mid-1950s, Grandma's youngest unmarried children, my Uncle Nate and Aunt Mazie lived in that house. My cousins Hayward and Marvin were my Aunt Vi's oldest children, but they also lived with my grandmother at one period of time. My Aunt Cassie's son James, lived there a few years when he was a young child. It had also been home to my Aunt Violet and Uncle Dan before they built their own home just behind our house. They moved back into Grandma's house again in the late 1950s while their house was rebuilt after being destroyed by fire. At one point or another, the house was probably home to family members and anyone else in the community that needed a temporary place to live. To the members of our family who were actually residents of Grandma Bert's house, it must have seemed like a family Grand Central Station. There were always people going and coming. When my mother sent me on an errand to purchase some necessity from the neighborhood store, I rarely took the closest and most direct route from our house to the store. I usually took the well beaten foot path from the rear door of our house that led to the unlocked rear door of Grandma Bert's house. I had no particular reason for detouring through Grandma's house other than to make my presence known, and just to see what was going on there. Once I checked things out, sometimes saying nothing, I would proceed straight through the dining room, the living room, out of the front door, and then across the highway to Vincent Leach's store, secure in the knowledge that everything was okay at Grandma's house; thus everything must be okay with the world.

The house served as our family gathering place. When family members had triumphs or tragedies, we usually met at Grandma's house to celebrate or commiserate. Early on, it was also our communication center. Long before other family members had telephones in their own homes, there was a telephone in Grandma Bert's house. During those years, long distance calls were very expensive. We did not text or telephone our loved ones living in faraway places on a daily basis as some of us are prone to do today. During the 1950s, you might get a call from a family member living in Philadelphia or New York perhaps once a year. Those of us receiving such a call would sprint to Grandma's house so the caller's long distance charges would be kept at a minimum while they waited for us to get to the phone. Whoever happened to be at Grandma's house at the time the call was received usually talked to the caller until the person for whom the call was intended finally arrived. Community members outside of the family also made and received that occasional important call on Grandma's phone. Her telephone was certainly the community phone, although I doubt that the community shared in the phone's considerable expense.

Grandma's house was also the family daycare center. When there was no work to be done on the farm or if children in the family were too young to work, we all stayed at Grandma's house. Some days during a typical week, there might be five or six children at Grandma's house while their parents worked. If your parents worked late and you were already asleep at Grandma's house when your parents came to retrieve you, quite often they just left you there for the night and you just started the routine over at her house the next day. If it was naptime during the day or even bedtime, it was not uncommon to see four or five kids sleeping in my Uncle Nate or my Aunt Mazie's bed. I have never been able to determine how Grandma managed all of those children with three and sometimes four adults living at that house, but mange us she did. We all were fed when we were hungry, and given a bed when we were sleepy. Where she got all of the food for us to eat or the space for us to sleep remains a mystery.

Sunday was a wonderful and grand day at Grandma Bert's. On Sunday afternoon, when church services were over, my aunts and uncles would bring their families to Grandma's house. The family members who lived nearby would of course be there, but it was a special treat to see our cousins from other neighborhoods that we didn't get to see on a daily basis. My Uncle Rob lived some forty-five miles away in Wilmington, North Carolina, and on special occasions, we would be delighted when he brought his family to visit on these Sundays.

Grandma's house on Sunday afternoons must have looked like one of those "Where's Waldo?" pictures. There were children everywhere. Adults were the primary occupants of the front porch. Grandma Bert usually sat in her rocking chair just right of the front door of the house while her children and their spouses sat on either side of her, but some of her grandchildren also mingled among them on the porch. The younger boys played under the porch of the house in what looked and felt like beach sand that had been placed there in stark contrast to the rich black soil of the adjacent surrounding areas. The older boys played baseball in a nearby yard or field while the girls who were too dainty for such activities, jumped rope and played hop scotch. With what must have seemed like inexhaustible energy, we climbed the big pecan tree by the side of the house, and darted about with breakneck speed to avoid the dreaded "It" label during the game of tag.

For the entire afternoon, there seemed to always be constant activity. Policing all of this activity and keeping the peace was Uncle Les. He was the oldest of Grandma's children so I guess being the person of authority at his mother's house was the responsibility of the oldest. Usually we required no more discipline from Uncle Les than a firm word and one of those stern troubled looks we were all accustomed to seeing on the faces of all the Hill family adults. It was a look that usually kept us from hurting each other, kept us from hurting ourselves, and although we played on and near the front porch, it also kept us out of grown folks' business.

I was either at my house or somewhere close by in the neighborhood when I heard the news that Grandma had died. I remember dashing toward her house as fast as skinny ten year old legs would carry me. By the time I reached her home, a gathering of family and neighbors had already filled the house and had spilled out into yard, so she must have died a half-hour or so before I got the news. I weaved my way through the mass of solemn men and wailing women in the yard and then in the house just in time to see Grandma being taken from her house. After Grandma Bert left that house for the last time, some of the adult men in the family began to disassemble her bed and remove it from the house. Removing the bed and clothing of the deceased was one of those unexplained southern African American customs that we followed back then in our family and community without real knowledge of its origination or knowledge of why we were following the custom. I have learned from older members of my sister-in-law, Judy Wilson's family in Jeffersonville, Georgia, and through my own research, that the custom dates back thousands of years to Mother Africa. In ancient times, the belonging of the deceased were removed and burned so any disease the deceased may have had would not be passed on to the living.

Burning the belongings of the deceased may have also served another purpose in some African cultures. A practice of some African tribes following the death of one of its members was to remove the person's body through an opening created in the wall of the owners hut or home instead of carrying the deceased through the door. This was done so the spirit of the deceased would be confused by the final exit through the wall and never be able to find its way back into the house again. In addition to lessening the possibility of transmitting disease, burning the belongings of the deceased could have also removed any material ties to the home that could attract the spirit of the departed. So not knowing where the door was located and having nothing to come back to, may have kept the spirits from returning to a place where they were not welcome. From the mélange of ancient African and southern Black traditions, burning the mattress and belongings of the deceased was one that survived and was widely practiced in our community when Grandma Bert died.

After the bed was taken down and removed with the mattress from the house, the entire room looked and felt so different. Never in my life had I seen that bedroom without Grandma's things. The room appeared stark and felt cold. It was no longer Grandma's room. It could've been anything then.

The house without Grandma Bert had the same effect on me as her bedroom without her bed, clothing and other belongings. Although the same pictures, the same fireplace and furniture were still there, the house felt empty to me. The succession of family members that moved into the house after her death were people that I loved and I'm sure they loved me, but they were not Grandma. I never felt the same way about the house without Grandma Bert being in it. After Grandma Bert's death, I never ate or slept there again. I no longer felt the need to detour through the house on my way to Vincent Leach's store. I never again felt the warmth of that fireplace on my face as I sat on the floor in front of it gazing at the grey oval picture of the distinguished looking Reverend Robert Luther Hill. I was in that house countless times after Grandma's death, but in reality I never returned to Grandma Bert's house.

Do You Have Everything You Need?

I deliberately chose the steps at the back of our house as the place that I would sit and wait until it was time for me to leave. My face was cradled in both hands and supported with the help of elbows resting on my knees. Directly in front of me were the flowering plum trees that I had planted many years earlier, my mother's garden and beyond that, Aunt Vi and Uncle Dan's house, but I gazed straight ahead looking at nothing. I was going to remain out there until my mother had left the house for work on the farm. Just before I had gone out onto the back steps, I had caught a glimpse of her crying and my father trying to console her. I was seventeen. I was leaving home to join the United States Air Force. I had to remain strong. I was a man, but I could not stand to see her cry again. I might have to be on the back steps for quite a while.

From our freshman to our senior year at high school, my friends and I spoke almost on a daily basis about our future plans. No one's plans included remaining in Whiteville. The students at the top of the class were all planning to attend college. Early on during the senior year, they had all been accepted at Fayetteville State, Johnson C. Smith, Shaw, A & T College or one of the other historically Black colleges in North Carolina. The ones at the bottom of the class were just happy to graduate. The students that ranked in the middle of the class had a multitude of dreams and aspirations. Some were planning to attend college, some were considering the armed forces, but almost every one also planned to follow the migration paths of sisters, brothers, and cousins that lead from Columbus County, North Carolina to Baltimore, Philadelphia and New York to get a good job. One friend, William "Toot" Betts had even dreamed of becoming a professional golfer. He had become proficient at the game while caddying at the Whiteville Country Club. His response to the question about what he was going to do with his life was always to same: "I plan to hit that little white ball long and straight." Toot really did not have a plan. What he had was a dream but I loved his dream. Even if he had had a plan, I don't know how one would have implemented such a plan in Whiteville, North Carolina, thirteen years before Tiger Woods was even born, so he was leaving the area also.

During our junior year in high school, my best friend, Isaac Shipman and I had devised a plan to attend The General Motors Institute. Neither of us had a particular love for cars nor did we even tinker with them as some of our friends loved to do. Like most boys living in rural areas, I had been driving since I was about twelve or thirteen years old, but my pal Ike, who lived in the city, didn't even learn to drive until our senior year. I had shared something that I had read about The General Motors Institute with Ike and we both thought that joining the program was a cool thing to do. I even wrote to GM about their program. We were really excited when GM responded. They sent me a personalized letter in a large package with glossy brochures that covered the opportunities the institute offered and the requirements for acceptance. After reading the information from GM we both realized that our plans would have to change. General Motors was offering a work-study program to transform young men who were gifted in the areas of math and science into automotive engineers. Math was my weakest subject. I had done so poorly in calculus that I dropped the subject and I barely passed the other required mathematics courses at Central. I was more of a history, English, geography kind of guy. Ike's math scores were even worse than mine, so wide-eyed enthusiasm was not going to get either of us into The General Motors Institute. We needed another plan.

By the time my senior year had rolled around, Ike and I still had no firm plans for the future. We were just breezing through the year. I entered the year with the required number of credits for graduation, but we were required to complete four years of English to graduate. Since I only had three years, English was the only subject I was required to take during my senior year. Theoretically, I could have taken only English and graduated on time. I wasn't about to do that. I liked school, and if I told my father that I was only required to study one subject the entire year, I'm certain that he would have found something for me to do on the farm to occupy my free time. Although my senior course load was easy, I made sure that I had a full day's schedule.

My friends and I went through our senior year enjoying the things apart from academic study that made high school such fun. We cut class. We took class trips. We took band trips. Ike and some of my other friends played varsity basketball. I played the short but exciting baseball season in high school. We gathered at the Sherwood and other hangouts in the Black sections of Whiteville to dance and wolf down fried chicken sandwiches, french fries and milk shakes. We got all dressed up for prom night held in our beautifully decorated gymnasium at Central. Since my friends and I had girlfriends at other schools, we also attended proms at nearby schools in Chadbourn, Lake Waccamaw, and East Arcadia. Before I knew it, graduation was approaching and I still was not sure of what I would be doing after high school. Several of my friends were in the same boat.

As graduation neared, it became increasingly clear to me that college was not going to be an option. Actually I never seriously considered going to college immediately after graduation to be an option. That was what my mother really wanted for me, but I couldn't burden my parents with the expense of college at that time. I still had vivid memories of the seemingly never-ending struggle they had endured when my older brother Jaye W was a student at A & T College in Greensboro. I did not want to put them through that again. One of our teachers, Marion Davis, who also coached the baseball team, did speak to me about a very small scholarship that might be available for me at Fisk University. I didn't even follow up with him to find out how much was being offered. I just assumed that it was a pittance. Besides I didn't even know where Fisk University was located so I didn't have any real interest in going there.

With few other prospects on the horizon, I decided that I would join the Air Force. I was not yet eighteen and I needed my parents approval, so I explained to them that after I had completed my four year military obligation, I could attend college and the G. I. Bill would pay my tuition. My father thought that it was a good idea. He said that I would be serving during a time of peace, and I could use those four years to determine what I wanted to do with my life. Although my mother really wanted me to go to college, they both consented that I could join the military. The advantage of the G. I. Bill was the hook for my parents, but that was really not my reason for wanting to join the Air Force. I wanted to see the world; all of it. I surmised the Air Force gave me a greater opportunity than anything else available to me to do just that.

My brother Jaye W said that he grew weary of the strain he was placing on family finances while he was in college. He did not want our parents to continue paying for his education when he knew they could not afford it. During his next visit home after he dropped out of A & T College, the family became aware of the decision he had already made and the action he had taken. He came home wearing a military uniform. I thought it was his R.O.T.C. cadet uniform from A& T, but what he was wearing was his Air Force uniform.

By my senior year in high school, my brother Jaye W had been in the Air Force for almost ten years. Much of that time he had spent out of the country. Every time he returned home with pictures and souvenirs from one of those exotic locations, my hunger for travel grew even more than it had been after I would read about those places in books at Central High School or in the discarded magazines my mother brought home from her employer, Mrs. Marks.

Soon after my parents agreed to sign the consent forms allowing me to join the Air Force, five of my friends and I headed to the military recruiters office in downtown Whiteville. The Army and Air Force recruiters shared the same office in what was then the post office building, and the excitement showed on both of their faces when six prospects showed up to inquire about joining. I guess they visualized their monthly quotas achieved in one fell swoop when we all walked through the door at the same time. Both recruiters were of course white.

The Air Force recruiter tried to reinforce our determination to join up by joking that he thought Whiteville was not just the name of our town, but it was also the attitude of its white citizens. They owned it, and they were not about to share it. The Air Force offers you opportunity: there is nothing for you here, he told us. We really didn't need to hear his sales pitch. Racial discrimination dominated our daily lives. We knew a lot more about the validity of those statements than the recruiter who made them could ever know. We were already convinced that we wanted to join the Air force and leave Whiteville.

The perception among my friends was that the Army would take just about anyone, but the Air Force was different. They were a lot more selective. If you wanted to enlist with them you were required to take a test to determine if you were Air Force material. I believed that the Air Force would also take just about anyone if they needed to fill a quota. Still, we were required to take a test if we wanted to join. On the day we were scheduled to be tested, my friends and I were picked up at our high school to be driven to the state capital of Raleigh where the test was being administered. We piled into two cars, and after a brief stop at a service station near the Columbus County court house to picked up a white kid who was also scheduled to be tested, we were on our way. In a couple of hours we were all at the testing facility in Raleigh.

The tests were lengthy and divided into categories to access your aptitude in areas such as administration, mechanics, electronics, and some areas that I can no longer recall. After we completed the test they gave us our scores, and we headed home. The ride back to Whiteville was not filled with the same horse play and frivolity as the ride to Raleigh had been that morning. The return trip was much more somber. We would once again have to change our plans quickly before graduation. My friend Ike and I would not be joining the Air Force together. Of the seven young men from Whiteville who had taken the test that day, only two of us had passed it; the white kid that we picked up the service station and me.

That period of time from the Air Force entrance examination to the graduation seemed almost like a blur, but even during this span of whirlwind activity, I still remember seriously contemplating the changes that were about to take place in my life. I began to realize how different my life was about to become. The daily interactions with people that I had loved and that I knew loved me would be no more. Some of the school friends that had been such an integral part of my life for the past twelve years, I might never see again. The familiar was about to be replaced with the unknown, but that was a choice that I made. I was about to begin my new season. It was somewhat of another rite of passage.

Two days after the pomp and circumstance of my graduation ceremony in Central High School's gymnasium, I was scheduled to raise my right hand, pledge to defend The United States of America against all enemies, foreign and domestic, and be inducted into the Air Force. My mother was still a little upset about the school ring that she and my father had made sacrifices to buy, and that I had lost even before I graduated. Despite the fact that I wasted their money by losing the ring, they scraped together even more money to purchase a graduation gift for me. They presented me with a beautiful blue box inscribed with the store name of Collier's Jewelers containing a watch. I loved it, and while that watch's value would not be significant by in today's dollars, the hard work my parents would have done for the money to purchase it made its sentimental value very significant. It remains to this day, a small but important symbol not only of their pride in my achievement but their sacrifice represented in this symbol of their love for me.

After my mother had regained her composure, she began to speak to me from the kitchen. I remained on the steps with my back to her. She wanted to know if I was sure I didn't want to go to college; couldn't you still get into college if you wanted to? No, it was too late at this point. Joining the Air Force is really what I want to do. She was still not understanding why I was leaving home with no suitcase. "Aren't you going to need a change of clothes?" she asked. "Do you have clean underwear?

My mother was obsessed with clean underwear. She always insisted that her boys be clean and have on clean underwear. "If you died I the middle of the night with dirty underwear, I'd be ashamed for the undertaker to come in here and get you." She would regularly quip before we went to bed.

"No, Ma, I am not allowed to bring a suitcase or any clothes. Tomorrow, the Air Force will give me all of the clothes and clean underwear that I need."

"Don't forget the box I fixed for you," she called out. The box meant the lunch box she had prepared for me. She fixed the same kind of box for every trip or school outing that I had ever taken; fried chicken sandwiches and a piece of cake neatly wrapped in wax paper and packed in a shoebox.

"Okay, I won't forget." As soon as I left the house I had planned to repackage everything into a paper bag. A guy with a paper bag lunch was a little more hip. A guy with a shoebox lunch was country! No way was I leaving home with my lunch in a shoebox.

"Lillie, we have to go," I heard my father say softly, but with an impatient tone, indicating that it was time for them to leave for work. My mother wasn't leaving until she finished questioning her knee-baby before he left home.

"Do you have any money?"

"Yes, I have few dollars."

"Do you need any more?"

"No, I won't need any money after tomorrow."

"Well okay then, we'll be leaving. Write as soon as you can."

Confident that the questioning and instructions were at an end, I assured Momma that I would. Glancing back over my left shoulder, I could see my father's arm around her, and I sensed that she was holding back tears as they turned to exit the kitchen. Before she left the kitchen however, she then asked one of those all-encompassing questions that only a mother could ask when she really wanted to be sure everything is right with her child. Her final question was, "Are you *sure* you have everything you need?"

Although I was just six months into the seventeenth year of my life, I have never forgotten that question and the many ways it could have been answered strengthened my spirit every day of my life since. Before she and my father left for work, and before I left home, I assured her in my agitated tone "Yes, I have all I need." I was seventeen years old with just a high school education, six dollars and a bus ticket to Raleigh in my pocket.

Hopefully, the life journey on which I was about to embark would be a long and successful one for me. If that journey was going to be long, just because it's on life's road, it was going to be difficult to travel. There would be dangers and challenges that could not possibly have been foreseen by a wide eye enthusiastic seventeen year-old with a serious case of wanderlust. I had no map to guide me on the journey. A map would have been useless anyway because I didn't even know where I was going. That road was far too dangerous and too difficult to travel by myself. I needed a lot of help, yet here I was, sitting on the steps, proclaiming that I was ready to go and that I had all that I needed. What was I going to need? What exactly did I have? In addition to the six dollar bills, my bus ticket, and my shoebox lunch, the only other material item I remember taking with me was a Bible. It had been a graduation gift given to me by the old widow, Miss Annie Smith. She lived mostly alone at the edge of the forest and stream where my young friends and I once loved to play cowboys and Indians, and near the cleared fields where we later played baseball. Occasionally, when we played near her house, we would torment her by raiding the fruit trees on her property until her incessant chastising and sometimes firing her double-barreled shotgun into the air, chased us away. Despite the fact that my young cousins and I often violated her peace and serenity, she still maintained a close relationship with my Hill family relatives. It was rumored that when she was a young and very beautiful woman, she had been in love with my grandfather, The

Reverend Luther Hill, so throughout the years she had an affinity for his descendants. I would see her on almost a daily basis as she walked the unpaved road from her home past our house to retrieve her mail from the neighborhood mail boxes grouped together on Highway 130. On one of those days just before my graduation, she called to me from the road. When I came out, she handed me a package wrapped in a thin piece of decorative paper with a purple ribbon loosely tied around it. She said, "This is your graduation present. It is the Lord's word. I want you to take this wherever you go. Read it. It will help you." I thanked her and assured her that I would read it although I had no intention of doing so.

For many years, although I would occasionally read the Bible that Miss Annie Smith had given me, I was never even a casual student of scripture. I was one of those "in case of emergency, turn to your Bible" kind of readers. I read that Bible when I was seeking an answer to one of life's questions that I had encountered on my journey, or if I sought solace when I couldn't understand the answer, or the answer was too difficult to accept. I am far from being a Biblical expert, but through the years I have obtained a far greater understanding of scripture than I had when I started reading the book Miss Annie gave me. Although I have also acquired many, many additional Bibles since the one Miss Annie gave me, hers is the only that has been with me in every location that I have lived since leaving home. I didn't realize it at the time, but that Bible was something that I really did need. Miss Annie's simple instructions to me tuned out to be far more prophetic than I could have possibly imagined at the time she gave them to me. She was right about the Bible. I read it, and it did help me.

Because I was about join the military, there were very few material necessities that I would need to begin my new life, but there were a lot of intangibles that I would surely need. I believed that I had them. What I had was an attitude that no work or any challenge would be too difficult for me. My perspective on hard work was developed in the hot North Carolina sun from the time I was a small child until that day. It was work that could not have been done by a lessor man or child. Whatever task I was about to face, in the words of my cousin Bobby Hill, I had already done something harder. I had the moral strength poured over and into me by the Sunday school lessons taught and the sermons preached at Cherry Grove and Mill Branch Baptist Churches. I had a strong sense of who I was. Central High School teachers who made an impact, like my eighth grade instructor, Novella Phifer, my history teacher, Lloyd Best and our principle R. Greyer Powell had convinced me that I was important, that I had something of value to offer, and that I was worthy of a decent life in spite of what the actions of the majority community were trying to tell me. I was convinced, that if someone spend so much time and energy focused on denying others opportunity based on their lack of whiteness, how could they have confidence in their value and abilities beyond their own whiteness? If they went to so much trouble attempting to deny me simple basic human rights, I must indeed be someone special. The very discrimination that was designed to kill my human spirit and confidence had just the opposite effect. I was strengthened and empowered by my circumstance. I knew I was not who they said that I was; I was who God said that I was. I felt that I was the physical and cerebral equal to any white person in my hometown. On issues of morality, I felt that I was their superior. I had the confidence that I could be successful. I knew other Black people had accomplished great things. Even members of my family had accomplished great things in the face of far greater adversity than I had ever seen. Why couldn't I also succeed?

Finally, I had the love of family. People who wanted me to do well. I had people who I loved and who loved me, praying on my behalf. I also had generations of family members going out in front of me praising God. Just as King Jehoshaphat's army had prevailed against insurmountable odds by having his people go out ahead of his army praising God, any battles that I needed to fight had been preceded by Melvin and Rebecca Jones, Henry and Mary Lewis, Esquire and Dolly Lewis, Henry and Fannie Hill, Peter, Nina and Sena Jones, grandparents, parents, siblings, aunts, uncles and cousins all going out in front of me praising God. My battles had already been won. I could answer my mother's final question with assurance: "Yes Ma. I have all I need."

Larry Carnell Jones
11/10/1948 – 9/23/2013
"Marcher to the beat of a different drummer"

Index

CPSIA information can be obtained at www.ICGtesting.com
Printed in the USA
LVOW06s0046040915

452577LV00001B/1/P